CONCORDIA UNIVERSITY
DS117.R2
HISTORY OF

HISTORY OF PALESTINE

VIEW OF JERUSALEM

HISTORY OF PALESTINE

by
ANGELO S. RAPPOPORT
Ph.D., B. ès L.

NEW YORK
E. P. DUTTON & CO., INC.

FIRST PUBLISHED IN U.S.A. IN 1931

All rights reserved
PRINTED IN GREAT BRITAIN BY
UNWIN BROTHERS LTD., WOKING

PREFACE

THERE is no other country in the world which can touch the hearts of nations as Palestine does. "Palestine" is a magic keyword which throws open the hidden gates of fancy and frees the prisoner imagination. It is a country which represents the birthplace of religion, of a fight and self-sacrifice for an ideal.

On the green hillocks of Judæa, on the flower-decked fields of Sharon, on the sun-scorched mountains and the golden sands of lake Genesaret lofty religions once evolved which have made an appeal to the human heart. For centuries the Holy Land has been the cynosure of Jewish and Christian eyes, a centre of attraction and veneration.

It is a strange country in many respects. It has seen far-flung empires crack and crumble and mighty peoples dwindle to naught, and its history cries to be told. Many of us are familiar with the Israelite period of the Promised Land, but few—unless they are historians—know the history of the country extending over forty centuries. Such a history is, in our opinion, a subject of topical interest, for Gentile and Jewish thoughts are now more than ever concentrated upon the country. Even while this book was in the press the limelight has been turned full upon Palestine.

On October 21, 1930, the Government published a White Paper (Cmd. 3692) which was a statement —or rather a restatement—of its Palestinian policy.

It contained a decision to take measures to check the excessive Jewish immigration to the Holy Land in order to protect the legitimate interests of the Arabs. This policy, to a certain extent based on the report of Sir John Hope Simpson (Cmd. 3686), aroused at once Zionist hostility. It led to vehement protests and to a debate in the House of Commons. The British Government thereupon declared that the White Paper had been misunderstood, and that Lord Passfield, the Colonial Secretary, did not mean what he said. Lord Passfield, however, never said what he really meant, and the effervescence in Zionist quarters is still very great.

We have written this *History of Palestine* in a spirit of perfect impartiality. It is not a book of propaganda, but the work of a humble student of history, trammelled in his researches by no prejudice or *parti pris*. We may perhaps be accused of having laid too much stress upon religion (in Chapter X), but it is our deliberate opinion that a national revival of the Jews in their ancestral home *without* the basis of religion has no *raison d'être*. A Jew whose heart does not beat faster and whose pulse is not quickened at the mention of Zion is lacking in sentiment and has no comprehension of the historic past of Judaism, but a Zionist who observes none of the fundamental laws of the Jewish religion manifests an even greater ignorance of both Judaism and Zionism.

Zionism stripped of religion, the Zionism of an

PREFACE

atheist, is an anomaly, a contradiction, an incomprehensible absurdity.

We are aware of the shortcomings of the present book, and do not pretend to have accomplished our task quite satisfactorily. We hope, however, to have rendered a small service to all those, Jews and Gentiles, who are interested in Palestine and its history. Our motto throughout has been: *Je ne propose rien, je ne suppose même rien, j'expose.*

A. S. R.

December 15, 1930
The first day of the Feast of Lights

CONTENTS

PART I

PRE-ISRAELITE PALESTINE

CHAPTER I
THE LAND — 19

Palestine, the land of the Philistines—The term "Palestine"—Kinahna—Eretz Israel—The Holy Land—Variety of climate and scenery—The Jordan Valley—The Ghor—Lebanon and Anti-Lebanon—Hoary Hermon—Samaria—The Negeb—The Jordan and the Nile—Merom, Tiberias and the Dead Sea—The Sea of Kinnereth—Beauty and grandeur—The Lake of Asphalt—Geology—Earthquakes—Variety of soil and climate—A land "flowing with milk and honey"—Picturesque Palestine—The majesty and sublimity of the desert—The howling wilderness—A land of contrasts—The Maritime Plain—The highway between Africa and Asia—Galilee—The ruins of Palestine—The Geographical position—Influence of Babylonia, Egypt and the Hittites

CHAPTER II
THE EARLIEST INHABITANTS — 34

The Excavations—Archæology and History—Religion and scientific investigation—The Palestine Exploration Fund—Flinders Petrie—Tell-el-Hesy—The fortress of Lachish—Eleven cities built one on top of the other—The Governor Zimrida—Macalister's researches—The city of Gezer—Prehistoric remains—Sellin's researches—Four ancient cities—Tell-el-Mutesellin—Schumacher's discoveries—The site of ancient Jericho—Archæological societies—Non-Semitic races—Palæolithic and Neolithic men—The troglodytes—The civilization of the men of the later Stone Age—Cremation of the dead—Semitic customs—The Horites—The caves of Seïr—The Kharu and the Hittites—Megalithic monuments—Menhirs—Cromlechs—Dolmens—Cup-marks and their functions—The earliest inhabitants a non-Semitic race

CHAPTER III
THE SEMITES — 51

The term "Semite"—The regions inhabited by the Semites—The Fertile Crescent—The home of the Semites—Winckler and Sprenger—Arabia the home of the Semites—Climatic changes—

Racial migrations—Four migrations—Babylonian, Amorite, Canaanite and Islamic—Sumerians and Akkadians—Professor Joseph Halévy—Semitic races in Palestine—Amorites and Canaanites—The term "Amorite" in the Old Testament—Amurru

CHAPTER IV

THE BABYLONIANS IN PALESTINE 58

Mesopotamia—The Sumerians—Cuneiform writing—Kengi, the land of canals and reeds—The city-states—Ur, Larsa, Erech—Nippur and Lagash—North and South Babylonia—Palestine and Babylonia—Imperialistic tendencies—The state in the Nile valley—Geographical position of Palestine—Trade-routes—The contest between Egypt and Babylonia—Civilizations of Babylonia and Egypt—Ur—Nina—King Lugalzaggisi—An Empire extending from the "rising to the setting of the sun"—The inscriptions of Lugalzaggisi—King Sargon of Agade—Gudea of Lagash—The Amorite migration—The rulers of Elam—Khammurabi—The fourteenth chapter of Genesis—Amraphel and Khammurabi—Babylonian influence—Babylonian culture—Egyptian and Hittite influences—The Tell-el-Amarna letters—Gezer and Taanach—Egypt and Palestine—The language and script of the Canaanites

CHAPTER V

FROM THE NILE TO THE JORDAN 74

Egypt covets Palestine—The copper mines of the Sinai peninsula—King Hu—The annals of Palermo—Seneferu's military expeditions—The "Wall of the Princes"—King Khufu, the Kheops of Herodotus—King Sahure—"Hail, Sahure"—The tomb of Inti—The siege of a Semitic town—Meri-Ra Pepi I—The land of the Herusha—The tomb of Una—The "sand-dwellers"—The land of the "Gazelle-nose"—The King's instruction for his son—The "Romance of Sinuhe"—Retenu—Description of Canaan—"Land handed me to land"—The tomb of Khnumhotep—Thirty-seven Asiatics visit Egypt—The arrival of Joseph's brethren in Egypt—The Kassite invasion—The Hyksos—The word "Hyksos"—The History of Manetho—Josephus—The Kingdom of Mitanni—Confusion in Palestine—The expulsion of the Hyksos—The conquests of Ahmose—Amenhotep I and Thutmose II—The campaigns of Thutmose III—The inscriptions on the walls of the temple at Karnak—The battle of Megiddo—The defeat of the enemy—The fugitives drawn up by garments—The siege of the city—The booty of Thutmose—The capture of the prince of Joppa—The policy of Thutmose III—Palestine an Egyptian province

CONTENTS

CHAPTER VI

THE TELL-EL-AMARNA AGE — 99

The successors of Thutmose III—A new danger in Palestine—The Hittites and the Khabiri—King Subbiluliuma—Professor Winckler at Boghaz-keui—The Tell-el-Amarna letters—The correspondence of Amenhotep III and Amenhotep IV—The heretic king—Akhetaten or "Horizon of Aton"—The governors of Palestine—The letters of Abdi-Khiba—The Khabiri and the Hittites—Babylon and Egypt—Pharaoh and the Kings of Mitanni—Burnaburiash, King of Babylon—Violence done to his servants — A diplomatic passport—Geography of Palestine—Jerusalem or Urusalimu—The tomb of Haremheb—The campaigns of Ramses I—Seti I and Ramses II—Egypt and the Hittites—The treaty of peace—A document written on silver tablets—A picture of Canaan—*The Travels of a Mohar*

PART II

PALESTINE, THE PROMISED LAND OF THE HEBREWS

CHAPTER VII

THE CONQUEST OF CANAAN AND THE AGE OF THE JUDGES — 117

Impossibility of independent national existence in Palestine—"The Canaanite was then in the land"—Phœnicians and Amorites—Egypt and the Hittites—Palestine an easy prey to invaders—Penetration by the Israelites—"Ibrim"—Moabites, Ammonites, Midianites and Edomites—The name "Hebrew"—Abraham—Nomadic Semites—"A wandering Syrian was my father"—Abraham and Khammurabi—The famine in Canaan—The pasture land of Goshen—The inscription on the tomb of Haremheb—Israel in Egypt—Ramses II builds Pithom and Raamses—The oppression of the Hebrews—The danger of an invasion—Merneptah, the Pharaoh of the oppression—The anti-alien policy of Egypt—The Khabiri—The Israel stele—The Apuru—The Exodus—Israel in the desert—Kadesh-Barnea—Moses and Joshua—The crossing of the Jordan—The Judges—Shophetim and Suffetes—The early Judges—Sisera—Deborah, Israel's Joan of Arc—The Song of Deborah—Jael, the wife of a Kenite—Barak—Jerubbaal—The raids of the neighbours—Gideon—Jephthah of Gilead—The tragic story of Iphigenia—The tribe of Dan—The image set up at Laish—The conquest of Canaan—National and religious bonds—The migration of tribes—The Philistines—The clamour for a monarchy—Samuel, the Warwick of early Israel—Saul

CHAPTER VIII

THE HEBREW MONARCHY 137

Saul, a democratic king—Attacks of the Philistines—On the mountains of Gilboa—The death of Saul—David's lament—"Ye mountains of Gilboa"—David King of Israel—The murder of Ishbosheth—The conquest of Jerusalem—The city of the Jebusites—Urusalimu of the Tell-el-Amarna letters—Mount Zion—Benjamin and Judah—The new metropolis—King Hiram of Tyre—The Messiah, a prince of the House of David—Solomon—An Egyptian army in Palestine—The town of Gezer—The reign of glory—New sources of revenue—Foreign markets—Horses for Hittite princes—The Temple—Expenses and heavy taxes—The discontent of the nation—The assembly of Shechem—The appeal of the tribes—The ill-advised monarch—The house divided—The two kingdoms—Jeroboam—Changes of dynasty—Sheshank, King of Egypt—The monument of Karnak—The Aramæans—The Kingdom of Zoba—The danger of Assyria—The Northern Kingdom—The house of Omri—The Tyrian princess—Ahab—Baal and Astarte—The protest of the Prophets—The battle of Aphek—Shalmaneser III—Biridri of Damascus and Ichrulini of Hamath—The battle of Karkar—The fall of Samaria—The Mesha stone—Jehu—The ambition of the King—King Joash—Jeroboam II—The beginning of the end—Menahem and Pekah—A vassal of Assyria—Sabako, King of Egypt—Tiglath-Pileser and Shalmaneser IV—The siege of Samaria—The captivity—The disappearance of the ten tribes

CHAPTER IX

ASSYRIANS, BABYLONIANS AND PERSIANS 152

Assyrians, Babylonians and Persians—The Southern Kingdom—Jehoshaphat, King of Judah—Jehoram and Athaliah—Joash—Invasion of the Aramæans—Azariah—The harbour of Elath—Material prosperity—Wealth and luxury—Pastoral life and mercantile pursuits—Social sins multiply—The Prophets—Enter Assyria—Assyria, the rival of Babylonia—Shalmaneser and Tiglath-Pileser—Assyria's Imperialistic policy—Ashur-nasir-pal and Ahab—Ashur-nasir-pal's boast—Shalmaneser III—His inscription—Raman-nirari and Tiglath-Pileser III—The city of Niniveh—Shalmaneser IV—Egypt the evil genius of Palestine—The broken reed—Sabako—The siege of Samaria—Sargon—The turning-point for Judah—King Ahaz—The commercial port of Elath—A vassal of Assyria—Isaiah—Ahimit and Yaman—The peoples of Philistia, Judah, Edom and Moab speak treason—Merodach-Baladan—Sennacherib—The battle of Altaku—

CONTENTS

PAGE

Tirhakah—The Old Testament and Herodotus—Esar-haddon—Hezekiah—Pharaoh Necho—Josiah—The Scythians—The decline of Nineveh—The independence of Babylon—Nabopolassar and Nebuchadrezzar—The fall of Jerusalem—The Babylonian captivity—Cyrus, King of Anshan—The overthrow of the Babylonian Empire—Zerubbabel—The state of Palestine—Danger of assimilation—The work of Ezra—Nehemiah—Politics and Religion—The *Torah*, the constitution of the Jews

CHAPTER X

RELIGION AND POLITICS—THE HOUSES OF PTOLEMY AND SELEUCUS 179

Persian rule—Satraps—Satrapy of Abar-Nahara—Rebellion under Artaxerxes Ochus—The restoration—Cultural individuality—Advance of the Arabs—Battle of Issus—The Diadochi—Ptolemy Lagi—Seleucus—Palestine a Greek province—Paganism in Palestine—Hellenization of country—Battle of Raphia—Seleucus IV—Antiochus Epiphanes—Religious persecutions—The Pro-Egyptian Party—Introduction of Hellenism—War on Jewish religion—Religion and politics—The Hasmonæans—Judas Maccabæus—Diplomatic relations with Rome—The Pharisees—Nation and religion—The *Torah* as charter of religion—Pharisees and Prophets—Religious vitality—Joppa a Jewish port—John Hyrcanus—Aristobulus I—Alexander Jannæus—The Nabatæans—Transjordania—Hyrcanus II—Aristobulus II—Antipater—Appeal to Rome

CHAPTER XI

IN THE TALONS OF ROME 199

The Romans—Pompey—The golden vine—Hyrcanus, High-Priest—The Roman protectorate—Hasmonæans and Idumæans—Scaurus—Gabinius—Division of Judæa—The Parthians—Antigonus—Herod and Antony—Palestine—Roman dependency—The Kingdom of Herod—Hatred of the Jews—The iron hand—The battle of Actium—Octavius—Native princes—Hordes of robbers—Anael, the High-Priest—Alexandra and Cleopatra—Sebaste—The Temple of Herod—The sons of Herod—A deputation to the Emperor—Archelaus—Herod Antipas—Administrative districts—Herod Philip—The "fox"—The Decapolis—Greek cities—The legate of Syria—The procurator—The *angariæ*—Agrippa I—The Birth of Christianity—The Redeemer—Judaism and paganism—The Romans and the Jews—The cruelties of the procurators—The war—Vespasian—Titus—The fall of Jerusalem

HISTORY OF PALESTINE

PART III
PALESTINE, THE HOLY LAND OF CHRISTENDOM

CHAPTER XII

PALESTINE UNDER ROMAN AND BYZANTINE EMPERORS (A.D. 70–634) . . . 221

The inhabitants of Palestine—Religious interests—Mixed population—Nabatæans andIturæans—Græco-Macedonian elements—Agriculture—The Edict of Milan—Constantine—Helena—Arius—The Council of Nicæa—Religious science—Bishop Macarius—The Holy Cross—Chosroes II—Heraclius—Persia and Byzantium—Native Syrians and Greeks—Siroes—Tiberias—Domitian—Hadrian—Persecution of the Jews—Bar Kochba—Jewish coins—Ælia Capitolina—Christian Jews—Jewish learning—Jamnia—Jochanan ben Zaccai—Antoninus Pius—The Patriarchate—The Mishna—Septimius Severus—Juda II—Græco-Roman influence—Julian the Apostate—Alypius—Justinian—Jews in Upper Galilee—The historian Theophanes—The Samaritans—Benjamin of Tiberias—The monks—The Fast of Heraclius

CHAPTER XIII

PALESTINE UNDER THE MOSLEMS (A.D. 634–1096) . . . 241

The invasion of the Moslems—A victory of Islam—Edomites and Nabatæans—Greek inscriptions—The penetration of Bedouins—Vassal states—Mar 'al Kais—The Ghassanidae—Mohammed—Liberty of conscience—Abu Bekr—Instructions to the army—Justice and toleration—Arabs settled in Palestine—Arabs in pay of Byzantium—Oppression of Jews and Christians—The fiscal screw—The spirit of unity—Capture of Damascus—Indifference of inhabitants—"Farewell, Syria"—The patriach Sophronius—The Caliph Omar—The Mosque of Omar—The Al Masjid al Aksa—Mohammed's night journey—The winged steed Al Burak—The five Junds—Property in Palestine—The Omaiyads—Mu'awiya—Abd-al-Malik—The Dome of the Rock—Hisham—Damascus and Bagdad—The Abbasids—The Fatimids—Nicephorus Phocas—Biamrillah—Persecutions—The Seljuks—Tutush and Malkshah—Sufferings of Christian pilgrims

CHAPTER XIV

PILGRIMAGES TO THE HOLY LAND . . . 261

Pilgrimages—Constantine—St. Helena—The Holy Cross—A cheque upon the Treasury—A splinter from the True Cross—St. Jerome and women pilgrims—Paula—Melania—St. Augustine—

CONTENTS

Piety, Adventure and Mercantile Pursuits—Relics a source of Revenue—Religion and business—Expiations for sins—Frotmond—Seigneurs troubling the public peace—A country which "devours its inhabitants"—Superstitious and educated pilgrims—The Bordeaux pilgrim—The Saracens—Bishop Arculf—The Church of the Holy Sepulchre—Willibald—Haroun-al-Rashid—Charlemagne—The Republic of Amalfi—An elephant and the keys of Jerusalem—Bernard the Wise—Pope Sylvester II—The Seljuks—Heavy taxes—Poor and wealthy pilgrims—Jewish pilgrims—The Wall of Lamentations—the ninth day of Ab—Byzantine sentinels—Visits to the Holy Land—Rabbi Zeira—The air of Palestine—The Resurrection of the Dead—Judah Halevy—Maimonides—The Karaites—The land of longing and yearning

CHAPTER XV

THE CROSS AND THE CRESCENT (A.D. 1096–1517)   278

The Crusades—Fanaticism—Popular indignation—Ambition and business considerations—The Norman Knights—The Republics of Pisa, Genoa and Venice—An ideal pretext—Godfrey of Bouillon—Penitence and prayers—Massacre and riot—A vassal of the Church—Feudal jurisprudence—An unwritten Creed—A mixture of races—Peace and prosperity—A *creatio ex nihilo*—Clericalism and militarism—A foreign civilization—Disadvantages of feudalism—A powerful enemy—Saladin—A leper, a child, a woman and a coward—"We shall all die of thirst"—Renaud of Châtillon—A cup of iced sherbet—Frederic II—The Carizmian Turks—General Beibars—Holagu—Kotuz—"Reign thou in his place"—The Abbasid Caliph—*Finita la tragedia*—Desolation and ruin—Six *mamlakas*—Yellow and blue turbans—The Bahrite and Burjite dynasties—Berkuck—Bertrand de la Brocquière—Jakmac—Mamelukes and Osmanlis—Selim I, the Grim—The Jews of Palestine

CHAPTER XVI

FOUR CENTURIES OF TURKISH RULE (A.D. 1517–1917)   300

The Ottoman Turks—The Pashalik of Falestin—A rotten régime—Heavy taxation—The Golden Age—Sultans Selim I and Suleiman II—Revenue and taxation—Inroads of Bedouins—An emir of the Druses—The ambitious chief—The Master of Galilee—Reforms and discontent—Petty tyrants—A powerful sheikh—Peace and security in Tiberias—Treaties of alliance—The tyranny of the pasha—Brutal despotism—Napoleon in Egypt—Visions of a World-Empire—The ambitious Bashibazouk—A dictator of Egypt—From the Nile to the Jordan—Revolutions and

HISTORY OF PALESTINE

PAGE

fights for freedom—The conquest of Palestine—Hopes and disillusions—Heavy taxation—Sympathy and hostility—A regenerator of the East—An unarmed Crusade—Churches and monasteries—Russian pilgrims—An asylum for the exiles—Jewish communities—A dreamer of dreams—Mysticism and Kabbala—Persecutions and oppressions—Messianic hopes—False Messiahs—The tragedy of Jewry—Jehuda Hassid—Disappointments—Ritual murder—European Consulates—A peaceful reconquest of Palestine

CHAPTER XVII

PALESTINE A BRITISH MANDATORY COUNTRY (A.D. 1917–1930) 324

The War of Liberation—Hopes and memories—Enthusiasm and imagination—The conquest of the Holy Land—The "Rise of Jerusalem"—A proclamation in seven languages—A national Home—Arabs and Jews—Nationalist dreams—Zionism—Diametrically opposed arguments—Religion and Economics—Capitalism and Democracy—Justice and Religion—The hopes of the Christian missionaries—Forcing the hand of Providence—A home for the spirit—The Jewish problem and the problem of Judaism—The opportunity of the Zionists—A Hebrew University—Arab claims and Zionist aspirations—The Balfour Declaration—A second Nehemiah—The constitution suspended—The Mandate and the National Home—A feverish activity—A phase of transition—Development of agriculture—Desolation and cultivation—Report of Sir Herbert Samuel—British policy—Broken pledges—Difficulties and obstacles—Riots and pogroms—A Commission of Inquiry—The Wall of Wailing—A land of destiny—A country of limited possibilities—A way of living—A mixed civilization

PRINCIPAL EVENTS AND IMPORTANT DATES IN THE HISTORY OF PALESTINE 353

BIBLIOGRAPHY 357

APPENDIX 359

INDEX 364

PART I

PRE-ISRAELITE PALESTINE

"For the Lord thy God bringeth thee into a good land, a land of brooks, of water, of fountains and depths, springing forth in valleys and hills; a land of wheat and barley, and vines and fig trees and pomegranates; a land of oil, olives and honey; a land whose stones are iron, and out of whose hills thou mayest dig brass."

Deut. viii. 7–9

CHAPTER I

THE LAND

Palestine, the land of the Philistines—The term "Palestine' —Kinahna—Eretz Israel—The Holy Land—Variety of climate and scenery—The Jordan Valley—The Ghor—Lebanon and Anti-Lebanon—Hoary Hermon—Samaria—The Negeb—The Jordan and the Nile—Merom, Tiberias and the Dead Sea—The Sea of Kinnereth—Beauty and grandeur—The Lake of Asphalt—Geology—Earthquakes—Variety of soil and climate—A land "flowing with milk and honey"—Picturesque Palestine—The majesty and sublimity of the desert—The howling wilderness—A land of contrasts—The Maritime Plain—The highway between Africa and Asia—Galilee—The ruins of Palestine — The geographical position — Influence of Babylonia, Egypt and the Hittites

PALESTINE means the land of the Philistines or Philistia, a name introduced only subsequent to the settlement of the Philistines in Canaan and during or after the period which marked their victories over Israel. Josephus[1] calls it Philistia. After a time the term "Palestine," first applied only to a part of the coast, spread inland. Both Josephus and Philo apply the name to the whole land of Israel, and it was employed by the Greeks[2] to distinguish South Syria, including Judæa, from Phœnicia and Cœlo-Syria. The Romans, who afterwards divided the country into four provinces, got the name Palestina from the Greeks.

It is somewhat an irony of history that the Israelites should be indebted to the Philistines, their hereditary enemies, for the very name of the country

[1] *Contra Apionem*, i. 22.   [2] Herodotus. 450 B.C.

which for four thousand years they have considered as their inheritance. The term "Canaan", *Kinahna*, used in the Babylonian inscriptions, would perhaps be more correct. This term, which may mean lowland, was at first applied to the Phœnician coast to distinguish it from the hills above. Later on the term extended to the Jordan Valley and the plain of Sharon. As the name of Palestine has, however, now become so familiar to both Jews and Christians, we are going to use it throughout this book. The modern Zionists prefer to call it Eretz Israel, or the land of Israel, while to Christians the country is known as the Holy Land. In Scripture it is only the prophet Zechariah who refers to Palestine as the Holy Land (Zech. ii. 12).

Palestine, or Canaan, is the southern portion of Syria, a narrow strip of land bounded by the Mediterranean Sea in the west, by the Jordan in the east, by the mountains of Lebanon in the north and by the desert separating Asia from Egypt in the south. In the east the River Jordan separates this strip of land from the district running parallel to it which is known as Transjordania. For many centuries these two strips of land stood in close relation, and later on were included by the Greeks under the general designation of Palestine. The whole of Palestine, situated between lat. $31°$ to $34°$ and long. $34°$ to $36°$, covered an area of nine thousand square miles.

The contour of the country is rather broken, and within its comparatively narrow limits there is a very great variety both of scenery and climate. One of the most important geographical facts in Palestine is the deep fissure of the Jordan Valley. This valley, called by Josephus the Great Plain, is now known as the Ghor, i.e. a long valley between mountains. The extraordinary depression of the Jordan Valley as well as the surface of the Dead Sea remained unproved as far down as the year 1836–7, when barometric observations were made. It was then demonstrated that the surface of the Dead Sea is far below that of any sheet of water on the surface of the globe.[1]

The country is naturally divided into four strips of territory running parallel, namely: the low plain along the coast, into which the northern end of the Carmel juts out; the hill country and the range of mountains west of the Jordan, extending from the Lebanon southwards throughout the land and intersected by the plain of Esdraelon; and the mountains and hill country east of the Jordan, extending southwards from the Hermon through Bashan, Gilead and Moab. This physical division of the country into four narrow parallel strips, having such a different elevation, also greatly affects the climate of Palestine. While the Ghor or the valley of the Jordan has a depression of several hundred feet below the level of the Mediterranean, the western plain rises slightly above it. Again, the hill country east of the Jordan reaches sometimes

---

[1] See E. Hall, *Memoir on the Geology and Geography of Arabia Petræa, Palestine and Adjoining Districts*, London, 1886, 12.

an elevation of 5,000 feet, while the western hill country around Hebron and Jerusalem rises only to a height of 2,500 or 2,700 feet.[1]

Palestine is pre-eminently a country of rugged and picturesque mountains, interspersed with a few tracts of fertile land. The Old Testament, when speaking of the visitors going on foot to Jerusalem, always employs the expression "going up". Whether one travels from Babylonia or from Egypt one always "goes up" to Palestine. To the north of Palestine the two great mountain ranges, the Lebanon and the Anti-Lebanon—hoary Hermon looking like a white cloud in the distance—raise their summits to a height of 10,000 feet. The Lebanon, which means the white mountain, takes its name from the cliffs of glistening limestone, while Hermon means the "consecrated". Majestic in its grandeur, with its snow-capped peaks, the Lebanon is famous for the cedars covering its slopes. Two ranges of mountains, offshoots of the Lebanon and the Anti-Lebanon, traverse Palestine from north to south and connect the two giants, Lebanon and Hermon, which stand sentinel in the north with Horeb and Sinai. Between them the Jordan flows, and they are intersected by plains and valleys. To the north the mountains are covered with trees and vegetation, while to the south they are barren rocks.

The plateau of Samaria, or the mountains of Ephraim, attain only moderate heights and are

---

[1] See Robinson, *Physical Geography of the Holy Land*, 269.

generally suited for agriculture, while the mountains of Judah, stretching southwards towards the Negeb,[1] are barren and inhospitable. The most savage slopes are to the east, looking towards the Dead Sea. To the west the hills of the Shephelah constitute a transition as far as the undulating plain of the land of the Philistines, continued in the south by the plain of Sharon.

The Jordan is the principal river of Palestine, and one might even say the only river in the true sense of the word. The Kishon, irrigating the plain of Megiddo, is nothing more than a large mountain stream, while the streams and streamlets that fall into the sea south of Carmel have little water in them, except in spring. The Jordan has often been compared to the Nile, both rivers dividing the countries through which they flow into two parts. While, however, the latter is the source of the fertility of the country and its principal artery of communication, the former divides Palestine into two strips of country which have often had an independent existence in history.[2] The Jordan, which means "Descender", has taken its name from its rapid fall, for in a course of about 200 miles it falls more than 4,000 feet. It has its source in several springs issuing from the western flank of Mount Hermon (Jebel es Sheikh), but the principal fountain is supposed to be a small pool a few miles

---

[1] The Negeb, or lowlands, is the region extending southwards from the Hebron.
[2] Robinson, *Physical Geography of the Holy Land*, 140.

north of Banias (Cæsarea Philippi). After descending over a rocky bed to the Lake of Huleh, the waters of Merom, 7 feet above the sea level, it issues forth from it and pursues a rapid course of 12 miles, when it enters the Lake of Tiberias. As the surface of this lake is 682 feet below the level of the sea, there is a total fall of 689 feet between the two lakes. On leaving the Lake of Tiberias the Jordan, one of the most tortuous of streams, pursues its winding course of 66 miles to the Dead Sea, the level of which is 1,292 feet below that of the Mediterranean. Issuing from the Lake of Tiberias the waters of the Jordan are clear, but as the river washes soft alluvial banks in its course, it soon becomes turgid. During February and March, owing to the melting of the snows in the Lebanon, the Jordan overflows its banks (Joshua iii. 15), but during the summer it is often fordable.

There are three lakes in Palestine, namely, Merom called Huleh, Tiberias and the Dead Sea. They form three singular depressions or troughs in the great natural groove or gorge. The Lake of Tiberias is called in the Old Testament the Sea of Kinnereth (harp), from its harp-shaped form (Num. xxxiv. 11; Joshua xiii. 27).[1] In the New Testament the lake is referred to as the Sea of Galilee or the Lake of Gennesaret (Luke v. 1; John vi. 1; Matt. iv. 18). While there is a subdued beauty about the Lake of Tiberias, there is grandeur

---

[1] "The Lord created seven seas, but the Sea of Kinnereth is his particular delight" (Talmud).

THE LAND

about the Dead Sea, and "the silvery sparkle of its waters gives a brightness to the scene enhanced by the dark shadows of the Mountains of Moab". The Dead Sea is also called the Lake of Asphalt on account of the bitumen floating upon its surface. It has no outlet, and it loses in evaporation all the water it receives from the River Jordan and its affluents. The Hebrew name of the Dead Sea is the Salt Sea (Gen. xiv. 3; Num. xxxiv. 3, 12), the Sea of the Desert (Arabah) or the Eastern Sea (Ezek. xlvii. 18; Joel ii. 20).

Palestine in general is not a well-wooded land, although trees have grown in abundance on the hills and there were forests of cedar trees on the slopes of Carmel and Lebanon. The kings of Babylon, of Egypt and of Assyria boast of having cut them down and brought them home for the construction of their temples and palaces.[1] The palm tree grew only in the valley of the Jordan and on the sea-coast, while the terebinth was so unfamiliar to the inhabitants that it became an object of worship to them.[2]

From the southern border of Palestine, where the hill country of Judah begins, to the extreme north, there is unvarying limestone. The great masses of rock which constitute the mountains of Palestine are Jura limestone; hard, compact and full of grottoes and caves. This rock is everywhere the basis on which have been deposited in some parts

---

[1] Barton, *A Sketch of Semitic Origins*, 145.
[2] Sayce, *Patriarchal Palestine*, 19.

extensive tracts of volcanic products; as also chalk and chalky limestone, dolomite, sandstone and marl.[1]

Palestine, being a country in which volcanic formations exist, is subject to earthquakes, although they are less frequent there than in Northern Syria. "Then the earth shook and trembled; the foundations of the hills moved and were shaken, because he was wroth", such is the poetic imagery in which the Old Testament describes an earthquake in the Holy Land (Ps. xviii. 17; lxviii. 8; Nah. i. 5, 6; Hab. iii. 10). The Book of Kings, as well as the prophets Amos and Zechariah, speaks of earthquakes in the country, and so does the New Testament. About the time of the Battle of Actium, 31 B.C., a violent earthquake occurred in Judæa and ten thousand people were killed by the fall of the houses, while the army encamped in tents was not harmed.[2] During the nineteenth century several earthquakes occurred in Palestine, the most terrific being that of 1837, when the town of Safed suffered terribly. The whole town was destroyed and four thousand people perished. The shocks were felt as far as Hebron.[3] In February 1930 earthquakes occurred at Hebron, and the superstitious Arabs considered them as a punishment for the sin they had committed in massacring the Jews of the town during the disturbances in August 1929.

Palestine is a land full of varieties, the difference

---

[1] Robinson, *Physical Geography*, 284.
[2] Josephus, *Antiquities*, XV. v. 2.
[3] Ritter, *Erdkunde*, xvi. 210, 287, 749.

of soil being intensified by the difference of climate. Its fauna and flora, too, are distinguished by a great diversity. Bare and secluded in one place, its soil is fertile and open in another, while the climate varies from the sub-tropical to the sub-alpine. There are sands and palms on the coast, wheat-fields in the plain of Esdraelon, oaks in Lower Galilee and bare peaks in Upper Galilee. This variety of soil and climate, as well as the geographical position of the country, explains to a certain extent the history of Palestine during five millenniums. "Just as the fauna and flora of the country represent many geological ages, and are related to the plants and animals of many other lands, so the varieties of the human race, culture and religion have preserved themselves through many ages side by side on different shelves and coigns of her surface."[1] On account of the diversified features of the land, snow-capped mountains and table-lands, tropical valleys and fruitful plains, the lives of the inhabitants have always differed as they still differ to-day. While cave-dwellers, or troglodytes, still existed in the hills of Palestine, agriculturists and Bedouins already flourished in the plains and in the valleys.

Palestine was once a land "flowing with milk and honey",[2] but for centuries the country has lain waste and desolate. The country has been lacking

---

[1] G. A. Smith, *Historical Geography of the Holy Land*, 58.
[2] The fertility of Palestine was famous in antiquity. Not only Josephus, but also Tacitus (*Hist.*, v. 6) praise the fertility of the Promised Land.

that beauty which cultivation alone could give it, the glory had departed from the "glens of Samaria" and the Judæan table-land became reputed for its stony dryness. And yet Palestine, even before its present renaissance by the Children of Israel, who are returning in thousands from their exile to their "National Home", has never ceased to be picturesque. There has always been beauty in Palestine, and, above all, majesty and grandeur, on account of the high position the land of Canaan occupies between the sea and the great desert. The desert itself is not without its majesty and sublimity. Deserts always influence imagination, and in the case of Palestine the desert has not failed to influence the imagination of Israel and to affect its literature. It gave to the people the sense of the awe of God, who made regions so contiguous and yet so different in character. The Hebrew prophets were greatly impressed by the howling wilderness. From the tops of the desert hills one catches a glimpse of the Dead Sea and its heavy mists, and the cold and grey mountains of Moab call forth memories of old. Our mind travels across centuries to the days when the wild, skin-clad prophets rushed down from the heights to rebuke the kings and the people. From these mountain summits the voice of Amos, the shepherd who haunted the heights and guarded his sheep on the slopes, speaks to us across the vast stretch of time—and his words have meaning even in our own age.

Contrasts are not without picturesqueness and

even beauty, and Palestine is a land of contrasts, just as the nation of Israel is full of contrasts. There is scarcely a land on the earth which combines such varieties of scenery as does the Holy Land.

It has been rightly pointed out that no other country was so well fitted for a people with a universal destiny, the possessor of a Book which has appealed to the intelligence of men universally.

On the one hand, the eye encounters in Palestine long ridges of grey limestone covered with grey heather, while on the other it passes over the line of purple-shadowed hills or luxuriant tropical foliage.

The whole Maritime Plain possesses a quiet and rich beauty, and the blue sea, the broken gold of the yellow sand, the fringe of foam, add colour and variety to it. Bees and butterflies fill the air, while glittering fire-flies, variegated flowers, roses and lilies of the valley, are scattered over the moorland and cornfields, and peace and fruitfulness seem to reign supreme over the whole Maritime Plain. In the Maritime Plain is the valley of Sharon. The country is undulating, with groups of hills between 250 and 300 feet high. It is largely wild moor and marsh to the north. The remains of a forest, the forest of Ashur, have given the name to the plain, which has often been designated as a forest. The southern part of Sharon, in front of the Gulf of Ajalon, can boast of a greater cultivation. Here are cornfields and orange groves, gardens, fields of melons and stately palms. There are numerous villages and towns once famous in history. Here is Lydda, once the seat of Jewish religious leaders, the centre of Jewish feeling, made pagan by the name of Diospolis under Septimius Severus in A.D. 202. Here is Ramleh, and Joppa, the ancient town we know from Jonah, who came to board a vessel in its harbour, sailing for Tarshish. From Joppa ships were plying the Mediterranean and trading to the islands of Kittim, Kaphtor (Cyprus and Crete) and Dedan (Gen. x. 4). They carried wheat and balm and oil and brought back cloth, purple and scarlet, silver and tin, lead and brass (Ezekiel).

The whole Maritime Plain is picturesque in its scenery, but for Europe, for Jews and Christians alike, it is full of memories. It is the continuation of that great historical highway between Africa and Asia. Along this highway marched the armies which repeatedly invaded Palestine. It is the real bridge between the two continents along which passed the hosts of Eastern and Western, ancient and modern, potentates and generals. Here was the pass crossing the hills, the Megiddo of the Biblical annals, which has witnessed the armies of Thutmose and Ramses, of Shalmaneser, Sargon and Sennacherib, of Cambyses and Alexander the Great, of Pompey and Vespasian, of Napoleon and Allenby.

The famous historical plain of Megiddo, or the plain of Esdraelon, encompassed by the hills of Carmel and Gilboa, is picturesque in the extreme.

THE LAND

The view from any of the hills which encircle it is an inspiring one. Before the eye of the spectator lies a flat expanse of red-and-black loam, very fertile and covered with corn and millet, cotton and tobacco.

But it is Galilee[1] which is undoubtedly the most beautiful and picturesque part of Palestine. From the plain of Esdraelon the green valleys and hills roll up to the foot of the snow-capped mountains of the Lebanon. Fair and verdant is the whole province and the shores of the Sea of Gennesaret, the Sea of Kinnereth, "the particular delight of God", whose waters, like silver threads framed by purple hills, are picturesque in the extreme. Palestine is picturesque also on account of its ruins. The ruins are perhaps not so numerous as they are in Egypt, Greece and Italy, but almost every hill-top is crowned with stones, heaps of stones, vestiges of ancient cities and fortresses, and remnants of diverse civilizations, Babylonian, Egyptian, Hittite, Amorite, Canaanitish and Jewish, Greek and Roman. To the Jews and Christians, however, Palestine appeals not only on account of its picturesqueness and its scenery, its charm and grandeur, but because it is full of memories of a glorious past, because its moral influence is immense and because it is the birthplace, the cradle and the stronghold, of an ancient race and a universal religion. Judæa has now ceased to be barren and Gilead is no

---

[1] Josephus is prolific in his hyperbolical praises of Galilee and of the country of Jericho.

longer deserted, but the country of Palestine has never ceased to be picturesque, and, above all, it has never lost its grip over races and nations and still strongly appeals to their hearts and imagination.

Now, a glance at the map will show us that geographically Palestine has a somewhat unique position. It has rightly been likened to a bridge, with the sea on one side and the desert on the other, connecting Asia with Africa. On account of its geographical position it has been the scene of many invasions and contending armies during several millenniums. Egyptians and Hittites, Babylonians and Assyrians, Persians, Greeks, Romans, Arabs and Turks, and in modern times English, French and Germans, have contested for the supremacy of the land.[1] Over this bridge the trade of the world passed, for in Palestine the traders of Babylonia and of the Far East could meet and traffic with those of Egypt and Ethiopia. Situated as it was between the great Empires of the Ancient World, the country was, however, not only the highroad of commerce, but also the meeting-place of civilization. The geographical position of the country has not only shaped its early history and civilization, but has also been to a certain extent responsible for the subsequent history of Israel and for its fate during the last twenty centuries. On the one hand, along the trade-routes were carried not only material merchandise but also intellectual products. Wherever there is an exchange of mer-

[1] A. Clay, *The Empire of the Amorites*, 51.

chandise there is also an exchange of ideas. Spiritual values are almost inseparable from the traffic of material goods. History furnishes us with numerous examples which corroborate this statement. Thus, while the civilization of pre-Israelite Palestine exhibits the influences of Babylonia, Egypt and the Hittites, the later civilization developed by Israel on the soil of the Promised Land is not free from foreign influences. On the other hand, the Exile of Israel and the Diaspora were also greatly due to the geographical position of the country. Jerusalem, "the gate of peoples" (Ezek. xxvi. 2), where the trade caravans of antiquity had constantly met, became later on the gate through which Israel passed when it started on its century-long wanderings across the world. Along the same trade-routes Israel, after the disappearance of its national existence, marched along in search of a new home. Thus it has marched and wandered till very recent times, when the trumpet-call of a return home has been sounded.

CHAPTER II

THE EARLIEST INHABITANTS

The Excavations—Archæology and History—Religion and scientific investigation—The Palestine Exploration Fund—Flinders Petrie—Tell-el-Hesy—The fortress of Lachish—Eleven cities built one on top of the other—The Governor Zimrida—Macalister's researches—The city of Gezer—Prehistoric remains—Sellin's researches—Four ancient cities—Tell-el-Mutesellin—Schumacher's discoveries—The site of ancient Jericho—Archæological societies—Non-Semitic races —Palæolithic and Neolithic men—The troglodytes—The civilization of the men of the later Stone Age—Cremation of the dead—Semitic customs—The Horites—The caves of Seïr—The Kharu and the Hittites—Megalithic monuments—Menhirs—Cromlechs—Dolmens—Cup-marks and their functions—The earliest inhabitants a non-Semitic race

It is only in the sixteenth century B.C. that Palestine enters into the full light of history, but from the recent excavations made in the country as well as from the Babylonian and Egyptian Records we are able to reconstruct to some extent the history of pre-Israelite Palestine. On the one hand, the excavations carried on in the Holy Land have proved the existence of primitive inhabitants, while, on the other, we gather from the documents of Babylonia and Egypt that as early as the third and even the fourth millennium B.C., in the dim and distant past, the rulers on the banks of the Euphrates and the Nile had entertained relations with Palestine, where they found a population. It will be necessary here to give a brief survey of the excavations carried out in Palestine.

From the ruins of the past, from the heaps

THE EARLIEST INHABITANTS

accumulated by centuries, the spade of the excavators has brought to light monuments and cities of bygone and forgotten ages. Majestic and elegant edifices and newly discovered documents have shed a dazzling light and revealed to the world the ancient civilizations of Egypt and Mesopotamia, of Anatolia and the Ægean Sea, the site where once the cradle of primitive Hellas stood.

For a long time, however, archæologists refrained from carrying on their researches in the Holy Land, the country which is not only the most illustrious in the East, but is most familiar to scholars and priests and where the faith and fervour, the dreams and hopes, of millions of believers are centred. It is precisely this latter reason which accounts for the reluctance of the archæologists. For a long time the religious spirit had prevented the scholars and archæologists from investigating the soil which the feet of the Patriarchs and the Prophets, of the Saviour, the Apostles and the Saints, have trodden. Times, however, have changed, and, in the nineteenth century, old superstitions had to yield to the modern craving for knowledge, to scientific investigation and research. After Egypt and Mesopotamia, the turn of Palestine has come, and archæologists have seriously turned their attention to the Holy Land.

In 1860 the Palestine Exploration Fund was established in London, and was followed by the German Oriental Society, and by the French Biblical School of Jerusalem. A special and abundant literature, dealing with the geography, the topography, the geology and the history of the Holy Land, soon grew up, and archæology soon followed suit. Practical work, however, was started only in 1890, when Flinders Petrie began his first investigations on the soil of Tell-el-Hesy, in Southern Judæa.

Under a hill Petrie discovered the site of the ancient fortress of Lachish, and found fragments of ancient pottery and other vestiges of a busy and active life. The first layer revealed the existence of a city which must have been destroyed and abandoned in the fifth century B.C. Under the first layer the British scholar discovered a second layer, which contained the vestiges of a still older city. Continuing his researches, Petrie thus successively discovered not less than eleven cities, built one on the top of the other, and belonging to a prehistoric civilization.

A comparative examination of the different strata of debris and of the pottery discovered in each layer enabled Petrie to establish the first methodical division of the civilizations of Palestine.

The first epoch of the town of Lachish—that is, the most ancient—comprises a period extending from 1760 to 1350 B.C. The city had a wall constructed in bricks, and among the remains were discovered debris of vases, of flint and also of Egyptian scarabs, one of which bears the name of Queen Taia, who lived about 1500 B.C.

A tablet on which the name of the governor, Zimrida, of Lachish is inscribed in cuneiform

THE EARLIEST INHABITANTS

writing, a name also mentioned in other documents, attests the Mesopotamian character of this first civilization.

On the top of these ruins there is a layer of ashes covering another city (at an altitude of 320 feet), which was finally destroyed by the Israelites (1300–1100 B.C.).

On the top of this stratum rise the remains of a massive wall built in square blocks and debris dating from the times of David and Solomon. The city was subsequently destroyed by a fire, but was rebuilt by the kings of Judah and remained until its destruction by the King of Babylon (in 590), never to rise again. The settlement of the Israelites is attested by ruins of public buildings, by remains of pottery, of objects of art and religious cult, among which is an Egyptian idol.

The excavations of Lachish must be considered as the prototype of archæological discoveries in Palestine. In a country which had to suffer so frequently from foreign invasions one had to expect the discovery of successive civilizations in the debris of the substratum and a succession of sediments and layers.

A more durable and better organized effort was made by the English scholar Macalister, who reconstituted the ancient city of Gezer[1] and confirmed this expectation. He availed himself of the

[1] Gezer was an old Canaanite city which remained in the possession of the Canaanites (Joshua xvi. 10). When the Pharaoh of Egypt, the father-in-law of Solomon, conquered the city he gave it as a portion to his daughter (1 Kings ix. 16).

previous researches of Clermont-Ganneau, who had ingeniously identified the site of Gezer with an Arab village.

Macalister started his excavations in 1902 and, continuing his researches almost with no interruption until 1909, discovered several strata, among which were found the following:

(1) The remains of a prehistoric city, either built upon the rock or cut into it. Flint and other objects dating from the neolithic age; primitive designs of animals, debris of pottery with simple lines were discovered. A cave serving as a place of cremation and a wall built of rough stones, protecting the open side of the rock, attest the transition from the Cave Age to that of dwellings.

(2) A first Semitic epoch (towards 2500–1600). Here the excavators established the presence of pottery similar to that of the Babylonians, the architecture reminding us of that of contemporary Egypt, a subterranean massive conduit, and remains of objects of a Semitic religious cult.

(3) The epoch of the Hyksos and of the Egyptian domination (1600–1200). During this period a strong Egyptian influence prevailed, but in its ensemble this period merges with the Semitic or Canaanite epoch.

The results of the excavations of Lachish, and particularly of those of Gezer, furnish us with all the essential elements and make it possible to classify the epochs and periods which accumulated and succeeded each other upon the soil of Palestine.

THE EARLIEST INHABITANTS

In spite of the numerous difficulties encountered, the excavations were simultaneously continued on various points. In 1902-3 the Austrian Sellin made researches at Taanach, a Canaanitish city mentioned by the King of Egypt, Thutmose III, and in the Song of Deborah. The result was the discovery of four ancient cities following each other. The first of these cities, the Semitic, is distinguished by its artistic technique. There are alabaster vases with geometrical figures, earthen huts, flint and bronze implements. There are no pagan miniature figures, while the flat pottery is red and not baked.

The second city corresponds to the Canaanitish period (1600-1300). We perceive a change in the religious and decorative conceptions. The slender vases become thinner at the bottom and are more supple; there are also geometrical designs wherein birds, fishes and the tree of life figure. Everywhere the influence of Cyprus and even of Egypt can be noticed. The basements of a citadel and of the dwelling of the prince have been found. Among the debris are scarabs of Thutmose III, gold ornaments and attire and miniature figures of Astarte. In the walls there are skeletons of children buried in large jars.

The written documents, the tablets in cuneiform writing, dating from the nineteenth century B.C., attest the relations which existed between the towns and the petty kings of the valley and those of the Phœnician coast.

Another part of the valley of Esdraelon, Tel-el-Mutesellin, the site of the ancient Megiddo, was explored by the German archæologist Schumacher. The importance of this bastion in the valley on the north side is referred to by the authors of antiquity. "The conquest of Megiddo is worth that of a thousand cities", proudly exclaimed Thutmose III. Schumacher discovered from six to nine cities one on the top of the other, among them:

(1) A prehistoric city, similar to that of Gezer and built against the rock. He found subterranean vaults, which served as habitations, and stone implements. The dead were cremated.

(2) A primitive Semitic city (2000–1500), built of bricks and stone. Egyptian influence is attested by the discovery of scarabs dating from the year 2000. There were also found remains of Asiatic pottery. The dead were buried.

(3) A city of the so-called Canaanitish type (1600–1000). Here one meets the same characteristics as noticed during the corresponding epochs in the discoveries of Gezer and Taanach, viz. pottery showing a Mediterranean influence, tombs containing bones and ashes; bones of animals in a well, miniature figures in stone, immured children, etc. Towards the end of this period both the use of iron and a Philistine influence are noticeable. The constructions resemble those of a modern Arab village. The city was evidently destroyed by the Israelites.

In 1908 Sellin undertook archæological researches

THE EARLIEST INHABITANTS

on the site which he supposed to be that of ancient Jericho. Here he discovered remains belonging to three epochs, the first being a Semitic or Canaanitish city. It was built of bricks and surrounded by a double belt of walls, the first of which has a width of 3 m. 70.

Under the present régime, inaugurated since the British Mandate of 1920, a new impetus has been given to archæological research in Palestine. Special attention is being paid to the conservation and protection of historical monuments, and measures have been taken to establish a National Museum.

Under the able and competent direction of Professor Garstang, of Liverpool, a special department of antiquities has been created with the assistance of a council consisting of representatives from the various religious communities in Jerusalem. New laws have been issued calculated to give greater facilities to the scholars and archæologists and to protect the common patrimony. A fresh impetus is thus given to archæological research, and new societies, such as the British School of Archæology, the Jewish Palestine Exploration Society and others, have been formed. The young and active Society Pro Jerusalem, inspired by the ardour and energy of the former Governor, Sir Ronald Storrs, undertook researches round the citadel known as the Tower of David and the walls of Jerusalem. Ancient monuments have been restored, and the Holy City has been embellished with new constructions. Two volumes, richly illustrated, published by this Society, attest its energy and activity.

Thus the recent archæological researches made in Palestine and the statements on the monuments of Babylonia and Egypt have disclosed to us the fact that already in the third millennium B.C. Palestine was inhabited by Semites, i.e. by races both ethnologically and linguistically related to the Hebrews. These Semites, however, were not the aboriginal inhabitants of the country, and there can be little doubt that in prehistoric times Palestine, like many other countries, was inhabited by other races. The excavations have laid bare the remains of a people who might be called aboriginal and who were of a non-Semitic origin. Man must have made his appearance in the land of Palestine at a very remote age. It is doubtful, however, whether we shall ever ascertain the date when the country was for the first time settled by man. According to some scholars (Dr. Max Blankenhorn), this happened more than ten thousand years B.C.

From the geological formation of the country and its surface we may conclude that during the tertiary period Palestine was still uninhabited by human beings, and that only during the later diluvial age it became possible for man to make his abode there.[1] He lived side by side with the cave-bear and the cave-lion, either fighting against them or seeking refuge from their attacks. In a cave on the Lebanon

---

[1] See Blankenhorn, *Ueber die Steinzeit und Feuersteinartefakte in Syrien und Palästina*, *Zeitschrift für Ethnologie*, xxxvii. (1905) 447, 465.

THE EARLIEST INHABITANTS

the bones of these animals have been found by the side of man.[1]

Sufficient evidence has thus been furnished by archæology entitling us to conclude the existence of palæolithic man in Palestine, i.e. from the far north of Canaan southwards down to the Negeb and the rocks of Sinai. Palæolithic flint implements have been discovered at Tell-el-Hesy, at Gezer and on the Maritime Plain.[2] In the fields around the ancient town of Gezer stone axes of the Chellean type have been found in great number.[3]

The earliest inhabitants of Palestine sought first the hills and the high plateaux, and only afterwards descended to the coast. The climate of the country seems to have enabled these palæolithic men to live under the open sky, although in later palæolithic times they sought also the caves—a fact which has been proved by the remains discovered. They were hunters and fishers living on the products of their expeditions. The skins of the animals they killed served them as garments, which they managed to sew together by means of needles made of bone, some of which have been discovered by archæologists. They found shelter in the numerous caves, or perhaps in rude huts made of branches and covered with the skins of animals. They knew neither the art of weaving nor that of pottery—and no

---

[1] Blankenhorn, *Z.D.P.V.*, 1892, 61; *Ztschr. für Ethnologie*, 1905, 458, 465.
[2] See Bliss, *A Mound of Many Cities*; Macalister, *The Excavation of Gezer*.
[3] Ibid., i. 6, ii. 121.

traces of either agriculture or breeding of cattle have been discovered. It is only with the neolithic age that the inhabitants of Palestine began to know something of pottery, rough work made by hand and exhibiting no signs of ornamentation. We know little of the civilization of Palestine in palæolithic times, the only records being the unwrought flint implements and weapons which have come down to us.[1] A flood of light, however, has been thrown on the customs and manners of the inhabitants of the country in the neolithic age. These men certainly belonged to a non-Semitic stock.

The excavations of Gezer, Taanach and Megiddo have yielded material enough enabling us to draw conclusions. On the rocky heart of the hill man had made his abode in caves—partly natural, partly artificial, and some of which were of large dimensions. The excavators who sifted the rubbish accumulated on the cave floors convinced themselves that the caves in the rocks had served as dwellings for primitive man in Palestine. Many of the caves of the Troglodytes were subsequently used also by the Semites, not as dwelling-places for the living, but as abodes for the dead, as cisterns or cellars. Whereas the men of the palæolithic or older stone age used only rude flint implements, which have been found on the surface of the plains of Palestine, the neolithic inhabitants of the country, or the men of the later stone age, availed themselves of worked and polished stone. If we know but little of the

[1] *Palestine Exploration Fund Quarterly* (*P.E.F.Q.*), 1912, xliv. 82 ff.

civilization of palæolithic man in Palestine, we can form some opinion as to the religion and the general civilization of the men of the later stone age. They cremated their dead and seem to have been addicted to cannibalism.[1] One of the caves discovered seems to have been used as a place for the burning of the dead, and the floor was covered with ashes. A hole had been pierced in the roof, which served as a chimney aperture to let the smoke out.[2] According to Professor Macalister, the cave-dwellers must have been a "non-Semitic race of slender build and small, but not dwarfish, stature, with thick skulls and showing evidence of great muscular strength".[3]

The fact that the inhabitants of Gezer burned their dead instead of burying them leads us to the conclusion that they were of a non-Semitic origin. The conception of the Semites of life and death made such a manner of disposing of the dead impossible. From the remotest times it has been customary among all Semitic peoples to bury their dead.

Not only was the custom of burying the dead prevalent among the Semites, but also among the Non-Semitic Akkadians in Babylonia. It is only among the Aryans, in Europe or in Asia, that cremation as a regular custom seems to have prevailed, although many Aryan tribes were also

[1] Macalister, *History of Civilization of Palestine*; see also *P.E.F.Q.*, 1913, 184.
[2] *P.E.F.Q.*, 1903, 50, 322–326.   [3] Ibid., 1902, 353–356.

burying peoples. "Son of a burnt father" is a reproach frequently hurled at the Hindu by a Moslem.¹

It has been suggested that the oldest inhabitants of Canaan, the cave-dwellers or Troglodytes, were the Horites, or Horim, the predecessors of the Edomites in the land of Seïr (Gen. xiv. 6; Deut. ii. 12, 22). Seïr is the limestone district south of the Dead Sea, full of caves, and a connection may have existed between the configuration of the country and the name of the inhabitants, Horim being derived from *hor* = hole or cave. Some scholars are therefore inclined to consider the Horites as the former possessors of the whole of Palestine.²

In Egyptian inscriptions the Kharu (Charu) are mentioned as the inhabitants of Palestine,³ a name which has been found in the form of Kharri or Charri at Boghaz-keui, the ancient capital of the Hittites. It has, therefore, been suggested that the Kharu or Kharri are identical with the Hittites, and that they constituted the primitive race occupying Syria and Palestine.⁴ Now the Old Testament mentions the existence of early pre-Semitic races in Canaan, such as the Rephaim,⁵ Anakim, Emim, Zuzim, Zam-Zummim and Horites, and there are indications of a people called Nephillim. It is possible that the Biblical indications show tradi-

---

¹ *P.E.F.Q.*, 1903, 179.
² Ed. Meyer, *Geschichte des Altertums*; Kittel, *Geschichte des Volkes Israel*, i. 36–37; *Revue des Etudes Juives*, ii. (1906) 32–51.
³ Meyer, l.c., 600.   ⁴ See against this theory Kittel, l.c., 38.
⁵ See note 1 in Appendix.

THE EARLIEST INHABITANTS

tions of primitive races who had actually occupied Canaan. The question, however, whether these races mentioned in the Old Testament are really akin to the early neolithic inhabitants of Palestine is one that cannot as yet be solved. The name of Rephaim has lingered on until a later period, used in connection with certain localities, such as the vale of the Rephaim, to the south-west of Jerusalem (Joshua xv. 8; xviii. 16; 2 Sam. v. 18, 22, etc.).[1]

In the absence, however, of accurate literary proof of an early pre-Semitic race in Palestine we have the existing megalithic monuments found in profusion in the country, particularly east of the Jordan.[2] The majority of these monuments are the work of the neolithic inhabitants of the country. They consist of *menhirs*, upright solitary blocks; *cromlechs*, or circles of stone;[3] and *dolmens*, stone tables formed by one flat slab being placed on two uprights.[4]

There is a divergence of opinion in regard to the object and purpose which the dolmens were meant to serve. Some scholars maintain that they were altars, while others are inclined to connect them with burial. Particularly puzzling are the cup-marks, or hollows, on the dolmens. These cup-marks dis-

---

[1] See also Knight, *Nile and Jordan*, 25–27.
[2] See Schumacher, *The Jaulan*, 123.
[3] *Gilgal*, a circle of stones, is the name of several localities in Palestine.
[4] Conder, *Heth and Moab*, 196–275; *Syrian Stone Lore*, 42, 43, 70; Perrot et Chipiez, *Histoire de l'Art dans l'Antiquité*, iv. 375; see also P. Thomsen, *Kompendium der Palästinischen Altertumskunde*, 1913, 12.

covered on the stones go back to the neolithic days. They were found on the table-stones of dolmens and in caves, upon the *Massebahs* or standing stones, and their functions seem to have varied. Some of the cup-marks were evidently put to profane uses, serving either as water-holders or as press and gathering cups for wine and oil. The majority of the cup-marks have been explained as being designed to receive the food and drink offerings so necessary for the welfare of the dead. Neolithic man in Palestine evidently believed that the departed spirits needed sustenance in the underworld. The custom of placing food on the graves of the dead is alluded to in Deut. xxvi. 4: "I have not given thereof to the dead." Professor Macalister ascribed the cup-marks found at Gezer to the Troglodytes. "All available evidence", he writes, "points to this peculiar feature being the work of the Troglodytes. Cup-marks were found in a good many parts of the mounds, and wherever they have any connection with other remains that can be definitely dated these remains are assignable to the cave-dwellers." That means to say that the neolithic men of Palestine are distinct from the Semites, who succeeded them in the country.[1] Now, the megalithic monuments, the dolmens, cromlechs and menhirs, are not peculiar only to Palestine. They are to be met with in the coastal districts of South India, in North Africa and as far as Lower Italy, the islands of the Mediterranean, the Pyrenean peninsula,

[1] *P.E.F.Q.*, 1913, 186.

THE EARLIEST INHABITANTS

France and Great Britain, and also on the shores of the North and East Seas. Everywhere they are considered as relics and products of the later stone age. Now India, Scandinavia, France and Great Britain are the chief homes of the Indo-German group of peoples. The mighty wave of migration of Indo-European peoples may also have touched Palestine and left behind them, for a longer or shorter period, a non-Semitic population. It is thus possible that the neolithic inhabitants of Palestine belonged to a race of European origin, the Celto-Libyan, which once occupied the entire coast of the Mediterranean.

The majority of scholars arrive at the conclusion that during the later stone age, i.e. from 3000 to 2500, the early inhabitants of Palestine were a tall, non-Semitic race who remained in the country all through the pre-Israelite Semitic occupation and whose power was ultimately broken only by the invading Hebrews. That these non-Semitic peoples disposed of their dead both by cremation and burial is no contradiction. The cremation cave at Gezer and the dolmens only tend to prove that they used concurrently both methods of disposing of the bodies of the dead. During the stone age the Indo-Germans had already adopted the custom of burying their dead.[1]

Apart from these megalithic monuments, the existence of an original non-Semitic race in Palestine is proved by the fact that many ancient names

---

[1] See Meyer, l.c., 736; see also Macalister, *History of Civilization*, 17; Kittel, l.c., 44, 46.

of places admit of no Semitic etymology and can only be explained as a survival of the pre-Semitic inhabitants.[1] One point, however, seems to be certain—that is, until further archæological researches prove the contrary, that the prehistoric inhabitants of Palestine belonged to a non-Semitic stock. Whether there were also Semites among them, especially in the south of Palestine, is a question which is still awaiting solution. These early inhabitants of Palestine knew not the art of metal-working, and used implements of bone and flint. They built no houses, but lived in the limestone caves which abound in many parts of the country. Under the rubbish of succeeding races and civilizations the excavators have discovered the buried remains of the skeletons and pottery of these early inhabitants of Palestine.

[1] Curiously enough there is also a Jordan in Crete, and the river Jordanus is mentioned by Homer. See *Expository Times*, xxi. 303.

CHAPTER III

THE SEMITES

The term "Semite"—The regions inhabited by the Semites—The Fertile Crescent—The home of the Semites—Winckler and Sprenger—Arabia, the home of the Semites—Climatic changes—Racial migrations—Four migrations—Babylonian, Amorite, Canaanite and Islamic—Sumerians and Akkadians—Professor Joseph Halévy—Semitic races in Palestine—Amorites and Canaanites—The term "Amorite" in the Old Testament—Amurru

THE term "Semite" is derived from Shem, the son of Noah (Gen. ix. 11). By Semites we understand a group of peoples known as Syrians (Aramæans) in the north, Babylonians and Assyrians in the east, Arabs in the south, and Phœnicians, Hebrews, Moabites, etc., in the west. The regions they inhabited or still inhabit are bounded by the Taurus, the Persian Gulf, the Indian Ocean, the Red Sea, Egypt and the Mediterranean. The whole area is called the "Fertile Crescent", because it forms a semicircle open to the south with the desert in front and the mountains behind.

For a long time there existed a divergence of opinion with regard to the cradle of the Semites, but it is now generally admitted that their original home was not Central Asia but the Arabian peninsula. "The home of the Semites", wrote Winckler, "is Arabia." His theory is based on geographical considerations, and on the fact that the purest Semites are even at present found in that land. Winckler also maintained that the migrations of the Semites were due to over-population and occurred periodically.¹ Already before Winckler, however, Sprenger had declared that "agriculturists do not become nomads and that all Semites are Arabs".²

Arabia is a land of barren and volcanic mountains, of broad stretches of dry, waste and unproductive soil and of wide areas of shifting sand, interrupted by an occasional oasis. Water, for the most part, being difficult to obtain, famine is always imminent.³ From time to time Arabia sent forth successive waves of immigration, for while producing immense populations it offers them but little sustenance. The nomads, therefore, who constitute the bulk of the population always quarrel for pasture, and when it becomes scarce the weaker are crowded out by the stronger and are compelled to seek new homes. The overflow penetrates into the adjacent more fertile lands. The Arabian peninsula is one of the great reservoirs of men on the face of the earth. It can breed and support vast masses of pastoral folk at certain times, i.e. when the supply of moisture is at its highest. At certain periods, however, in consequence of climatic changes, this moisture fails, and then the men and their flocks of sheep and goats must perish unless they escape. There is safety in numbers, and when the moment comes, the whole desert population, like a human

---

1 Winckler, *Geschichte Babyloniens und Assyriens*.
2 Sprenger, *Das Leben und die Lehre Mohammeds*, 1861, 241; see also Barton, *A Sketch of Semitic Origins*; A. Clay, *The Empire of the Amorites*, 28.
3 Doughty, *Travels in Arabia Deserta*, i. 56.

THE SEMITES

flood, breaks forth, penetrating into districts where there is pasture. These pulsations of climatic change apply to all the great inland steppes upon the earth's surface, periods of maximum moisture being followed by long intervals of comparative aridity.[1] These climatic changes are the cause of the great racial migrations issuing from Central Arabia which have given their inhabitants to many countries of North Africa and Western Asia, including Palestine.[2]

Four times in history the Semitic nomad tribes left the pasture lands of Northern Arabia and like a roaring wave spread over the neighbouring countries. The first migration was when the Semites overran the valley of the Tigris and the Euphrates and gained a position of pre-eminence in Northern Babylonia, where the Sumerian had finally to yield to the Semite. It is known in history as the Babylonian migration. The second great migration is that of the Amurru or Western Semites, which gave to Canaan its Semitic inhabitants. The third great migration is known as the Aramæan, which took place in the fourteenth century B.C. and resulted in the establishment of the kingdom in Syria with the capital Damascus. The fourth great Semitic migration took place in our own era, namely, in the seventh century, when Islam conquered Western Asia, Northern Africa and South-Western Europe.

Thus in the fourth millennium B.C. a Semitic

[1] E. Huntington, *The Pulse of Asia*, 1907.
[2] See also King, *History of Babylon*, 121.

invasion had taken place and occupied Mesopotamia, while in the third millennium another Semitic wave had swept over the country and modified the Semitic element there.

We do not know exactly when the Sumerian colonies first entered the Euphrates Valley, and it is even possible that Sumer and Accad are identical. Many scholars regarded, and still continue to regard, the Sumerian and the Semitic Babylonian on the cuneiform inscriptions as two different languages. The Sumerians are supposed to have invented the cuneiform system of writing.[1] Professor Joseph Halévy, however, was the first to maintain that the so-called Sumerian was only an allographic way of writing Semitic, and that the cuneiform system of writing was consequently an invention of the Semites. The scholars who have adopted this theory urge that no Sumerians are mentioned in the historical inscriptions as the Elamites, Kassites, etc., and that no such people ever existed.[2]

With regard to Palestine, until quite recently scholars were of opinion that before the invasion of the Hebrews the country was inhabited by *one* Semitic race. It is now, however, admitted that there were at least two kindred Semitic races, the Amorites and the Canaanites, from whom the Hebrews later on wrested the land of Palestine.[3]

---

[1] See L. W. King, *History of Sumer and Accad*.
[2] See Barton, l.c., 164–165.
[3] See Böhl, *Kanaaniter und Hebräer*, 1911; Procksch, *Die Völker Altpalästinas*, 1914.

THE SEMITES

In the early part of the third millennium a tide of migration, issuing from Arabia, swept over Asia and settled in Canaan, or, as it became known later on, Palestine. These Semitic nomads were of the same stock as those who had overrun Babylonia. They were more vigorous and taller than the neolithic inhabitants of Canaan, and either learnt the use of metal after having settled in the country or had brought the knowledge with them. They had no difficulty in gaining predominance over their predecessors, for with their flint arrows and knives the latter could not long fight against the new invaders, who availed themselves of weapons of copper and bronze. The Western Semites who had settled in Canaan intermarried with their predecessors, and produced a race whose speech was Semitic, but in whose veins ran also the blood of a lower dark-skinned Mediterranean race. Palestine, therefore, although Semites had existed there since the fourth millennium, assumed its proper Semitic character only towards the middle of the third millennium.

As for the much-discussed question of the terms "Amorites" and "Canaanites", two theories are possible. Either the Canaanites were the first Semitic inhabitants of the country, encroached upon and driven back by later invaders, the Amorites, or vice versâ. The Amorites were the earlier inhabitants and the Canaanite migration dislodged them. The Canaanites subjugated the Amorites or drove them into the hills, and the land derived its name from the conquering race.

In the Old Testament the Amorites are regarded as the pre-Israelite inhabitants of Palestine. The term "Amorite" is used as having an ethnic signification, but frequently it is also employed in a collective and geographical sense. The Canaanites are said to have lived along the coast, while the Amorites dwelt in the hills or on high ground (Joshua v. 1, etc.). In several passages of the Old Testament (Gen. xviii., xxii., etc.) the terms "Amorites" and "Canaanites" are used synonymously, and in some instances *all* the inhabitants of Palestine are designated as Amorites. Again, in Genesis xiv., the Amorites are said to have occupied the land to the extreme south, while at the time of the Hebrew invasion they are represented in the Old Testament as possessing only a portion of the land.

Now, while it is clear from Egyptian Records that as early as 2500 Palestine was inhabited by a Semitic race, it appears from Babylonian Records that this race was called Amurru, the Amorites of the Old Testament.[1] In Babylonian inscriptions "Amurru" is the name applied to the whole of Syria and Palestine in the time of Khammurabi. We now possess abundant evidence that the Amorites entered Babylonia at the same time as they entered Palestine, and that the result of their invasion was the foundation of the so-called first dynasty of Babylon.[2]

One may, therefore, justifiably hold the view that the Amorites were the first Semitic inhabitants of

---

[1] Meyer, *Geschichte des Altertums*, i. 465.   [2] Meyer, l.c., 465, 544.

Palestine, and that the Canaanites represent a later wave of immigration. These Canaanites were a kindred race of the Amorites, but not identical with them. The Amorites were driven northwards, while the later immigrants took possession of the coast and of the entire country.[1]

As early as the third millennium a mighty Amorite Empire, that of Amurru, existed in Syria, including Palestine. The Amurru or Amorites possessed a civilization of their own, and exerted their influence upon the peoples with whom they came into contact. According to some scholars, in opposition to the so-called Pan-Babylonian school, it was Amurru which not only furnished Babylonia with its Semitic inhabitants, but also influenced its civilization.[2] The migration termed the Canaanite, on the other hand, took place at about 1700 B.C. The appearance of the Canaanites may be connected with the advent of the Hyksos and their subsequent expulsion from Egypt.[3]

[1] See Kittel, l.c., 24 and 57; Böhl, *Kanaaniter und Hebräer*, 12.
[2] See A. Clay, *The Empire of the Amorites*, 19–20.
[3] See Paton, *Early History of Syria and Palestine*, 68, 70.

CHAPTER IV

THE BABYLONIANS IN PALESTINE

Mesopotamia—The Sumerians—Cuneiform writing—Kengi, the land of canals and reeds—The City-States—Ur, Larsa, Erech—Nippur and Lagash—North and South Babylonia—Palestine and Babylonia—Imperialistic tendencies—The state in the Nile Valley—Geographical position of Palestine—Trade-routes—The contest between Egypt and Babylonia—Civilizations of Babylonia and Egypt—Ur—Nina—King Lugalzaggisi—An Empire extending from the "rising to the setting of the sun"—The inscriptions of Lugalzaggisi—King Sargon of Agade—Gudea of Lagash—The Amorite migration—The rulers of Elam—Khammurabi—The fourteenth chapter of Genesis—Amraphel and Khammurabi—Babylonia's influence—Babylonian culture—Egyptian and Hittite influences—The Tell-el-Amarna letters—Gezer and Taanach—Egypt and Palestine—The language and script of the Canaanites

At the head of the Persian Gulf there is a valley known as Mesopotamia, i.e. between two rivers (Tigris and Euphrates). Here, several millenniums before the Christian Era, civilization began, due to a people known as the Sumerians. The majority of Assyriologists are of opinion that the Sumerians were the original inhabitants of the country, and that to them is due the invention of the cuneiform system of writing. Before the dawn of history, however, the Semites invaded the country and conquered the original inhabitants. Although the Semites had broken the Sumerian power long before any mention of them could be made in the inscriptions of Babylonia, the conquerors were, nevertheless, compelled at first to resort to the

THE BABYLONIANS IN PALESTINE

Sumerian script and writing, mingling with it their own idiom.[1]

At the dawn of history, more than four thousand years before the common era, the country was called Kengi, land of canals and reeds. Following up the course of the river northwards the aboriginal inhabitants built cities, such as Ur, Larsa, Erech, Nippur and Lagash. City-States, each with a king, were established, but they were continually at war with each other. The strongest cities or city kings extended their sway one over the other, trying to dominate them. Some of the city kings became masters of whole districts, while others even claimed the titles of "King of the World", or of the "four regions". As early as 4500 B.C. some of these kings claimed to be kings of Elam in the east and also of the lands of the Western Sea, i.e. of Phœnicia and Palestine. In about 4000 B.C. the Semites appeared in the central part of the valley, established themselves in the north and contested the valley with the Sumerians in the south. The battle went on until *c.* 2800 B.C., when the Sumerians disappeared. For more than two milleniums the city kings had not only practised a policy of unification, but had also made attempts to carry their authority beyond the borders of Babylonia to the shores of the Mediterranean and the northern mountains.

From a political point of view Palestine claimed the attention of Babylonia as the hinterland of the

---

[1] See Radau, *Early Babylonian History*, 145–147; Barton, *A Sketch of Semitic Origins*, 166–167.

Mediterranean coast of Phœnicia and as the highroad for commerce between Mesopotamia and the Nile land, the two centres of old Oriental political and cultural development. Every State on the banks of the Euphrates and Tigris with Imperialistic tendencies was, on account of its geographical position, compelled to make an effort and to reach the coast of the Mediterranean; in other words, it was bound to think of conquests and to extend its sway, not only over the Phœnician coast of the Mediterranean, but also over north-western Syria and Palestine, which it could not allow to remain in foreign hands. The same necessity existed also for the State formed in the Nile Valley. The Delta coast is too small and too poor in ports to be sufficient for the requirements of Egypt and Nubia. The Phœnician coast and the districts or countries situated behind it were thus predestined by their geographical position to become the apple of discord between Mesopotamia and Egypt. So it happened, not only in the old Orient but also in the Hellenistic period, as well as in the days of Napoleon I. and in more recent times. It must also be borne in mind that from the very earliest times of their existence both Egypt and Mesopotamia depended greatly on commercial intercourse, which made Palestine a transit region. In addition to the caravan routes from Damascus to Egypt, which touched only the fringe of Palestine, the land of Dan, several trade-routes led right through Palestine. One of these routes, the shortest, led from Damascus through

THE BABYLONIANS IN PALESTINE

the East Jordan district, the later land of Manasseh and Gad, passing over the Jordan north of the Dead Sea and crossing Southern Palestine through Jericho and Jerusalem and ultimately joining the caravan route a little to the north of Gaza. Thus in very ancient times, when travel overland was incomparably more important than travel by sea, Palestine as a transit land was of the highest importance for both the Powers on the Euphrates and Tigris and on the Nile. The result of such a situation was the constant contest between the two Powers for the possession of Palestine, a contest waged either by peaceful means or by the aid of arms. As long as a peaceful understanding existed between the two Great Powers the safety of the trade-routes could easily be ensured. Given, however, a state of hostility, Egypt was compelled to assert her power against either Babylon or Assyria in Palestine, which thus became a bulwark against the enemy advancing from the north. Politically the result was that an independent State in Palestine could only be formed with the permission of the two Great Powers, which could scarcely be expected at a time when they were in a flourishing condition. Only at a period of decline of the Great Powers could Palestine rise to an independent position and form a strong State, otherwise it was always compelled to submit and be tributary either to Egypt or to the Mesopotamian Power.[1]

[1] Cf. Jeremias, *Das alte Testament im Lichte des alten Orients*.

If, however, its geographical position had, so to say, doomed Palestine to a state of political dependence, from the point of view of civilization and culture it had its advantages. The products and results of civilization are carried, together with other merchandise, along the routes of commerce. Palestine, just on account of its geographical position, has thus from time immemorial been impregnated by the civilizations of both Mesopotamia and Egypt. Here, either in succession or simultaneously, the streams of culture which issued from the valleys of the Nile or the Euphrates and the Tigris discharged their roaring waves, fructifying the soil where the cradles of two great religions were destined to stand. Long before the first Hebrew had set his foot on the soil of Canaan a powerful settled population, the Canaanites, lived in Palestine, where they had developed a civilization of their own.

Politically, Babylonian influence had prevailed in Palestine since the fourth millennium B.C. The Sinaitic peninsula and Midian were known to the Babylonians under the name of Magan, and the copper-mines were coveted by the Babylonians just as they were coveted by Egypt, although the road from Babylonia was long and difficult, while it was only a short journey from Egypt.

At about 3200 Ur-Nina boasts of having brought cedarwood for his temples from the Lebanon. More certain, however, is the fact that King Lugalzaggisi kept up relations with the West. Lugalzaggisi, son of Ukush, the *patesi* of Umma, had made an end of the prosperous reign of Uru-Kagina and of the power of the City-State of Lagash in 2897. His empire, as has now been gathered from extant cuneiform records, extended "from the rising of the sun to the setting of the sun". "He straightened his path from the Lower Sea of the Tigris and the Euphrates to the Upper Sea."[1] This king ruled over Syria and Palestine, his kingdom extending from the Persian Gulf to the Mediterranean Sea. The name of Lugalzaggisi has been found on a number of fragments of vases made of white calcite stalagmite discovered at Nippur. By piecing the fragments together it was possible to obtain an almost complete copy of the records engraved upon each of them. Lugalzaggisi described himself as "King of the World", the god Eulil having bestowed upon him great power and granted him success. Two centuries later King Sargon of Agade,[2] who conquered Elam and Babylonia, extended his dominion over Amurru or the land of the Amorites, and exercised his control over Syria. Sargon, it has been maintained, was only a legendary ruler and his great deeds had no historical value, but the discovery of several of his inscriptions show that he had actually existed. His son, Naram-Sin, King of

[1] Hilprecht, *Old Babylonian Inscriptions*, ii. 53; Radau, *Early Babylonian History*, 135.
[2] Agade, no doubt identical with Akkad (Gen. x. 10), the residence of Sargon, was in the vicinity of Sippar, north of Babylon. When Sargon called himself King of Sumer and Akkad he meant South and North Babylonia.

the four quarters of the earth, maintained his father's empire in the West.

Other Babylonian records show that Gudea of Lagash carried on an extensive commerce with the West. "He opened his way from the Upper Sea to the Lower Sea and procured cedars which he brought down out of their mountains." Thus from 3000 to 2500 B.C. Syria and, evidently, Palestine were ruled by Babylonia, forming part of the Babylonian world.

At about 2500 a new wave of Semitic migration, pouring out of Arabia, spread over Babylon, and also overran the valley of the Nile and Canaan. This new wave of Semitic migration overflowed Western Asia from Babylonia to Egypt and from Syria to South Arabia. Ethnically the results of this immigration were not the same in Egypt and Babylonia as they were in Syria and Palestine. Whereas in the first two countries where the population was crowded the immigrants were quickly absorbed by the older race, the contrary was the case in Syria and Palestine. Here the invaders found no dense population, and, outnumbering the older inhabitants, they imposed on them their language and customs. Politically, however, the invasion had weakened Babylonia, so that she lost control over Syria and Palestine. In 2200 the rulers of Elam were the masters of Babylonia. They continued to extend their sway over the West. In 2150 Kudurmabuk called himself Adda, or ruler of the land of the Amorites. This

THE BABYLONIANS IN PALESTINE

statement coincides with a passage in Genesis (xiv. 1), according to which the Elamites ruled for twelve years over Palestine. A little later Khammurabi, who became ruler over the entire country of Babylonia, had no doubt extended his sway as far as the Mediterranean. The great similarity existing between the Code of Khammurabi[1] and the Law of Israel proves in any case to what an extent Babylonian culture had penetrated into Syria and Palestine.

In the fourteenth chapter of Genesis we are told that in the days of Amraphel four kings of the East, after the five kings of the vale of Siddim had rebelled against Elam, invaded the land and fought them. Hearing of their victory and that his brother's son Lot had been taken prisoner, Abraham, who was dwelling in the plain of Mamre, gathered his trained servants and his allies and pursued the kings Chedorlaomer, Tidal, Amraphel and Arioch as far as Dan. He routed them at night and pursued them unto Hobah, near Damascus. The fourteenth chapter of Genesis has been under fire for a long time. Scholars declared this narrative to be the work of a later Hebrew writer, who was anxious to magnify the martial valour of Abraham. Some maintained that he was the fictitious father of the Hebrew race, while others saw in him the name of a clan. Light, however, from the East has now dissipated the mist. The decipherment of the cuneiform inscriptions has compelled some of the

[1] See note 2 in Appendix.

Biblical critics to change their views. It is now being generally admitted that Amraphel, King of Shinar, is identical with the great Khammurabi, Ammurabi or Ammurapi. It was no new thing for the armies of Babylonia to make a conquest of the kings of the West. A precedent had already been set by Sargon and Naram-Sin, who, centuries before, had made expeditions into the West-land. The date of Khammurabi has been fixed by Assyriologists at 2250 or 2100 B.C. The latter date is borne out by a statement of Nabonidus, according to which Khammurabi lived seven hundred years before Burna-Buriash, who reigned about 1400 B.C.[1] As for Chedorlaomer, although no cuneiform records mention his name, it is, nevertheless, of genuine Elamite origin, a number of Elamite kings bearing names the first part of which consists of Kudur—such as Kudur-Nankhundi, Kudur-Mabuk. It does not enter within the scope of this book to discuss the question whether Genesis xiv. displays any accurate knowledge of early Babylonian history. For our present purpose it will suffice to say that at the beginning of Khammurabi's reign in Babylon Elam had extended its dominion over Western Asia, and the hegemony of Babylonia, carrying with it the rule not only of Mesopotamia but also of Syria and Palestine, was broken. This Elamite supremacy in Babylon as well as in the West did not, however, last very long. It was put an end to by Khammurabi, who, after casting off the Elamite

---

[1] See Rawlinson, *Inscriptions of Western Asia*, i. 69*b*, 4–8.

THE BABYLONIANS IN PALESTINE

yoke, united Babylonia under his rule. Babylon became the holy city of the ancient world, from which civilization went forth. The long reign of Khammurabi, which lasted fifty-five years, marked an epoch in Babylonia. From being a vassal of Chedorlaomer (Kudur-Lagh-ghamar) he became the ruler of a united and independent Babylonia. He cleared the country of its enemies, fortified its cities and built temples and walls. Along with the sovereignty over Babylonia the supremacy over Western Asia passed to Khammurabi, and he gained control over Syria and Palestine, as is proved by an inscription.[1]

Thus for centuries Babylonia had made conquests in Palestine. Her generals and officials lived in the country and administered her affairs. An active trade was being carried on between the Euphrates and the Mediterranean coast.[2] The influence of Babylonia in Palestine lasted for several centuries, continuing almost uninterruptedly from 2600 to 1950. Khammurabi had called himself king of the country of the Amorites as well as of Babylon, and so did his great-grandson. When Babylonia was conquered by the Kassites, Palestine recovered her independence, which, however, was of no long duration, for Thutmose III, of the XVIIIth Egyptian dynasty, made it a province of Egypt. Egyptian supremacy succeeded that of Babylonia: Palestine seems always to be doomed to have a

[1] See Winckler, *Altorientalische Forschungen*, i. 146.
[2] See Sayce, *Early Israel*, London, 1899, 73.

foreign master. All through history, for forty centuries one may say, its ruin has been and still is the want of union. In ancient times the cities of Canaan were continually fighting with one another, and even the strong hand of the kings of Egypt could not keep them at peace. When they united at rare moments it generally was under a foreign leader. The period of Hebrew occupation of Canaan is marked by constant quarrels and a want of union, while racial hatred and quarrels are still ruining Palestine now as they did forty centuries ago. Palestine is, indeed, the "Unchangeable East".

With regard to the much-discussed question of Babylonian spiritual and cultural influence in Palestine, it will be dealt with in a subsequent chapter on the Civilization of Pre-Israelite Palestine. For the present a few general remarks will suffice. Without denying the fact that Babylonian culture and civilization had penetrated deeply in Palestine, we are far from adopting the theories of the so-called Pan-Babylonian school.

The whole history of Palestine, political as well as cultural, is the result of its geographical position. Situated as is the country at a point where Asia and Africa meet, lying between the three civilized lands which dominated the ancient world, namely, Babylon, Egypt and the Empire of the Hittites, Palestine was from time immemorial under the influence of these three civilizations, Babylonian, Egyptian and Hittite. Too small a country, con-

THE BABYLONIANS IN PALESTINE

stantly an apple of discord between mighty empires, it was too poor to develop any civilization of its own, and for a comparatively short period only could it boast of an independent political existence. The only significance of Palestine lies in the fact that it has given the world two great religions.

As far as civilization is concerned Babylonians, Egyptians and Hittites have left their indelible marks. The great influence of the Babylonian civilization is amply proved by the Tell-el-Amarna letters.[1] Here we see a number of small Palestinian and Syrian princes who write to their sovereign, the Pharaoh of Egypt, not in his own language, but in that of the lands of the Euphrates, in cuneiform characters and in the Babylonian language. Babylonian seems to have been not only the diplomatic language of both Asia Minor and Egypt, but also the speech used in private correspondence. The new discoveries made at Boghaz-keui show that the kings of Asia Minor employed the Babylonian language. The fact that Babylonia had exercised a cultural influence in Canaan has been proved by excavations in Palestine itself, where clay tablets were unearthed at Lachish, Taanach and Gezer. The tablets found at Taanach, a Canaanitish town allotted to Manasseh and mentioned in the Song of Deborah (Judges v. 19), furnish evidence that the small rulers of the cities corresponded one with the other in Babylonian. Among the numerous objects in clay, dating from the earliest times, there is a

[1] See Chapter VI.

letter from the Prince of Megiddo, who wrote in Babylonian. Thus Babylonia had in the earliest times introduced into the land of Canaan its language and writing, its religion and *Weltanschauung*, its cult and its culture.

With the exception of those discovered at Gezer (seventh century B.C.) the tablets belong to the Amarna period, i.e. 1400 B.C. From the Amarna letters we knew already that Babylonian was the diplomatic language in the whole Orient, while the tablets discovered in Palestine itself, which contain the private correspondence of Canaanitish chiefs, tend to prove that the only script known in the country was the cuneiform system. There was no reason for the chiefs and petty princes of Canaan to avail themselves of the cumbrous cuneiform system had they been in possession of the alphabet. Thus both the Tell-el-Amarna letters and the tablets discovered in the country itself clearly prove how deeply Babylonian civilization and culture had penetrated into Palestine. Language and culture are indissolubly interwoven, the former being the characteristic trait of the latter. It shows to what an extent Palestine had been permeated by Babylonian culture if, in spite of the fact that the country was then an Egyptian province, the vassal princes, nevertheless, wrote in Babylonian and not in hieroglyphics.[1] The Tell-el-Amarna letters further show that the Egyptian scribes at the Court of the Pharaohs found it necessary to learn cuneiform

[1] Gressmann, *Die Ausgrabungen in Palästina*, 1908, 15.

so as to be able to correspond with the governors in Palestine.[1]

And yet it would be an exaggeration to imagine that Babylonia and Babylonia alone had exercised a cultural influence upon Canaan and that Egypt had left there no traces whatever. Recent excavations at Gezer and Taanach have proved the contrary. During the reign of Thutmose III the interrelations between Egypt and Palestine were of the closest. While on the one hand wealth was pouring into Thebes and the commercial cities of the Delta, Egyptian products were brought to Syria and Palestine, and together with the material goods came also the civilization of Egypt, its art, thought and mode of life. The policy adopted later on by Thutmose III shows that he had made some effort to Egyptianize Palestine, while the great religious reformer, Amenhotep IV, the heretic king, cannot have omitted to avail himself of every possible opportunity to introduce his ideas and his cult into his Asiatic dominions.[2]

It has been suggested that the Canaanites, who had neither script nor language of their own, had adopted those of Babylonia. In reality, however, the Canaanites not only had their language, but also their own method of writing it. As the Babylonians had long dominated Palestine, their system of writing was well known to the inhabitants, and there is no wonder that in order to express them-

[1] See Jastrow, *The Civilization of Babylonia and Assyria*, 1911, 116.
[2] See E. Schrader, *Die Keilinschriften und das Alte Testament*, 1903, 192.

selves in writing they had recourse to the Babylonian script and language, mingling their own idioms with those of the foreign tongue.[1]

Most scholars do not admit that the Western Semites had a script of their own prior to 1000 B.C., when the Phœnician alphabet is supposed to have been introduced. If, however, writing is not mentioned in the Old Testament until the time of Moses, it does not prove that writing was not practised. The fact that no evidence has been found does not entitle us to this conclusion. The absence among the antiquities is no proof whatever. They may have had a script of their own which they used upon perishable material. It is also quite possible, nay probable, that, while the Amarna letters are written in Babylonian, the language of the country was Canaanite. Side by side with the Babylonian words there are glosses in the tablets in the Canaanite language. No doubt the scribe was afraid that the reader would not understand the meaning of the word, or perhaps he was not quite sure that he had used the right word.[2]

To conclude, it seems probable that while the Canaanites availed themselves of Babylonian script and language, they may have had a language and even an alphabet of their own. Further, one may venture to express the view that side by side with the cultural influence of Babylonia, Egypt, as will be shown in subsequent chapters, has made her

---

[1] See Barton, l.c., 167.
[2] See A. T. Clay, *Light on the Old Testament from Babel*, 1907, 263.

influence felt in Palestine, both politically and spiritually. Not only from the banks of the Euphrates, but also from those of the Nile, currents of civilization had flowed into that strip of country which was destined to become the Holy Land of Jew and Christian.

CHAPTER V

FROM THE NILE TO THE JORDAN

Egypt covets Palestine—The copper-mines of the Sinai peninsula—King Hu—The annals of Palermo—Seneferu's military expeditions—The "Wall of the Princes"—King Khufu, the Kheops of Herodotus—King Sahure—"Hail, Sahure"—The tomb of Inti—The siege of a Semitic town—Meri-Ra-Pepi I—The land of the Herusha—The tomb of Una—The "sand-dwellers"—The land of the "Gazelle-nose"—The King's instruction for his son—The "Romance of Sinuhe"—Retenu—Description of Canaan—"Land handed me to land"—The tomb of Khnumhotep—Thirty-seven Asiatics visit Egypt—The arrival of Joseph's brethren in Egypt—The Kassite invasion—The Hyksos—The word "Hyksos"—The History of Manetho—Josephus—The kingdom of Mitanni—Confusion in Palestine—The expulsion of the Hyksos—The conquests of Ahmose—Amenhotep I and Thutmose II—The campaigns of Thutmose III—The inscriptions on the walls of the temple at Karnak—The battle of Megiddo—The defeat of the enemy—The fugitives drawn up by garments—The siege of the city—The booty of Thutmose—The capture of the prince of Joppa—The policy of Thutmose III—Palestine an Egyptian province

THE Babylonians never were the undisputed masters of Palestine in olden times, even when their sway over the country was predominant. The old empire of Egypt had made repeated efforts to reach the gold and ivory country of Punt southwards along the Red Sea, although it was more on account of trade and commerce than for the sake of annexation. There were, however, other districts and lands which Egypt was anxious to acquire, namely, Palestine and Syria, with the roads leading to Babylonia and the Far East. Palestine was, therefore, a country which was coveted by Egypt in the past, as it is being coveted by the European nations in the present. The Egyptian kings of the Ist dynasty enumerated by Manetho had already come into conflict with the Asiatic Semites on the Sinai peninsula. Here the Pharaohs exploited the rich copper and turquoise mines. The mines were, no doubt, worked by the Semites of Sinai long before the Ist dynasty of Egypt, but from the days of Hu, the seventh king of the Ist dynasty, they were in the possession of the Egyptians. On a rock at Wadi Magharah there is a scene sculptured representing Hu in the act of slaying a native. At the time of Lugalzaggisi, of Sargon and Naram-Sin, Egypt was ruled by the kings of the IVth and Vth dynasties, those great builders of the Pyramids (*c.* 2840–2680 and 2680–2540 B.C.). In the annals of Palermo we are informed that Seneferu, supposed to have been the founder of the IVth dynasty, undertook military expeditions and pushed his operations as far as Palestine. He worked the copper-mines of Sinai for the metal and the turquoises, and in a large relief cut on the rocks he is represented as slaying a Semite, a native of the country. He boasts of a victory over the Semitic nomads. Forty ships laden with cedarwood came from Syria. It was at that time also that the "Wall of the Princes", destined to check the invasion of the barbarians, was erected. Thus in those early days already Egypt seems to have tried to make her influence felt in Canaan or Palestine. The fact that Seneferu sent a fleet of forty vessels to the coast of Phœnicia to procure cedar beams from the Lebanon shows that Egypt was entering into commercial relations with the Asiatic territories. The merchant, however, is usually followed by the arrival of the soldier, and while the timber was being brought by sea the armies were advancing on land. King Khufu, the Kheops of Herodotus, the second king of the IVth dynasty, the builder of the Great Pyramid, is represented on a relief as slaying Bedouin captives. Sahure of the Vth dynasty undertook an expedition into the region of the Lebanon. In his pyramid temple various gods are shown in the act of leading Asiatics before the king, while on his tomb Syrian bears are represented.[1] A relief of Sahure represents the Egyptian fleet returning from an expedition to the Lebanon district, and the sailors are seen compelling the Semite captives to join in the shout: "Hail, Sahure, God of the living who witness thy beauty." A representation in the tomb of a Vth dynasty noble named Inti shows an attack of Egyptian warriors on the walled settlements of Semites, which seems to be in Southern Palestine. There is a vivid representation of the siege of one town. The Semites are in despair, while Egyptians are making a breach in the wall or are scaling it. The inhabitants are being massacred, while others are being led away as captives. Una, the last king of the Vth dynasty, also worked the copper-mines in Sinai, as also did Meri-Ra-Pepi I, the third king of the VIth dynasty.

[1] Borchardt, *Das Grabdenkmal des Königs Sahure II*, 18–2

This king sent expeditions into the interior of Palestine, and his triumphs are recorded in the inscription on the tomb of Una.[1] The king, we are informed, made war with the Asiatics (Amu) and Bedawin(Heru-Sha) and gathered an army of many thousands, placing Una at the head of this army. The army destroyed the land of the Herusha, cast down their strongholds and cut down their fig trees and their vines. It slew many thousands of the enemy and brought back a great multitude captive. Una was sent five times to chastise the "sand-dwellers". It seems that he landed north of Mount Carmel. "When it was said there were revolts because of a matter among the barbarians in the land of the Gazelle-nose, I crossed over in troop-ships with the troops, and I voyaged to the back of the height of the ridge on the north of the sand-dwellers." Thus in the olden times already Palestine was being conquered and ruled not only by Babylonia, but also by Egypt. After Naram-Sin's reign Babylonia must frequently have had to defend her possessions, and only Khammurabi succeeded in strengthening Babylonian power in Palestine. The Babylonians exercised their political authority only from time to time, and were compelled to strengthen it by frequent campaigns and invasions. What was permanent, as will be shown in a subsequent chapter, was the Babylonian civilization and culture which permeated Palestine and left its mark, not

---

[1] Birch, *Records of the Past*, ii. 1 ff.; Maspero, *Dawn of Civilization*, 419; Erman, *Zeitschrift für Aegyptische Sprache*, 1882, 1–29.

only under Egyptian supremacy, but also after Israel had established itself in Canaan.

In 2056 B.C. began the IInd dynasty of Babylon, and contemporaneous with it were the XIth and XIIth dynasties of the Middle Empire in Egypt. Although intercourse with Palestine and Syria must have been frequent, as is proved by the common use of Semitic names for imported articles, no conquests were as yet undertaken.[1]

There is, however, a document described by Gardiner[2] which shows that even the kings of the IXth and Xth dynasties never lost Palestine out of their sight. King Meri-Ka-ra, King of Upper and Lower Egypt, left an instruction for his son, wherein he advised him to build fortifications on the northern frontier of Egypt against the Palestinians. He further described the nature of the country, which he seems to have visited. It is just the opposite of the rainless and flat land of Egypt, namely, humid and mountainous. "Behold the wretched Amu, toilsome is the land wherein he dwells; a land troubled with water, made difficult by many trees, its ways made toilsome by reason of the mountains."

Anyhow, portions of Palestine had been tributary to Egypt before the VIth dynasty, although there is evidence enough to show that during the political weakness of Egypt, from the VIIth to the XIth dynasties (2500–2000 B.C.), independent States had in the meantime arisen in Syria. On the one hand, the monuments of the XIIth dynasty make no

---

[1] Müller, *Asien und Europa*, 34.   [2] *Journal of Egyptian Arch.* 1914.

mention whatever of Egyptian influence in Palestine, while, on the other hand, in the *Romance of Sinuhe* the writer speaks rather respectfully of the Syrian princes.[1]

The story of the adventures of Sinuhe, very popular throughout the Theban period, is still considered to be, if not one of the world's masterpieces of literary skill, at least a classic of Egyptian lore. Sinuhe, a noble of high rank, was in the western Delta with the army commanded by the young co-regent, Prince Usertsen (Sesostris), engaged on a campaign against the Libyans. Laden with spoil, the army was returning home when a message announcing the death of the king reached the camp. Usertsen, without making the news public, immediately returned to the royal palace so as to establish himself firmly on the throne of Egypt before any pretender could precede him. Sinuhe, however, who had been standing by, overheard the news and was seized with fear. Being a son of the king, he no doubt felt that, as the old king had died, the heir might see in him a possible rival, and that his life would consequently be in danger. He therefore fled the country, making Palestine his goal. He informs us in his tale that he fled to Upper Retenu, which was the term used for Palestine during the Empire.[2] He went south, slept the night in an open field, then got to Gizeh,

---

[1] Jeremias, *Das Alte Testament im Lichte des Alten Orients*, Leipzig, 1904, 193.
[2] See Müller, *Asien und Europa*, 38–47.

where he ferried himself over the river. In his flight Sinuhe reached the "Wall of the Princes", the famous wall built by Amenemhat I to keep off the Bedouin encroachments. He spent the day hiding in a thicket, and during the night passed the fortifications and reached Petny in the early morning, and then came to the island of Kem-wer, where he fell in with some Bedouins, who treated him kindly, and he remained with them for some time. He then set forth towards Byblos and came as far as Kedem.

"Land handed me to land. I set forth to Byblos, I pushed on to Kedem." Here he spent half a year. Then Enshi, son of Amu, prince of Upper Retenu, Canaan proper, took him, married him to his daughter and gave him a tract of land called Yaa, rich in fruits of all kinds and growing both wheat and barley, where Sinuhe lived for many years as the prince's chief counsellor and general. He performed mighty deeds, killed a giant in dual combat and led the Syrians to battle against the princes of the nations. Sinuhe, however, longed for Egypt, and having received a letter of pardon from the Pharaoh, returned to Egypt following the "way of the land of the Philistines".[1]

In this tale Sinuhe, on the one hand, describes the pastoral life which at that time prevailed in Southern Palestine. The chief possessions of the people among whom Sinuhe dwelt were cattle and flocks of sheep and goats. "Figs were in it and grapes, and its wine was more abundant than its

---

[1] A. H. Gardiner, *Notes on the Story of Sinuhe*, Paris, 1916.

water. Plentiful was its honey, many were its olives, all manner of fruit were on its trees. Wheat was in it, and limitless cattle of all kinds." The life of the tribe with whom Sinuhe lived was evidently not nomadic or half-nomadic, usual on the borderlands between cultivation and desert. Some authors maintain that the conditions of life which Sinuhe describes, and which the author must have seen and been familiar with, were those of the half-nomadic tribes of Southern Palestine, and not of Northern Syria. It is further evident from the story that a lively interrelation existed between Egypt and Asia. "The messenger who fared north, or south to the Residence, tarried with me."

The tale of Sinuhe is preserved in a hieratic papyrus of the Middle Kingdom, now in Berlin.[1] It is the oldest account of pre-Israelite Palestine, and appears to be essentially true to fact, showing the superiority of the Egyptians of the time over the Bedouins of Palestine.[2]

Although the story is only a romance, it nevertheless gives us what may be considered to be a correct picture of Palestine about 2000 B.C. The land which, according to the Old Testament, was "flowing with milk and honey", was indeed a "good land", a prosperous country. It was rich in vine, figs and olives, in wheat and barley, in milk and cattle. "The wine was more plentiful than water,

---

[1] See Breasted, *Ancient Records of Egypt*, 1906, i. 233.
[2] Erman, *Aus den Papyrus des Königlichen Museums zu Berlin*, 20–29; Maspero, *Contes populaires*; Petrie, *Egyptian Tales*.

and there was abundance of game." It is also evident from the tale that the Bedouin tribes in Palestine stood in close relation with the land of Egypt and that the sheikhs sometimes visited the Court of the Pharaohs. These Asiatic Bedouins were, therefore, not at all barbarians.[1]

A glimpse of the state of Canaan under Usertsen II (or Senusert) can also be obtained from the figures inscribed on the walls of the tomb of Khnumhotep, prince of Oryx Nome. There, thirty-seven Asiatics, men, women and children, under the leadership of Abishua, are depicted. They are arrayed in true Syrian garments and are carrying Canaanite weapons. Their whole appearance suggests that they are people of importance. The painting, which was supposed by some to represent the arrival of Joseph's brethren in Egypt, conveys the information that Canaan possessed in those days much barbaric wealth, that the people knew the arts of weaving and of fashioning arms. It shows that the rich Palestinian merchants affected a high degree of magnificence and even of culture.[2]

Thus politically Palestine in those days seems to have witnessed a continual struggle between Babylonia and Egypt for the supremacy of the country. There was a constant clash between the influences of the Great Powers on the Euphrates and the Tigris and on the Nile. It was natural that the

---

[1] Jeremias, l.c. 195; see *Frazer's Magazine*, 1865, 185–202; *Records of the Past*, vi. 131–50.
[2] See Chabas, *Etudes sur l'Antiquité historique*; Knight, l.c., 81.

power and influence of Egypt should have made itself felt more in the south of the country while Babylonia exercised her sway over the north. During the earlier period, however, the balance had been in favour of Babylonia, the latter being ethnically related to the Amorites. When the central power of the Great Empires weakened, the petty local potentates at once raised their heads, made an effort to shake off the foreign yoke and established small principalities or City-States of their own. "One country handed me to another", writes Sinuhe. This assertion tends to prove that the petty kinglets of Canaan lived in harmony among themselves, united by their common suffering and misery and their common opposition to the foreigner.

Such was the state of Palestine about 1700 B.C. At that time a new invader appeared in Babylonia and overran the country. From the steppes of Central Asia came a non-Semitic race, somewhat akin to the Tartars of a later age, the Kassites or Kashshu. Their leader, Gandash, founded a new dynasty, which retained power in Babylon for six centuries. These new invaders were totally different from the Babylonian Semites as well as from the Indo-Germanic races, and at first the conquerors ruled over the subdued population with fire and sword and destroyed the ancient civilization. The invaders naturally had the advantage over the old subdued population. Agum II, one of the early rulers of the Kassite dynasty, styles himself

King of the Kashshu and Akkadu, that is, of the Kassites and the Accadians. The Kassite invasion had not the same results as the Semitic invasion before. After two centuries of possession the barbarous Kassite mountaineers were imbued with the Babylonian spirit and culture. The difference between conquerors and conquered disappeared, for the invaders had fallen under the spell of the ancient civilization of Babylon and adopted its language and customs. Once more the Semitic type reappeared, and the gods of Babylon, Marduk and Sapanit, who had been exiled to Khani in Media, were brought back, and the splendour of their temples was restored.

Contemporaneous with the rule of the Kassites in Babylonia was that of the Hyksos in Egypt. The kings of Egypt in those days were too weak to defend the country against attacks of foes, and the country was soon invaded by a host of nomad Semitic tribes. The Asiatic hordes, in search of a home, had chosen Egypt as their goal, overrun the valley of the Nile and held the country in subjection for several centuries.

The word "Hyksos" is derived from the Egyptian Hiku-Khasut, which means "princes of the deserts", the appellation for Bedouin chiefs. These Bedouins were also called Shasu, or shepherds, since the chief occupation of the Arabs living on the borders of Egypt was the breeding and herding of flocks of sheep. The invasion of the Hyksos has been traced to the confusion caused by the first appearance of the Indo-Europeans in the Near East. Babylon was taken and sacked by the Hittites, who carried off their spoil to Anatolia. The Kassites had founded a new dynasty, which lasted six centuries. Other Aryan tribes entered Mesopotamia farther north. The State of Mitanni was set up in the region of the Khabur and Balikh. A confusion was caused in Syria and the native population flowed into Palestine. Then waves of the mingled population passed the Princes' Wall, and flowed into and overwhelmed Egypt. From the Sinai Peninsula, from Syria and Palestine, the invaders came, and the native Egyptians were powerless to resist them. They settled in the Delta, and very soon became masters of Lower Egypt. Manetho calls them the Hyksos, and they became known as the Shepherd Kings. They were also known as "Aat-t", that is, "foreigners", "rebels", "invaders" or "pestilence". It will be interesting to quote the passage from Flavius Josephus, who gives a description of the invasion of the Hyksos after the Second Book of *The Egyptian History of Manetho*:

"There was a king of ours, whose name was Timaus. Under him it came to pass, I know not how, that God was averse to us, and there came, after a surprising manner, men of an ignoble birth out of the eastern parts, and had boldness enough to make an expedition into our country, and with ease subdued it by force, yet without our hazarding a battle with them. So when they had gotten those that governed us under their power, they afterwards burnt down our cities, and demolished the temples of the gods, and used all the inhabitants after a most barbarous manner; nay, some they slew, and led their children and their wives into slavery. At length they made one of themselves king, whose name was Salatis; he lived in Memphis, and made both the upper and lower regions pay tribute and left garrisons in places that were most proper for them. He chiefly aimed to secure the eastern parts, as, foreseeing that the Assyrians, who had then the greatest power, would be desirous of that kingdom and invade them; and as he found in the Sethroite Nome a city very proper for his purpose, and which lay upon the Bubastite channel, but with regard to a certain theologic notion was called 'Avaris', this he rebuilt, and made very strong by the walls he built about it, and by a most numerous garrison of 240,000 armed men whom he put into it to keep it. Thither Salatis came in summer-time, partly to gather his corn and pay his soldiers their wages, and partly to exercise his armed men, and thereby to terrify foreigners. When this man had reigned 13 years, after him reigned another, whose name was Beon, for 44 years; after him reigned another, called Apachnas, 36 years and 7 months; after him Apophis reigned 61 years, and then Jonias 50 years and 1 month; after all these reigned Assis 49 years and 2 months. And these six were the first rulers among them, who were all along making war with the Egyptians, and were very desirous gradually to destroy them to the very roots. The whole nation was styled 'Hycsos', that is Shepherd Kings."[1]

The Hyksos are generally considered to have been a race of Semitic origin and related to the Amorites. Before invading Egypt they had conquered Palestine, where they built Hebron. In Egypt their favourite residence was Tanis (the Biblical Zoan), and their stronghold was Auaris, on the eastern frontier.[2] The invaders are said to have been barbarians, to have spread "terror, ruined the temples, massacred the priests, and burned the cities of Egypt—in a word, to have ruled in the midst of desolation over a terror-stricken nation. Some scholars, however, are of opinion that the Shepherd Kings, on the contrary, furthered commerce, and that under their rule art and literature and civilization in general flourished both in Palestine and in Egypt.[3]

Now, whatever the attitude of the Hyksos was at the beginning of their invasion, it is clear that Egyptian culture proved too strong for them and that they ultimately fell under its spell. In course of time the former chiefs of savage hordes became in almost every respect like the Ancient Pharaohs. Once more art and literature began to flourish. The difference of religion alone prevented an

---

[1] See Josephus; see also E. A. Wallis Budge, *A Short History of the Egyptian People*, 67–68.
[2] See Müller, *Mitteilungen der vorderasiatischen Gesellschaft*, 1898, iii. 22.
[3] See Paton, l.c., 70.

amalgamation of the invaders and the conquered race as in Babylon.

Contemporaneous with the Kassite and Hyksos invasions there took place the migration into Mesopotamia of a new race known as that of the Mitanni. They established a kingdom of their own, which in time became very powerful and was considered as one of the four Great Powers, the other three being Babylon, Egypt and Assyria.

The result of all these migrations and invasions with regard to the political fate of Palestine was important. It was natural that the establishment of the Kingdom of Mitanni in Mesopotamia and the rule of foreigners both in Egypt and Babylon should have its effect in the country where both Babylon and Egypt were trying to gain supremacy.

The Kassite dynasty of Babylonia was rather weak, and from the sixteenth century onwards Babylonia was no longer able to oppose Egyptian control over Palestine. The only strong power the Egyptians had to face were the Hittites in North-eastern Syria, who offered resistance to the advance of Egyptian arms. Babylonia, aware of her weakness, no longer contested the possession of the strip of land along the Mediterranean, and was content to live in peace with her old rival, Egypt.

In consequence of her calamities Babylon had lost her grasp over Palestine, as her foreign dependencies could not long survive the invasion. For a time Babylon, cut off from her trade with the

West, lost her commercial prosperity. Released of the Babylonian dominion, the petty States of Syria and Palestine made themselves independent, but, unable to form a political confederacy, fell into a state of confusion, which soon afterwards helped Egypt to establish her supremacy.

For two hundred and sixty years the Hyksos had ruled over Egypt, while the native Egyptians were secluded in the south and the heirs of the Thebes Pharaohs still survived as princes of Thebes. Religion, as has been pointed out, and pride of race had prevented a fusion between the two peoples, and it came about that when the power of the conquerors began to decline the hopes of the princes revived and their pretensions increased. They defied the invaders and established a native dynasty in Upper Egypt. The strangers were pushed back as far as the north-eastern corner of the Delta until their favourite residence, Zoan (Tanis), fell into the hands of the Pharaohs of Upper Egypt. The former conquerors were dislodged from point to point, and the rulers of the ancient race regained the possessions of their forefathers. The Shepherds at last retired to Auaris, the stronghold built by their first monarch. Besieged by the Egyptian prince, Ahmose, the stronghold was ultimately taken and the Hyksos were expelled from Egypt and driven back to Asia. Ahmose founded the XVIIIth dynasty, and it was he who renewed the policy of the former Pharaohs, namely, the conquest of Palestine, a policy extending over three centuries, and made Palestine an Egyptian province.

It is quite probable that at first Ahmose had no intention whatever to inaugurate a policy of conquest in Asia. He had at first only continued his war against the enemy. The latter had retired to Sharuhen, later on in the portion occupied by the tribe of Simeon (Joshua xix. 6). Bent on revenge, or anxious to make a return of the Hyksos impossible in the future, Ahmose pursued them and inflicted on them a crushing defeat. In order to do his work thoroughly he pursued the Hyksos, who had retired to the north. Success produced ambition and thirst for conquest in the heart of the Pharaoh, and the New Empire once more energetically raised its claims to Syria and Palestine. The struggle for freedom and the war of independence crowned with success soon became a war of conquest. Amenophis (Amenhotep) I, the son of Ahmose I, also led expeditions into Asia, and Thutmose I, his successor, penetrated to the Euphrates as far as Carchemish. He returned to Thebes laden with booty. Under Thutmose II the Asiatics thought of throwing off the Egyptian yoke, and they were in open revolt when his son, Thutmose III, became lord of Egypt. Thutmose III ruled from 1501 to 1447, and under his reign Babylon lost her power over Canaan, which became an Egyptian province, the whole country having been reduced to subjection. Flushed with his victories, Thutmose thought of conquest and revenge. As the Asiatics had done unto Egypt, so would he do unto them. His predecessors, the Pharaohs of the former dynasties, had only paid flying visits to Canaan and simply collected tribute. From time to time Egyptian troops had raided the trade-routes and penetrated to the Negeb and the Shephelah, but the Pharaohs had not really endeavoured to establish a permanent rule in Palestine. Thutmose III decided otherwise.

Upon the walls of the Temple of Amen at Karnak are inscribed the annals of the campaigns of Thutmose III. This document gives us a glimpse of the state of Syria and Palestine in those days. Northern Palestine and the whole of Syria had evidently once more rebelled against Egypt, although Southern Palestine had remained loyal Thutmose assembled an army at the city of Zalu, on the border of Palestine, set out across the desert and in nine days reached Gaza. This well-known city of the later Philistine territory was generally loyal to Egypt and the last to revolt. Marching northward by the regular caravan route along the coast, the Egyptian army reached the plain of Sharon at the fortress of Yehem. Here the King of Egypt assembled his troops and commanded that a discourse be pronounced to them, informing them of what he had learned. Word had, namely, been brought to him that at Maketa (the Biblical Megiddo), in the plain of Esdraelon, the King of Kadesh had assembled a coalition, the chiefs of all the countries from Naharina or Northern Syria, the land of the

Amorites and Northern Palestine, and had decided to defend Megiddo against the forces of Egypt. Now an army marching from Sharon to Esdraelon could be led along one of the three passes. The first, leading over Mount Aluna, was narrow and very dangerous. The foe encamped on the overhanging heights was sure to attack the army before the rear would come up. The second pass, leading from Ziftha to Megiddo, and the third, some miles to the south, the circuitous road from Aluna to Taanach (the modern Tannuk), were much safer. It seems that the king's generals were in favour of caution and advised him to choose the longer but safer road. Thutmose, however, announced that he would show no cowardice, but proceed by the more dangerous pass. Those who were ready to brave the danger could follow him, while the others might take the other road. The result was that the soldiers enthusiastically declared that they would join their king and follow him wherever he went. The passage was effected safely, although there were skirmishes with the enemy.

The sun declined when the whole army was in the valley, and the king therefore commanded his forces to prepare for battle on the following morning. The Egyptians, occupying a rather advantageous position on the slopes overhanging Megiddo and Taanach, encamped for the night. On the morning the line of battle was formed; the right wing of the Egyptian army occupied the hill above Taanach to the south of the water of Qina, while the left extended to the north-west of Megiddo. The enemy was in the plain below.

"The south horn of the army of His Majesty was at the shore (of the lake of Kaina), the northern horn (extending) to the north-west of Maketa, His Majesty being in the midst of them, the god Amen being the protection in his active limbs. . . ."[1]

The king himself went forth, riding "in a chariot of gold, distinguished by the decorations, like the terrible Horus, the Lord who makes things, like Mentu Lord of Uas, like his father Amen-Ra."[2]

The Egyptians advanced, presenting a solid, orderly front, and as soon as they came into close quarters with the enemy, the latter was stricken with terror and in a panic fled from the field of battle. The Syrians hastily retreated towards Megiddo, leaving behind them their chariots of silver and gold.

"His Majesty prevailed over them before his army. They saw His Majesty prevailing over them, they fell prostrate on the (plains) of Maketa on their faces through terror, they left their horses, their chariots of gold and silver which drew them, and were drawn in their clothes to that fortress."[3]

The gates of Megiddo, however, had been shut by the townsmen, who were afraid of opening them to their protectors in presence of the Egyptians. Luckily for the fugitives the Egyptian soldiers, instead of pursuing the enemy, turned their atten-

---

[1] S. Birch, *Records of the Past*, ii. 43.
[2] Ibid.   [3] Ibid.

tion to the booty left behind. In their eagerness to escape the Syrians had left behind their chariots of gold and silver, their horses, the furnishings and arms. The spoil detained the Egyptian soldiers and gave the enemy time to escape. The fugitives were drawn up by garments or ropes lowered from the battlements.

"The men shut up in that fortress took off their clothes to haul them up to that fortress."[1]

The King of Egypt now issued a command to lay siege to Megiddo. Within its walls were shut up all the kings of the country, "the capture of the city would be as the capture of a thousand towns".

"Inasmuch as every Chief of the countries and places came rebellious into it, inasmuch as the fulness of a thousand fortresses is the fulness of Maketa."[2]

Trees in the neighbourhood were cut down and a thick wall was erected surrounding the town. This wall was called by Thutmose Ramen-Kheper-Uah-Sat (Holder of the plains of the Sati).

Megiddo was the key of Syria from a military point of view, and it was natural that the enemy should resist with obstinacy. The siege, however, lasted only a few weeks, as the Syrians, threatened with hunger, submitted. The city surrendered, and the rebellious chiefs came forth to sue for peace, prostrating themselves before the victorious Pharaoh.

On his return to Egypt Thutmose ordered the

[1] S. Birch, *Records of the Past*, ii. 43.   [2] Ibid., 44.

names of the cities he had captured to be engraved on the pylons of the Temple of Karnak.[1] One hundred and nineteen towns are mentioned, many of which are familiar to us. In this list we read the names of the following places: Beroth, Beth-Amoth, Gilboa, Cana, Hazor, Laish, Kadesh, Megiddo, Merom, Kinnereth and the ports of Acre, Beirut, Joppa and Damascus, the rulers of which Thutmose had shut up in Megiddo.

The fall of Megiddo was followed by the surrender of almost the whole of Syria and Palestine. Tribute was brought from all sides, and the entire harvest, amounting to 150,000 bushels of grain, was placed at the disposal of the Pharaoh before he left the plain of Jezreel. Carrying a vast amount of booty, the army returned home.

During his campaign against Megiddo Thutmose III carried away to Egypt vast spoil. The booty included animals and skins, metallic works of art, jewels, temple furniture and warlike material. The list enumerated by the Pharaoh of Egypt mentions horses and foals, bulls and cows, buffaloes and goats. There were also 280,000 bushels of corn from the plain of Megiddo and also mulberries, figs and vines; incense, honey and logs of sycamore, silver statues and an ark of gold.[2]

The booty further included two hundred suits of

---

[1] See *Proceedings of the Soc. of Bibl. Arch.*, 1893, 255; Müller, *Asien und Europa*, 157 ff.; Maspero, *Recueil des Travaux*, ii. 48–56, 139–150; *Quarterly Statement* of the Palestine Exploration Fund, 1876, 90–97, 140–148.
[2] *Records of the Past*, ii. 45.

armour of brass or bronze, bows and swords with precious stones, shekels or weights of gold, lapis-lazuli, gold dishes and vases; a sceptre of gold inlaid with jewels and tables studded with gems; there were further chairs of gold, ivory, ebony and cedar inlaid with gold.[1]

Thutmose undertook no fewer than seventeen campaigns into Palestine,[2] and finally established his rule over the country. Canaan and Syria recognized the overlordship of Egypt, and Egyptian domination left its mark also on the civilization of the country. Recent excavations in Palestine have now brought to light many traces of Egyptian influence by the side of that of Babylonia. The spade of the excavators has turned up at Gezer and at Tell-el-Safi (Gath) numerous objects such as scarabs of Thutmose, jar-handles, vases, beads and amulets, which were either direct importations from Egypt or the work of Syrian artisans.[3]

There is a romance, composed during the XIXth dynasty, which relates the capture of the city of Joppa by Tehutia, a general of Thutmose III. The general trapped the prince of Joppa and, having felled him with the stolen royal sceptre, he introduced five hundred soldiers sealed up in large jars. He captured the city and led away the inhabitants bound in ropes.[4]

---

[1] See Conder, *Syrian Stone Lore*, 1886, 40–41.
[2] Hall, *Ancient History of the Near East*, 244.
[3] *P.E.F.Q.*, 1904, 224; ibid., 1899.
[4] Maspero, *Contes populaires*, 149; Goodwin, *Soc. Bibl. Arch.*, iii. 340; see also Chabas, *Mélanges Egyptol.*, 1862, 42–54.

A new policy was now inaugurated and a permanent Government was established. Canaan was ruled by tributary princes, vassals of the Pharaoh, or by viceroys appointed by him. Fortresses, garrisoned with Egyptian troops and commanded by Egyptian officers, were erected all over the country. The representatives of the king had to maintain order, collect the annual tribute and quell disorder or rebellion.

Thutmose, however, was clever enough to understand that he could not govern the country otherwise than by the native chiefs, and he consequently reappointed all the kings and chieftains who had submitted to his authority after the fall of Megiddo. The Pharaoh was also careful not to interfere in the existing laws and customs of Palestine and Syria. The king, nevertheless, tried to place at the head of the petty kingdoms and countries of Canaan those chieftains of whose loyalty he had been able to convince himself. He furthermore caused hostages to be taken among the sons of the rulers of the subdued provinces. These hostages were brought to Egypt, where they were educated, all due honour being paid to their rank. Imbued with love of Egyptian learning and ideas, and having adopted Egyptian manners and customs, they were then sent home, there to occupy the places vacated in consequence of either death or rebellion. Although the loyalty of the provinces was thus being assured, additional precautions were taken. The native rulers were surrounded by Egyptian officials, whose duty it was not only to advise but also to observe the ruler. All the Egyptian officials were answerable to a general governor appointed by the king.

What the king mostly insisted upon was the payment of the annual tribute. A refusal, or even a delay in the payment of this tribute, was tantamount to rebellion, and was severely punished. The princes of Syria and Canaan paid the tribute rather reluctantly. Bearing the Egyptian yoke very unwillingly, they were never slow in seizing an opportunity to rebel.

New expeditions were undertaken by Amenhotep II, Thutmose IV, Amenhotep III and Amenhotep IV, under whose reign the Egyptian Empire fell to pieces, while her power in Syria was threatened by the Khati or Hittites under Subbiluliuma and by the Khabiri nomads. As for the internal state of Palestine, the Egyptian records enable us to reconstruct a picture of the country in the first half of the second millennium B.C. It was evidently a civilized country with cities and fields, kings and soldiers, scribes, artisans and traders, with temples and priests. There were chariots and horses, nomads and brigands.

CHAPTER VI

THE TELL-EL-AMARNA AGE

The successors of Thutmose III—A new danger in Palestine—The Hittites and the Khabiri—King Subbiluliuma—Professor Winckler at Boghaz-keui—The Tell-el-Amarna letters—The correspondence of Amenhotep III and Amenhotep IV—The heretic king—Akhetaten or "Horizon of Aton"—The governors of Palestine—The letters of Abdi-Khiba—The Khabiri and the Hittites—Babylon and Egypt—Pharaoh and the Kings of Mitanni—Burnaburiash, King of Babylon—Violence done to his servants—A diplomatic passport—Geography of Palestine—Jerusalem or Urusalimu—The tomb of Haremheb—The campaigns of Ramses I—Seti I and Ramses II—Egypt and the Hittites—The treaty of peace—A document written on silver tablets—A picture of Canaan—*The Travels of a Mohar*

THE successors of Thutmose III were unable to maintain the dominion of Egypt in Asia. On the one hand, the princes of Canaan, feeling the weakness of Egypt, whose power was falling to pieces, once more made an attempt to shake off the Egyptian yoke. The native governors were fighting with one another or intriguing with the enemies of Egypt. On the other hand, a new danger had arisen in the appearance of the Hittites and the Khabiri. This happened during the reigns of Amenhotep III and Amenhotep IV (fourteenth century B.C.).

The greatest trouble in Palestine at that time was the encroachment of the Hittites upon the north. They were an Anatolian people, who had at first probably formed a collection of semi-independent tribes, loosely united by the bond of common extraction. About this time, however, there arose among them a powerful chief, named Subbiluliuma, who was king of a city named Kussar. His reign lasted for forty years (1385–1345 B.C.). Having succeeded in binding the Hittite clans into a strong confederation, he began a career of conquest and created a powerful empire. His capital city was called Hati, east and north of the river Halys, in the district later known as Cappadocia. The site of this ancient city is marked by the modern village of Boghaz-keui, where Professor Winckler discovered the Hittite archives, consisting of a number of tablets written in cuneiform, either in the Babylonian or in the Hittite language.[1]

Much light has been thrown over this period by the discovery of the Tell-el-Amarna letters. In 1887 about three hundred baked clay tablets in cuneiform characters and in the Babylonian language were unearthed in a chamber to the east of the palace of Amenhotep IV, eighty miles south of Cairo, near the modern Tell-el-Amarna. The mounds of Tell-el-Amarna mark the site of a city once called Akhetaten, built by Amenhotep IV, one of the later kings of the XVIIIth dynasty. This king, a heretic, having broken with the Theban priesthood of Amon, abandoned his capital, Thebes, and his royal residence and determined to found a new city which would be devoted exclusively to the service of the new solar god, Aton. He suppressed the existing religion of Egypt and introduced a sort

[1] Cf. C. T. Burney, *Israel's Settlement in Canaan*, London, 1917, 60.

THE TELL-EL-AMARNA AGE

of monotheism associated with the worship of the solar disk. Deserting Thebes, he selected a site for his new city at about one hundred and sixty miles above modern Cairo, on the east bank of the Nile. Here he built Akhetaten or Horizon of Aton, now known as Tell-el-Amarna (a corruption of El-Amarieh), which had a brilliant though brief existence.[1] To his new capital Amenhotep transferred the official records of his own and his father's government as well as the diplomatic correspondence with the kings of Babylon, Assyria and Mesopotamia, and also the dispatches from Egypt's Asiatic provinces, Syria and Palestine.[2]

The letters written to the Pharaoh of Egypt by the vassal kings of Canaan throw a light over the history of Palestine from the close of the fifteenth to the latter half of the thirteenth century B.C. The writers make it clear that Egypt was losing her hold over Palestine and that the governors of the different cities could not stand against the growing power of the Hittites and the Khabiri. Egypt's Asiatic dominion was crumbling away, although Babylon in the meantime held aloof, preoccupied rather with commerce than with conquest. Reference is made in these letters to the Hittite power in the north of the mountains of Anatolia. The Hittites, who were coveting the plains of Northern Syria but were not strong enough to challenge Egypt directly, were trying to stir up a rebellion in Canaan among the native princes. The latter, therefore, especially

[1] Petrie, *Tell-el-Amarna*, 2.   [2] Breasted, l.c., ii. 391.

those who had remained loyal to the King of Egypt, implored the Pharaoh for help, attempting at the same time to quell rebellion and hold back the invading tribes.

The most interesting letters in this collection, as far as the history of Palestine is concerned, are, therefore, those written by the governors and vassal princes of Canaan. They informed the Pharaoh of the invasion of the Khabiri, and appealed to him to send troops or come himself and crush the enemy. "The land of the King has revolted." The Pharaoh is advised "to send hired soldiers", for "if there be no hired soldiers the land of the King will go over to the Khabiri." "The cities of Askalon, Gezer and Lachish have supplied the enemy with provisions." The most interesting letters are those written by Abdi-Khiba, which we will give *in extenso* after the translation of Knudtzon. Abdi-Khiba was the vassal king of Jerusalem and a rival and enemy of Su-Ardata.

"To the King, my lord, the Sun-god," he writes, "thus speaks Abdi-Khiba thy servant. At the feet of the King, my lord, seven times seven I prostrate myself. Behold, the King has established his name at the rising of the sun and the setting of the sun. Slanders have been uttered against me. Behold, I am not a governor, a vassal of the King, my lord. Behold, I am an ally of the King, and I have paid the tribute due to the King, even I. Neither my father nor my mother, but the arm of the Mighty King, established me in the house of my fathers.

There have come to me as a present thirteen (women) and ten slaves. Seti, the Commissioner of the King, has come to me: twenty-one female slaves and twenty male slaves captured in war have been given into the hands of Seti as a gift for the King, my lord, as the King has ordained for his country. The country of the King is being destroyed, all of it. Hostilities are being carried on against me as far as the mountains of Seïr and the city of Gath-Karmel. All the other governors are at peace, but there is war against myself, since I see the foe, but I do not see the tears of the King, my lord, because war has been raised against me. While there is a ship in the midst of the sea, the army of the mighty King shall conquer the countries of Naharaïm (Nahrima) and Babylonia. But now the Khabiri are capturing the fortresses of the King. Not a single governor remains among them to the King, my lord, all have perished. Behold, Turbazu, thy military officer, has been killed in the great gate of the city of Zelah. Behold, Zimrida of Lachish has been murdered by the servants who have revolted against the King. Jephthah Hadad, thy military officer, has been slain in the great gate Zelah. May the King, my lord, send help to his country. May the King turn his face to his subjects and may he dispatch troops to the country. Behold, if no troops come this year, all the countries of the King, my lord, will be utterly destroyed. They do not say before the face of the King, my lord, that the country of the King, my lord, is destroyed, and that all the governors are destroyed, if no troops come this year. Let the King send a commissioner, and let him come to me, even to me, with auxiliary troops and we will die with the King, our lord. To the secretary of the King, my lord, speaks Abdi-Khiba, thy servant. At thy feet I prostrate myself. Let a report of my words be laid before the King, my lord. Thy loyal servant am I."

"To the King, my lord, thus speaks Abdi-Khiba thy servant: At the feet of the King, my lord, seven times seven I prostrate myself. Let the King know that all the provinces have united in hostility against me, and let the King send help to his country. Behold, the country of the cities of Gezer, of Askalon and of Lachish have given them food, oil, and whatever they wanted; so let the King send troops against the men who have committed a sin against the King, my lord. If troops come this year then there will remain both provinces and governors to the King, my lord, but if no troops arrive, there will remain no provinces or governors to the King, my lord. Behold, neither my father nor my mother has given this country of the city of Jerusalem unto me; it was the arm of the mighty King that gave it to me, even to me. Behold, Melehiel and the sons of Labai have given the country of the King to the Khabiri. Behold, O King, my lord, be just towards me as regards the Babylonians. Let the King ask the commissioners whether they have acted violently. They have taken upon themselves a very grievous sin. They had abundance of food, abundance of oil and abundance of clothes until Pauru, the commissioner of the King, came up to the country of the city of Jerusalem, and Adai revolted, together with the garrison. Let thy favour be towards me; I have sent to the King, my lord, 5,000 prisoners and tribute-bearers. The caravans of the King have been robbed in the field of Ajalon. Let the King, my lord, know that I am not able to send a caravan to the King, my lord, according to thy instructions. Behold, the King has established his name in the country of Jerusalem for ever, and he cannot forsake the territory of the city of Jerusalem. To the Secretary of the King, my lord, Abdi-Khiba, thy servant, at thy feet I fall: I am thy servant, make a clear report of my words to the King, my lord, that I am the vassal of the King. Abundance of good fortune to thee! Thou hast performed deeds I cannot enumerate against the men of the land of Cush.

"To the King, my lord, thus speaks Abdi-Khiba thy servant. At the feet of the King, my lord, seven times seven I prostrate myself. What have I done against the King, my lord? They have slandered me before the King, my lord, and said that Abdi-Khiba has revolted from his lord, the King. Behold, it is neither my father nor my mother who exalted me in this place; it was the arm of the King that made me enter the house of my father. Then why should I have committed a sin against the King, my lord? By the life of the King, what I said to the Commissioner of the King was this: Why dost thou love the Khabiri and hate the governors? Continually are they slandering me before the King, my lord, because I say that the provinces of the King are being destroyed. Let the King, my lord, consider, since the King, my lord, has established the garrisons which have taken the fortresses. May the King send help to this country. The cities of the King, my lord, are lost which Elimelech is destroying, even all the country of the King; so let the King, my lord, send help to his country. I said unto myself: I will go down to the King, my lord, and shall I not see the tears of the King, my lord? But the enemy is so strong against me and I have not been able to go down to the King, my lord. So let the King incline his face towards me and send a garrison to me, and I will go down and see the tears of the King, my lord. When the Commissioner departed I said: The provinces of the King are being destroyed, but thou dost not listen to me. All the governors are destroyed, and no governor remains to the King, my lord. May the King turn his face to his men and send the troops of the King, my lord. The Khabiri have wrested all the provinces and no provinces remain to the King, my lord. If troops come this year the provinces of the King, my lord, will be preserved; but if no troops come, then the provinces of the King, my lord, will be destroyed. To the Secretary of the King, my lord, Abdi-Khiba, thy servant: make a clear report of my words to the King, my lord, that the provinces of the King, my lord, are being destroyed by the enemy."

We thus see that the native princes or governors who wrote the letters were subject to Egypt. The authority of the land on the Nile was declining, and the requests of the governors and their appeals for reinforcements were disregarded. The Hittites and the Khabiri were making inroads into the land, and a number of the princes were in league with them, while others, though protesting their loyalty, were only waiting for an opportunity to shake off the Egyptian yoke. While in the letters written from the north of Palestine the invaders are referred to as the Hittites, in the south it was "the Khabiri". In a word, the picture we gain from the Amarna letters is of Palestine in a state of restlessness. The Canaanite princes had realized that the Government in Egypt was weak in consequence of the disaffected priesthood whom King Amenhotep IV had alienated by the introduction of a new religion. Even those princes who wished to remain loyal to Egypt soon gave it up as hopeless. The same disturbed condition prevailed in the north of Palestine, as is shown by the letters of Rib-Abda, governor of Byblos.

It is not certain whether Amenhotep, busy with his religious reforms, did send any troops against the Khabiri, but it is clear that the latter extended their sway over Southern Palestine. For a time Egypt lost her Asiatic Empire. Both the Khabiri and the Kheta, or Hittites, continued to grow in power. Egypt made no attempt to save the situation and the result was that in the confusion many of the princes of Canaan shook off the Egyptian yoke and became independent. Politically Egypt had failed to establish a firm government in the country, while from the point of view of civilization she had not been able to eradicate or even supersede the influence of Babylonia, which continued even while Palestine was an Egyptian province.

As for Babylon, she no longer disputed the power of Egypt in Palestine, while friendly relations existed between Egypt and the Asiatic kings. A number of the Amarna letters are addressed to the Pharaoh of Egypt by the rulers and kings of Mitanni, of Babylonia and Assyria and of the Hittites. The relations entertained seem to have been friendly. The letters written by Burnaburiash, King of Babylon, are particularly interesting. In one of his letters Burnaburiash wrote as follows to the King of Egypt: "In the time of Kurigalzu, my father, the Canaanites unitedly wrote to him: Against the border of the land we will march and make an insurrection. With thee we will make an alliance. My father wrote them as follows: Seek no alliance with me. If you are hostile to the King of Egypt, my brother, and make an alliance with one another, I will surely come and plunder you, for he is in alliance with me. My father, for the sake of your father, would not listen to them."[1] The same Burnaburiash even complained to King Amenhotep IV because

[1] Knudtzon, *Die El-Amarna-Tafeln*, No. 7.

his representatives had been molested by the people of Acco at Hinnatouni (the Biblical Khannaton, Joshua xix. 14). "Canaan", wrote the Kassite king, "is *thy* land and its kings are *thy* servants. In *thy* country I have suffered violence. Suppress thy subjects and give me back the money they have taken from me, destroy the men who have killed my servants and revenge their blood. If thou wilt not act thus, then they will start to kill either my caravans or thy own messengers, communication between us will have to be stopped, and the Canaanites will fall away from thee."[1]

An interesting document mentioned in the letters of Amarna[2] furnishes a further proof of the power which Egypt had hitherto exercised over Palestine, a power which was acknowledged by the kings of Asia. It is a sort of diplomatic passport handed over by a king of Asia to one of his envoys who had to traverse the land of Canaan. It runs as follows:

"To the Kings of Canaan, the servants of my brother" (the King of Egypt being the brother and the kinglets of Canaan his servants). "Behold, I have sent Akia, my representative, to the King of Egypt, my brother, to express my sympathy to him" (condolence on the occasion of the death of Amenhotep III). "Let no one stop him. Send an escort to accompany him and bring him safely and speedily to Egypt." It clearly proves the utter dependence of the kinglets and princes of Canaan on the Pharaoh of Egypt. The Asiatic potentate

[1] See Knudtzon, l.c., viii. 25–34.   [2] See Knudtzon, No. 30.

requests them to protect his envoy, who carries a message to their sovereign.

Through the Amarna letters we also gain a good many data for the geography of Palestine. About one hundred and fifty cities are mentioned in these letters, and of these about one hundred have been identified. The letters also throw much light upon places mentioned in the Old Testament and reveal an interesting fact with regard to Jerusalem. The name of the city prior to the time of David was supposed to have been Jebus, but from the Amarna letters it is evident that the older name was Jerusalem, which is spelt "Urusalimu." The district of which Jerusalem was the capital extended as far as Carmel of Judah. Thus the name of Jerusalem, or Urusalimu, the city of the god of peace, was already known in Babylonian times.

Under Amenhotep IV, Northern Syria was conquered by the Hittites, while the Phœnician towns had made themselves independent, Southern Palestine remaining under the sovereignty of Egypt. It was in these days of confusion that many Palestinians took to the hills or sought refuge in Egypt. From the tomb of Haremheb, the general of Amenhotep IV, we learn that starving Asiatics poured into Egypt, begging the Pharaoh for protection. "They have been destroyed and their town laid waste, and fire has been thrown into their grain. Their countries are starving, they live like goats of the mountain. A few of the Asiatics,

THE TELL-EL-AMARNA AGE

who knew not how they should live, have come to beg a home in the domain of the Pharaoh."

Affairs in Palestine remained almost unchanged during the reign of Ramses I, but his successors, Seti I and Ramses II, partly restored Egyptian prestige in Syria and Palestine. In his campaigns Seti followed the method of Thutmose III. He marched first through Southern Palestine, then moved northwards and subdued the Lebanon district. Having secured the Phœnician coast and thus established a connection with Egypt by sea, so that reinforcements and supplies might be landed at one of the Phœnician harbours, he moved upon the interior of Syria, especially the Orontes Valley. The war was now continued between the mountains of Lebanon, and here, for the first time, Egyptians and Hittites met in battle.[1] Among the cities which Seti captured he enumerates those of Beth-Anoth, Kirjath-Anab, Januamu and Kadesh on the Orontes. The struggle against the Hittites was continued by Seti's son, Ramses II. The Hittites had grown in power and upon Ramses II had fallen the task of checking their advance and thus saving Egypt's conquests in Asia. The conflict between Egypt and the Hittites lasted for nearly twenty years. Ramses II, who is supposed to be the Pharaoh of the oppression,[2] has left in his inscriptions a detailed account of his victory over the Hittites at the battle of Kadesh. Here the Hittite king Kheta-Sar had mustered his allies from

[1] See Breasted, l.c., iii. 40.   [2] See Note 3 in Appendix.

various lands and threatened to put an end to Egypt's power in Syria and Palestine. A fierce battle was fought, but was far from being decisive. Although the Hittites were routed and Kheta-Sar himself had been compelled to seek asylum in Kadesh, the losses on the side of the Egyptians were so heavy that Ramses II accepted the proposal of a truce. Eight years later a revolt broke out in Galilee, and a year later the Shephelah, bordering on the Egyptian frontier, followed the same example. In spite of the various victories of Ramses the Hittites remained unconquered, and a treaty was finally concluded between Egyptians and Hittites, putting an end to their struggle in Canaan. By this treaty, written on silver tablets, the Babylonian original of which has been discovered by Winckler at Boghaz-keui, on the site of the old Hittite capital, the Kheta promised not to invade Egypt, while the Egyptians bound themselves not to make inroads into Hittite territory. The latter retained power over Canaan as far as the Carmel.[1]

In this famous treaty the two parties promised friendship and concord between one another. "It was the agreement of the great Prince of Egypt in common with the great King of the Hittites that the god should not allow enmity to exist between them, on the basis of a treaty." They promised one another good friendship and a good understanding for ever. "He shall be my ally; he shall be my friend. I will be his ally; I will be his friend for

[1] See Breasted, l.c., iii. 163.

THE TELL-EL-AMARNA AGE

ever. Never let the great King of the Hittites invade the land of Egypt, and never let the King of Egypt overstep the boundary of the land of the Hittites." From this unique document, which was engraved on the walls of Karnak and the Ramesseum, it is evident that Egypt's power in Asia had greatly diminished. The Hittite Empire was as strong as the Egyptian and the two rulers treated on equal terms. They pledged themselves not only to abstain from hostilities in the future, but also to render aid one to the other if ever one of the allies was attacked by a third party.[1]

Of Canaan in the days of Ramses II we possess a picture in a satirical literary production, the curious and interesting papyrus, Anastasi I. It is the work of a *littérateur* of the age (Ramses II, 1275–1208) and is called *The Travels of a Mohar*. The author draws a picture of Canaan and sketches an imaginative tour through Palestine. Once more, after the conquests of Thutmose III, interrelations between the land on the Nile and Canaan were renewed and communication between the two countries became easy and frequent. For a short time, after the fall of the XVIIIth dynasty, the intercourse between Egypt and Palestine had been interrupted, but it was soon resumed. Once more messengers and travellers went to and fro, from the Nile to the Jordan and from the Jordan to the Nile. *The Travels of a Mohar* is a kind of geographical

---

[1] *Records of the Past*, 1st series, iv. 25; *Mitteilungen der vorderasiatischen Gesellschaft*, 1902; see also Sayce, *The Hittites*.

romance and was composed during the reign of Ramses II. It is the facetious story of the adventures which a tourist travelling to Palestine would, in the opinion of the author, meet with. The author of *The Travels of a Mohar* pretends to have travelled in Palestine and to have traversed the country from end to end, although he had never left Egypt. He knew, however, so much of the country, and was so well acquainted with its geography, that to a stay-at-home friend he could display his intimacy with things and places in Palestine. With a rare skill he compiled not only a guide-book to the geography of Palestine in the fifteenth century B.C., the age of the XIXth dynasty, but he also painted a picture of Canaan, describing the anarchy and confusion prevailing there and showing what an unpleasant and dreadful place it was.[1]

The reign of Ramses II was the last glimmer of Egypt's greatness, and under his successor, Mineptah, the decline and fall of the empire began. A Syrian like the Hyksos of old gained power in Egypt. It is from this time that the history of Palestine becomes linked up with that of the Israelites.

[1] See Chabas, *Voyage d'un Egyptien en Syrie, en Phénicie, en Palestine, au XIV siècle avant notre ère*, 1866; also Sayce, *Petriarchal Palestine*, 209; see also Lauth, *Moses der Ebraer*, Munich, 1868.

PART II
PALESTINE, THE PROMISED LAND OF THE HEBREWS

CHAPTER VII

THE CONQUEST OF CANAAN AND THE AGE OF THE JUDGES

Impossibility of independent national existence in Palestine—"The Canaanite was then in the land"—Phœnicians and Amorites—Egypt and the Hittites—Palestine an easy prey to invaders—Penetration by the Israelites—"Ibrim"—Moabites, Ammonites, Midianites and Edomites—The name "Hebrew"—Abraham—Nomadic Semites—"A wandering Syrian was my father"—Abraham and Khammurabi—The famine in Canaan—The pasture land of Goshen—The inscription on the tomb of Haremheb—Israel in Egypt—Ramses II builds Pithom and Raamses—The oppression of the Hebrews—The danger of an invasion—Mineptah, the Pharaoh of the oppression—The anti-alien policy of Egypt—The Khabiri—The Israel stele—The Apuru—The Exodus—Israel in the desert—Kadesh-Barnea—Moses and Joshua—The crossing of the Jordan—The Judges—Shophetim and Suffetes—The early Judges—Sisera—Deborah, Israel's Joan of Arc—The Song of Deborah—Jael, the wife of a Kenite—Barak—Jerubbaal—The raids of the neighbours—Gideon—Jephthah of Gilead—The tragic story of Iphigenia—The tribe of Dan—The image set up at Laish—The conquest of Canaan—National and religious bonds—The migration of tribes—The Philistines—The clamour for a monarchy—Samuel, the Warwick of early Israel—Saul

In the previous chapters we have seen that the development of an independent national existence in Palestine was almost impossible on account of the geographical position of the country. The rivalry between the two empires on the Euphrates and the Nile continued for centuries. At first, Babylon had extended her sway over the country; when her power had been weakened, in consequence of the Kassite invasion and of the ascendancy of Assyria, it was the turn of the Empire on the Nile to assert its domination and for a period extending over

250 years Palestine was more or less an Egyptian province. The land was inhabited by the Canaanites, who were "then in the land", as well as by other tribes. The Egyptians found in Palestine a welter of peoples, a native Semitic population with aboriginal pre-Semitic elements.

On the coast were the Phœnicians, seafarers and wealthy traders. The Amorites were settled inland, and to the north of them were the Hittites, who were descending not only into Syria, but also into Southern Palestine. We have seen how Egypt established her authority over Palestine and how she subsequently lost it. The Empire on the Nile could not hold the country permanently. On the one hand, the Hittites proved dangerous rivals, while the invading barbarians from the northern coasts of the Mediterranean were causing trouble in Palestine. It was a time of restlessness and confusion. The motley crowd of peoples occupying the country and the weakness of the controlling power, the Empire on the Nile, rendered Palestine an easy prey to invaders. It was at this moment that Israel appeared on the scene, prepared to conquer the land of Canaan.

The penetration of the Israelites into Palestine or Canaan was a return to a land where once their forefathers had dwelt, a return to an ancestral home. To the Semites, wandering about in the desert and drifting into Canaan, belonged also the "Ibrim." "Ibrim"[1] meant "men from the other side

[1] See Note 4 in Appendix.

of the river", which was originally applied to the Euphrates, but afterwards also to the Jordan. We do not know exactly to what branch of the Semitic family the Hebrews belonged, but there is no doubt that they were closely related to the Aramæans. To the Hebrews were also related the Moabites, Ammonites, Ishmaelites, Midianites and Edomites, who were afterwards called Idumæans. Long before the conquest of Canaan by the Israelites, a branch which had separated itself from the common Semitic stock had settled in Canaan. The name "Hebrew" is mentioned in the Bible for the first time in connection with Abraham (Gen. xiv. 13), where the legendary life of the Patriarch is told.

In the light of the newly discovered monuments the narratives in the Bible concerning Abraham and the other patriarchs gain reality and may be considered as records of historical events.[1] The way which Abraham is said to have travelled is the same road along which the numerous nomadic Semites of antiquity had marched when they decided to pass from the nomadic to the settled life. The ancestors of the Israelites were nomads, wandering about in the desert with their flocks, leading the life of the Bedouins of the present day. "A wandering Syrian was my father" (Deut. xxvi. 5). The Hebrews had first wandered into the eastern point of the "fertile crescent", which is now known by the name of Mesopotamia, and

[1] See Note 5 in Appendix.

Abraham is said to have dwelt in Ur-Kasdim, Ur of the Chaldees. From here Abraham and his clan proceeded to the town of Harran, thus approaching the frontiers of Syria, where other Semitic groups were already dwelling. Wandering farther and farther, Abraham and his clan came to the Negeb, or the south of Palestine. Here the wanderers were drawn into great political movements, which occurred during the reign of Khammurabi. The appearance of the group of the Hebrews in Southern Palestine may thus be dated in the twentieth century B.C.

Then a great famine broke out in Canaan, and the Hebrews, harassed on all sides and death staring them in the face, decided to fold their tents and to seek other abodes. Towards 1400 B.C. these Hebrews, from whom the nation of Israel was to develop later on, left their old home in the south of Palestine and wandered to the neighbouring pasture land of Goshen. There was food and drink in abundance in the lands of the Nile, both for the men and the flocks. The migration of nomadic Semites from the desert to the fruitful land of the Delta was a regular occurrence in those days, and the Egyptian Government was quite ready to offer hospitality to the immigrants. An inscription on the tomb of Haremheb, general of Amenhotep IV, who afterwards ascended the throne of Egypt, informs us of one of these immigrations. "Asiatics whose lands are suffering from famine and are living like goats on the hills; whose children are crying for bread . . . some of

THE CONQUEST OF CANAAN

these Asiatics who did not know how to live have come and asked the Pharaoh to grant them a home. Their dwellings have been occupied by others and destroyed, fire has been set to their grain."

Thus the Hebrew shepherds struggled into the pasture land of Goshen, where they settled down. Here they remained what they had been before, namely, shepherds of sheep and goats. Living on Egyptian soil and surrounded by the culture and civilization of Egypt, they nevertheless retained their patriarchal mode of life, their old habits and their language.[1] For some time the immigrants were allowed to live in peace, the Egyptians being too busy with their own affairs and engaged, as has been related above, on a desperate struggle against the Hittites. The great Ramses II, however, having in the end concluded a treaty with the Hittites, had now leisure to turn his attention to the administration and the internal organization of the country. Seized with the desire to build palaces and huge temples as monuments to himself and the gods of Egypt, he built, as we read in the Bible, on the road leading to the Sinai peninsula, the cities of Pithom (house of Atom) and of Per-Raamses (house of Ramses). For his huge constructions Ramses required numerous slaves, and without hesitation he took the Semitic shepherds into slavery. The oppression of the Hebrews served also another purpose. It was calculated to crush the

[1] Wellhausen, *Israelitische und Jüdische Geschichte.*

spirit of the aliens and to prevent them from joining the enemy in case of war. The danger of an invasion was always near, and Egypt had never forgotten the disastrous period of the Hyksos. In fact, Mineptah, the son and successor of Ramses, had to fight against Palestinian and Syrian invaders, as is related in the famous Israel stele.

The enslavement of the Hebrews was thus, after all, a natural occurrence and in keeping with the policy of the Egyptian Government. Ikhnaten had introduced into Egypt, not only the Asiatic faith, but also the influence and even the dominion of Asiatic officials. The XIXth dynasty adopted another policy, a national policy. The rulers of this dynasty decided to prevent a repetition of the Hyksos period, and all Asiatics who were still dwelling in Egypt had to be kept down and made incapable of ever becoming formidable. In modern times Governments pass laws and restrictions against aliens, but in the ancient Orient they resorted to enslavement. The means employed may differ, but the causes are identical. They are the result of religious and race hatred, of a grudge against the foreigner. Everything foreign was tabooed in Egypt, the Babylonian language was no longer employed and the national party triumphed.

Thus the free sons of the desert, the nomads who considered themselves to be aristocrats in comparison to the peasants living on the land, suddenly found themselves reduced to a state of slavery. To work on the brickfields of Egypt under the lash of

THE CONQUEST OF CANAAN

hard taskmasters was unbearable to those men used to freedom and independence. Eagerly they longed for deliverance from bondage. The oppression lasted for many years, and the slaves were clamouring for permission from the Pharaoh to leave the country. They were anxious to rejoin their brethren in the desert, where they could sacrifice to their god. Pharaoh hardened his heart, but a favourable opportunity soon offered itself which the Hebrews under their leader Moses soon seized. After the death of Ramses II the power of Egypt had begun to crumble. Hordes of barbarians had once more begun to invade the Delta land, and great distress prevailed in the country. In the midst of this confusion the Hebrews got away. The exact time of the Exodus of the Israelites from Egypt is still a point upon which opinions differ. When the Tell-el-Amarna letters were discovered, scholars were inclined to place the time of the Exodus in the fifteenth or sixteenth century B.C. The Khabiri mentioned in the Amarna letters were supposed to have been the Hebrews who were invading Canaan. Scholars such as Hommel and Böhl were in favour of this earlier date, and their arguments were based, not only on certain passages in the Bible, but also on the contents of the famous Israel stele discovered by Flinders Petrie in 1896.

The Israel stele is an inscription engraved on a slab of granite, by order of Mineptah, son of Ramses II, and placed in a temple at Thebes. It is a song of triumph over the defeat of the invaders from the Greek seas and the Libyans, which took place in the fifth year of the King's reign. It is for the first time that the name of Israel is mentioned in inscriptions. "The chiefs", we read in the inscription, "are overthrown and speak only of peace. None of the Barbarians lifts up his head. Waste is laid the land of the Libyans, the land of the Hittites is tranquillized; captive is the land of Canaan and utterly miserable; carried away is the land of Askalon; overpowered is the land of Gezer, and the land of Innuam is brought to naught. The Israelites are spoiled so that they have no seed, and like the widows of Egypt the land of Khar has become."

Israel therefore, it was argued, had already left Egypt by that time and settled in Canaan. Against this date other scholars invoked the fact that the narrative of the Bible with regard to the construction of Pithom and Ramses is corroborated by Egyptian papyri, where the Apuru are said to have been employed to carry stones for the construction of the city of Ramses-Meri-Amon. The Apuru may, of course, not be identical with the Hebrew-Israelites, but the fact nevertheless remains that Asiatics were made to work under the lash of Egyptian taskmasters, as is described in the Bible. The majority of scholars are therefore in favour of the later date as far as the Exodus is concerned, namely, the end of the thirteenth century B.C. (between 1230 and 1215). As for the mention of Israel in the Israel stele, it must be borne in mind that the Israelites

THE CONQUEST OF CANAAN

are the only people enumerated which had no locality. They may already have fled from Egypt but not yet reached Canaan, wandering about in the wilderness, near Kadesh-Barnea, where they joined other tribes related to them.[1]

After their escape from Egypt the Israelites, instead of marching towards the near coastland of the Philistines, took the way of the desert. On the one hand, they were not prepared to face a fight with the powerful and warlike inhabitants of Canaan, while, on the other, it was necessary at first to join their brethren, the clans and tribes related to them, who were either wandering in the desert or dwelling in the south of Palestine, for several tribes related to the Hebrews had remained in Canaan. It was out of the question for the moment for the escaped labourers on the brickfields of Egypt to venture a direct attack upon Canaan. Their goal from the very beginning was this country, the land once inhabited by their ancestors, the Promised Land, as it became known later on, but they were not yet prepared to conquer it. Long slavery and oppression had broken their spirit, crippled their bodies and crushed their souls. Many a time and oft, during their wanderings in the desert, faced by hardships and misery, the escaped slaves yearned for the "fleshpots of Egypt". More than once the desert-wearied tribes clamoured for a return to the land of slavery, and their courageous and God-inspired leader had to use

[1] See for discussion on date of Exodus Note 6 in Appendix.

all his authority to keep them from running back.

One of the most important halting-places of the tribes wandering in the desert was Kadesh-Barnea (to be distinguished from Kadesh on the Orontes), a plain surrounded by hills. In all probability, this rich oasis must have served as a centre for the dispersed tribes. From Kadesh-Barnea, and no doubt soon after the Exodus, spies were sent out to explore the land of Canaan. The report was unfavourable and the account of the land "evil". It frightened the timorous generation who had escaped from bondage, and the panic-stricken mood of the tribes convinced the leader that the moment had not yet come for an invasion of a country where they would have to fight against the fierce and hardy inhabitants. The slave generation would have to die off and a tougher, more courageous and desperate generation to arise.

For forty or thirty-eight years the Israelites wandered about in the desert, suffering hardships innumerable, before they could muster up courage enough to march into Canaan. They passed into Transjordania and were at the gates of Canaan. Moses died in the meantime in the plains of Moab, and upon his disciple Joshua fell the task of conquering the Promised Land. The great warrior for freedom was no more, but his spirit remained alive among his people for ever. The Israelites crossed the Jordan at a point near the city of Jericho, the first place to succumb to the onset of the conquerors.

THE CONQUEST OF CANAAN

Gilgal was selected as the central camp, a base from which a further campaign was organized against the Canaanites. The Israelites had to fight for every inch of the land, the tribes fighting their way separately into the country and settling in different localities. A powerful coalition had in the meantime been formed in Northern Palestine under the leadership of Jabin, King of Hazor in Galilee, but the enemy was prevented from joining the southern princes, thanks to the rapidity of Joshua's movements. With his army, the leader fell upon Jabin, taking him by surprise. The Canaanites were routed and fled in all directions. The battle near the waters of Merom (or Maron) was the crowning achievement of Joshua's life. It gained for the Israelites the possession of Northern Palestine. Joshua died at the age of 110 years, and before his death the Tabernacle was erected at Shiloh in Mount Ephraim, which became the national centre of the newly conquered territory (Joshua xviii. 1).[1]

The conquest lasted several centuries, and the former inhabitants of Palestine, the Canaanites, were far from being exterminated or completely repulsed by the Israelites. A considerable portion of the land was still in the possession of the enemy, and there were large tracts which the foot of the invaders had not yet touched. In many districts the conquerors had succeeded in getting a footing without, however, gaining supremacy. In central Canaan the towns and strong fortresses were still

[1] See Note 7 in Appendix.

in the possession of the old inhabitants. Thus the plain of Jezreel, girded by the strongly fortified cities of Acco to Beth-Shean and the entire coast plain, the Shephelah, remained in the possession of the Philistines and the Phœnicians. The Israelites had conquered the mountains of Ephraim with the exception of towns like Jebus and Sichem, and the Negeb or the south of Palestine. For the rest of the country they had still to fight, and for three centuries the invaders had to contend with powerful enemies on all sides. This age, before a monarchy was finally established, is known as the age of the Judges.

The Age of the Judges

In the Bible the Judges or "Shophetim" are the deliverers raised up from time to time; valiant chieftains who placed themselves at the head of the tribes in times of need. They remind us of the Suffetes of Carthage, but differed from the latter inasmuch as they were not elective. Although the judges enjoyed a moral influence on account of their successful exploits and military achievements, their powers and authority were never recognized by the whole nation, nor were they ever invested with any regular power or dignity.

The Canaanites who had recovered from the effects of the early victories of Israel renewed their efforts, trying hard to repulse the invaders and regain possession of their native land and their old

THE CONQUEST OF CANAAN

supremacy. On the other hand, the nomad peoples like the Moabites, Midianites and Amalekites were pressing on Israel, while the Philistines were a constant danger. Some of the earlier judges like Othniel, Ehud and Shamgar succeeded in checking the raids of the enemy, but no decisive blow had been dealt. A confederacy of the northern Canaanites had in the meantime been formed, prepared to fight against Israel. The leader of the Canaanitish host was Sisera, evidently, to judge by his name, a Hittite, assisted by Jabin, King of Hazor. The latter, the possessor of nine hundred chariots of iron, had oppressed the northern Israelites for twenty years. Sisera occupied the strongholds of Taanach and Megiddo in the plain of Jezreel, and from there the confederate kings and their hosts made repeated raids upon the north and the south, hindering at the same time the tribes from joining their brethren in the south. In the plain of Jezreel, the famous battleground, the enemy awaited the invaders for a decisive fight. The Israelites were badly equipped and but poorly armed. How destitute of weapons they were is indicated in the Song of Deborah, where it is said that the forty thousand fighting men had neither spear nor shield in their possession. The misery of Israel was great, and only a miracle could save them. But what the Hebrew peasants lacked in weapons and strength was made up by their enthusiasm. The impulse this time was given by a woman, Deborah the prophetess, Israel's Joan of Arc, if we may be allowed to make this comparison. Issuing from the tribes of Issachar and dwelling between Ramah and Bethel in Mount Ephraim, she was able to gauge the danger, as the tribe of Issachar was occupying the plain. Deborah, moreover, understood that only a religious impulse was calculated to inspire the tribes with enthusiasm and to encourage them to fight desperately. She summoned the chiefs or princes (Sarim) of her tribe, and particularly Barak, the son of Abinoam, and induced them to rally to her standard. At Deborah's inspired call the tribes dwelling on both sides of the plain, Ephraim, Manasseh and Benjamin in the south, and Zebulun, Naphtali and Issachar in the north, sent detachments. Barak concentrated his forces on Mount Tabor, overlooking the plain, where he awaited his opportunity. Between Taanach and Megiddo the Hebrew peasants met the well-equipped Canaanites and their cavalry. The tribes of Reuben, Gad, Asher and Dan had sent no help; they were not suffering from the Canaanites as did their brethren. Enthusiasm and religious fervour triumphed over brute-force. In a panic the enemy fled before the onset of Barak and wild confusion set in among the cavalry of Sisera. "The stars in their courses fought against Sisera."

A storm had broken out, a pouring rain had come down and the River Kishon had risen. On the foaming waves of the swollen river the fugitive Canaanites were swept away. Sisera himself left his chariot and fled from the battlefield. He sought refuge in the tent of Jael, the wife of a Kenite, an

Arab tribe which was evidently friendly disposed towards the Israelites. While the Canaanite general was asleep in her tent, the Kenite woman slew him treacherously.

The victory, however, was far from being complete, for a number of the fugitives must have escaped. In the Song of Deborah the tribes who had not hurried to take part in the contest are bitterly denounced, and a curse is uttered against the inhabitants of Meroz, who had not come to share the peril "to the help of Jehovah, the help of Jehovah among the heroes". Although the towns in the plain still remained in the possession of the Canaanites, and the tribe of Issachar became tributary to the enemy, the immediate danger had nevertheless been averted. The power of the Canaanites had been broken, and for a long time Israel had peace. The enthusiasm of the Israelites and the heroism of Barak are commemorated in the famous Song of Deborah, one of the most ancient fragments of Hebrew literature. Apart from its poetic beauty, the song, which is evidently the work of a contemporary author, is of great historical, value as it depicts the political and spiritual situation of Israel in that barbarous and rude age.

One of the most famous judges was Jerubbaal named Gideon. He was a peasant of the tribe of Manasseh. It happened that "when Israel had sown, the Midianites came up, and the Amalekites and the children of the East, they came up against them and destroyed the increase of the earth, till thou come unto Gaza, and left no sustenance in Israel, neither sheep, nor ox, nor ass". Now Gideon, with a little band carrying torches and trumpets, attacked the camp of the Midianites in the middle of the night. Seized with terror, the panic-stricken soldiers slew one another. The tribes were overjoyed with Gideon's exploits and offered him the title of King.

"Rule thou over us," they said, "thou and thy son, and thy son's son also, for thou hast saved us out of the hand of Midian."

Gideon, however, in his modesty declined the royal dignity. "I will not rule over you, neither shall my son rule over you; Jehovah shall rule over you."

After Gideon's death one of his sons, Abimelech, succeeded in proclaiming himself King, thanks to the support of his kinsmen, the Shechemites. The result was a civil war and the destruction of Shechem.

Another famous judge was Jephthah, a man of Gilead. The Ammonites had encamped at Gilead and attacked the tribe of Manasseh, whose territory lay on both banks of the Jordan. The elders of Gilead fetched Jephthah from the land of Tob and appointed him their chief. He was successful in his exploits. The story of Jephthah's vow and of the subsequent sacrifice of his own daughter greatly resembles the Greek tradition of the tragic story of Iphigenia. Did Jephthah really offer his daughter as a burnt-offering or was she only vowed to perpetual celibacy as some maintain?[1] The age of the Judges was thus one of constant fight against outside foes and one of lawlessness, confusion, civil wars and merciless reprisals.

Two narratives in the Book of Judges cast a somewhat melancholy light both on the morals of the Israelites in those days and the state of confusion. The tribe of Dan, harassed and pressed by the Philistines, decided to seek another territory to dwell in. They discovered the town of Laish, slew the inhabitants and settled there. When passing through the hill country of Ephraim they found, in the house of a certain Micah, an ephod and a graven image in the charge of a Levite. They took the graven image and the ephod, and carried off the Levite to serve them as chaplain. At Laish they set up the graven image, while the house of God was at Shiloh.

Another more melancholy story is the narrative of the Levite of Ephraim, whose wife had been murdered at Gibeah by a band of men of the tribe of Benjamin. The husband cried for revenge and appealed to the other tribes. As the Benjaminites refused to deliver up the culprits, war was declared upon them and nearly the whole tribe was wiped out.

The conquest of Canaan was not accomplished in five years, but only very gradually in the course of two or three centuries. The complete subjugation of the Canaanites was achieved only during the reign of Solomon. Towards the end of the period of the Judges, before the establishment of the mon-

[1] See Munk, *Palestine*.

archy, the Israelites were settled in the midst of the Canaanites, but their position was not everywhere the same. While in some districts the inhabitants had been exterminated, in others they remained in the possession of the land. Only on payment of a tribute were the Israelites allowed to settle there. In some places it was a state of armed neutrality. Whenever an opportunity arose, the old inhabitants were not slow in seizing it, subjugating or expelling the invaders. Canaanites, Amorites and Philistines were constantly watching for such opportunities, which were many.

The bond uniting the Israelites was neither political nor national, but religious, and even religion had not yet taken a strong hold over them. On the contrary, the sojourn among other tribes and peoples made it grow weaker every day. "It came to pass that they turned back and dealt more corruptly than their fathers, in following other gods to serve them, and to bow down unto them, they ceased not from their doings, nor from their stubborn way." The result was a disunion of the tribes, and when the foe attacked a weak tribe, the stronger ones never hurried to his aid. The tribes of the east were continually striving with the Ammonites and the Midianites, while the tribes of the north were being harassed by the Canaanites and were more or less successful in maintaining their independence. Much more formidable, however, was the foe whom the tribes in the south had to face.

THE CONQUEST OF CANAAN

In the closing days of Israel's sojourn in Egypt an enormous migration of tribes from the Mediterranean coast had taken place. Among these new invaders was a people known in history as the Philistines. They had come from the shores and the islands of the Mediterranean and settled permanently in Canaan. During the entire period of the Judges the Philistines had continually made border raids and harassed Israel, but now they began a more formidable struggle, which called for a united effort on the part of the new settlers.

Israel seemed to have little chance of success in its struggle against the formidable foe. The Philistines were united and well organized, while the tribes were continually engaged in internal strife. At Aphek near Mizpah the ark of Jehovah was captured by the enemy. The Philistines established their sway over the centre and the south of Canaan, and prevented the people from availing themselves of weapons. It was a critical moment for Israel, and the tribes at last realized the fact that only by organizing the tribal communities under one ruler could an end be put to disorder and disunion which resulted in constant defeat. The people began to clamour for a monarchy—that is, for a permanent ruler and a leader in war, whose dignity would be hereditary. The emergency called for a leader who would prove the right man in the right place, a man of influence and courage, a chieftain whom the people would trust and on whom they could rely. Samuel, the political prophet, the Warwick of early Israel, understood that the theocracy could no longer be upheld and that the establishment of a monarchy was the crying need of the moment. His choice fell on Saul, a native of Gibeah, of the tribe of Benjamin. The awakening of the national sentiment was, however, more the result of a revival of religious zeal than of political union. It is a trait peculiar to the Semites as to all Eastern nations and may be witnessed among the Arabs even in our own century.[1] The fight against the Philistines was the fire in which the Kingdom of Israel and the Empire of David and Solomon were forged. The Philistines were instrumental in bringing about, not only a union of the tribes, but a return to the worship of Jehovah. The triumph over the enemy was to be the triumph, not only of the people of Israel, but of their religion.

[1] Cf. Ménard, L., *Histoire des Israélites*, 1883, 48.

CHAPTER VIII

THE HEBREW MONARCHY

Saul, a democratic king—Attacks of the Philistines—On the mountains of Gilboa—The death of Saul—David's lament—"Ye mountains of Gilboa"—David King of Israel—The murder of Ishbosheth—The conquest of Jerusalem—The city of the Jebusites—Urusalimu of the Tell-el-Amarna letters—Mount Zion—Benjamin and Judah—The new metropolis—King Hiram of Tyre—The Messiah, a prince of the House of David—Solomon—An Egyptian army in Palestine—The town of Gezer—The reign of glory—New sources of revenue—Foreign markets—Horses for Hittite princes—The Temple—Expenses and heavy taxes—The discontent of the nation—The assembly of Shechem—The appeal of the tribes—The ill-advised monarch—The house divided—The two kingdoms—Jeroboam—Changes of dynasty—Sheshank, King of Egypt—The monument of Karnak—The Aramæans—The Kingdom of Zoba—The danger of Assyria—The Northern Kingdom—The house of Omri—The Tyrian princess—Ahab—Baal and Astarte—The protest of the Prophets—The battle of Aphek—Shalmaneser III—Biridri of Damascus and Ichrulini of Hamath—The battle of Karkar—The fall of Samaria—The Mesha stone—Jehu—The ambition of the King—King Joash—Jeroboam II—The beginning of the end—Menahem and Pekah—A vassal of Assyria—Sabako, King of Egypt—Tiglath-Pileser and Shalmaneser IV—The siege of Samaria—The captivity—The disappearance of the ten tribes

SAUL, DAVID AND SOLOMON

A MONARCHY had been established, but it was a monarchy in name only. Saul was a democratic ruler upon whom the title of King had been bestowed. He was merely a judge and a chieftain whose authority had been acknowledged, not by one tribe, but by the whole of Israel. All through his life Saul remained modest and democratic. Like Cincinnatus, he was fetched from his farm from behind the plough to come and save the tribes from the attacks of the Philistines. Soon after his election Saul had opportunities to give proof of his valour. He conducted expeditions against the Amalekites and in particular against the Philistines. In the course of time, however, the Philistines prepared for a decisive struggle and marched into the plain of Esdraelon. Saul's army awaited the attack on the slopes of Mount Gilboa. The Israelites gave way and fled in confusion, and Saul's three sons were slain. Saul, determined not to survive the defeat of his army, killed himself, and the throne became vacant for David. The King-elect's lament over the death of his predecessor is famous:

"Ye mountains of Gilboa, let there be no dew, neither let there be rain upon you, nor fields of offerings. For there the shield of the mighty is vilely cast away, the shield of Saul." "Ye daughters of Israel, weep over Saul who clothed you in scarlet with other delights; who put ornaments of gold upon your apparel. How are the mighty fallen in the midst of the battle."

David did not become King of Israel at once. He had succeeded in establishing an independent sovereignty in the territory of the tribe of Judah and was reigning at Hebron, while Saul's younger son, Ishbosheth, reigned over the other tribes. A murder, however, no doubt welcome to David, even if not instigated by him, at last removed the rival from his path. While the son of Saul was taking his midday rest, he was murdered "on his bed". The murderers hastened to bring the King's head to David at Hebron, but he had them both hanged. David, a popular hero, was now raised to the throne of all Israel.

The two outstanding achievements of David were his decisive and crushing defeat of the Philistines and the capture of Mount Zion, the Jebusite city. The Philistines who had settled themselves in the heart of Palestine, in the plain of Esdraelon, were driven back to the coast, where they remained for centuries. The second political act on David's part was to fix his residence in the city of Jerusalem, situated in the territory of Benjamin, and to transfer thither the tabernacle and the Ark of God. When Saul had been elected King, it was the tribe of Benjamin which had thus taken the lead, but with the ascension of David the place was taken by the tribe of Judah. In order to reconcile the offended tribe of Benjamin, David purposely fixed the royal residence in his territory. To Jerusalem, the place of worship, all the tribes of Israel would now have to "go up".[1] The town of Jebus, situated on the frontier of Benjamin and Judah, had the advantage of giving the King ready access to the plains of Jericho below, without separating him from his own tribe. The hills and ravines surrounding the town constituted a natural defence. The Jebusites were confident of their safety, but the city was actually captured by David's general Joab and became

[1] See Note 8 in Appendix.

henceforth known as Jerusalem, although the name of Urusalimu is already mentioned in the Tell-el-Amarna letters. Judah and Jerusalem are thus David's creations, and while the tribe of Judah grew to be the most powerful one in Israel, Jerusalem became, not only the political, but also the religious metropolis of the kingdom, the holy city where the Ark came to rest. David continued to distinguish himself by his military achievements, and broke for ever the power of the Philistines. Emboldened by his successes, he also attacked and subdued Moab, Ammon and Edom, and even Damascus was made tributary. With Hiram, King of Tyre, he made an alliance. All these successes produced a deep impression upon Israel, and David appeared to the tribes as the ideal prince, the popular hero. A cluster of legends was subsequently woven round the first national King of Israel, and henceforth in all its sufferings and misery the people grew accustomed to expect salvation from the house of David. The Messiah, destined not only to deliver the people of Israel from oppression, but to spread the name of Jehovah over the earth, was to be a descendant of the house of David.

David's son and successor Solomon enjoyed the fruits of David's achievements. Being a wise king and a prince of peace, Solomon turned his attention to the internal organization and administration of his inheritance. He never extended the empire which his father had created, nor could he prevent the rise of a new Aramæan kingdom in Damascus, while Edom regained its liberty. As for Tyre, with whose king, Hiram, David had concluded an alliance, Solomon seems to have been dependent on it. The payments he made to Hiram of Tyre and the cession of twenty cities could not have been a voluntary act on the part of Solomon. The payments were no doubt a sort of tribute. During Solomon's reign Egypt once more began to take an interest in the affairs of Palestine. Already under David we see the Empire on the Nile, after many centuries, turning its attention to its former Asiatic possession. During the first years of Solomon's reign an Egyptian army came to Palestine. For the moment, however, Egypt's appearance on the scene was of no immediate danger. It was the land of the Philistines that the Pharaoh had in view, as the important trade-route towards the Euphrates was running through Philistine territory. Solomon, however, seems to have recognized the suzerainty of Egypt. He must even have rendered some service to the Pharaoh of Egypt, who made him a present of the town of Gezer, which he had captured.

Solomon was animated by a desire to reign in glory and to imitate other Asiatic potentates. He wished, however, that all his magnificence should be displayed in the honour of his own and his father's God Jehovah. He built a temple and palaces for himself and his wives. What his father had done by war he decided to do by commerce—that is, to open for himself new sources of revenue and gain. He found a ready market for the products of the land of Israel, wheat and barley, wine, oil and honey, timber and wool, among the neighbouring Phœnicians. With Egypt, too, he opened up commerce, and imported chariots and horses for the Hittite princes who were still dwelling independently among the Israelites. Solomon used his wealth principally for building purposes, among his numerous edifices being, besides the temple, his own palace and that of the queen, a law-court, a porch of judgment and a house in the Lebanon. For the construction of his edifices the king required both wealth and workmen. As the revenues of his trade and his domains were not sufficient to meet his vast expenses, the king did not hesitate to lay the burdens of taxes and work upon the shoulders of his subjects. While Solomon was reigning peacefully, avoiding wars but spending money lavishly and thus sowing discontent among his people, clouds were gathering on the horizon. Rezon, a revolted servant of Hadadezer, had become master of Damascus and founded a kingdom which soon became formidable and a constant danger later on, particularly to the northern kingdom. On the other hand, the wealth displayed by Solomon, his splendour and his glory, were calculated to excite the envy and the cupidity of the neighbouring Powers. During his own lifetime Solomon's Empire was not actually impaired, but the symptoms of disruption and decline already began to appear.

THE HEBREW MONARCHY

After a reign which had lasted forty years, Solomon died (in 933 B.C.), leaving behind the reputation of a wise and glorious king but no contented country. The spirit of discontent and bitterness which had been brooding, excited by the oppressive régime and the extravagant tastes, at once burst into flame. At a popular assembly held at Shechem the northern tribes made an appeal to Solomon's successor, Rehoboam. They besought him to lighten their burdens, but the ill-advised ruler was foolish enough to "answer the people roughly". A disaster which a more astute monarch might have averted was thus precipitated. The ten northern tribes openly revolted and elected Jeroboam as their king, the tribes Judah and Benjamin alone remaining faithful to their allegiance and to the Davidic dynasty.

The House Divided

The house was now divided and the political power of Israel had come to an end for ever. Never again, except in the days of Herod the Great, did Israel enjoy the undisputed possession of Palestine, the Promised Land. The tact and patience which David had displayed in his endeavour to unite the tribes under one sceptre had been in vain. The hopes of a united Israel and of a Palestine as the undisputed home of Israel were shattered for ever. The two brother kingdoms were henceforth seldom at peace one with the other, but engaged in constant wars. Now and again either the one or the other excited a third kingdom to attack his rival, and the neighbours were not slow to take advantage of such a state of affairs. The northern tribes were more numerous, but upon them fell the burden of a constant defensive warfare against foreign foes, and particularly against the growing power of Syria.

Suffering as it also did from the repeated changes of dynasty, the northern kingdom could not maintain itself for any length of time. More exposed to the onset of foreign foes than was the southern kingdom, it perished, unable even to save its nationality and its type of religious life and worship, which, by the way, were no longer pure. The southern kingdom, more secluded and consolidated by the stability of the Davidic dynasty and the Temple, both politically and religiously, enjoyed its tranquillity a little longer. The inhabitants lost their land and their national independence in the end, but they had the advantage of saving their religion and national consciousness, and this enabled the two tribes of Judah and Benjamin to live on.

Soon after the disruption, the consequences of the disaster made themselves felt. Sheshank I, King of Egypt, the Shishak of the Bible, undertook an expedition against Palestine, took Jerusalem and pillaged the treasures of the temple. From a monument celebrating the victories of Sheshank in the temple of Karnak we learn that he had captured 156 cities, not only in Judæa, but also in the north, and that he had penetrated as far as Galilee. Any-

THE HEBREW MONARCHY

how, it was in Egypt's interest to widen the gulf between Israel and Judah. It has been suggested that Sheshank may have captured several northern cities which Rehoboam had taken possession of and returned them to Jeroboam, whom he had supported[1] in order to encourage the split and thus prevent a reconciliation and a renewal of a single national empire of the Israelites in Palestine. Another power which was delighted at the division of Israel was that of the Aramæans. Apart from the various Semitic tribes and the Philistines, who were constantly threatening Israel, the Aramæans proved in the course of time the most formidable foes of both Israel and Judah.

Advancing from the east and the south-east, the Aramæans, who, like the Arabs, are perhaps the purest representatives of the Semitic race, had penetrated since the second millennium into Mesopotamia and Syria. They were at first repelled by the mighty Hittites, but when the latter's power was on the ebb the Aramæans succeeded in settling permanently in Syria, and towards the ninth century B.C. they occupied almost the whole of Syria, with the exception of the Phœnician coastland.[2] Saul and David and the later kings of Israel had to engage in warfare against the Aramæan Kingdom of Zoba. A still greater danger, however, which threatened the Kingdom of Israel, came from Assyria. Palestine, as a united kingdom,

[1] See Lehmann-Haupt, *Die Geschichte Judas u. Israels*, 48.
[2] See Kraeling, *Aram and Israel*.

was at best only a buffer State between Egypt and Assyria. The trade-route from Assyria to Egypt ran through Damascus, along the plain of Esdraelon, crossing the low mountains which join Carmel with the range of Southern Palestine. It then passed southwards through the land of the Philistines, by Gaza and Lachish to the desert. Judæa and Jerusalem lay on the hills and may have been advantageous to an Assyrian army anxious to maintain communications with the Delta land, but Samaria was absolutely indispensable to them. Samaria therefore fell first, while Judah was allowed to enjoy her independence a little longer.

The entire history of the Kingdom of Israel, that is, of the northern tribes, is a succession of wars, of changes of dynasty and of violent usurpations. Jeroboam, the founder of the new kingdom, died, and his son Nadab was assassinated by Baasha, who reigned twenty-two years. His son Elah was assassinated by Zimri, but the army which was then in the land of the Philistines proclaimed their general Omri as king.

Omri was a powerful personality and an astute ruler. He was clever enough to realize the fact that the kingdom of the south possessed a great advantage, namely, a strong capital situated on a height. Omri therefore built himself the city of Samaria, which, on account of its position on a height in the territory of Ephraim, was calculated to become a centre of resistance. He furthermore concluded an alliance with the King of Tyre, which proved very valuable for him in his struggle against the growing power of Syria. In order to cement his friendship with Ethbaal, King of Tyre, Omri asked and obtained the hand of the Tyrian princess, the famous Jezebel, for his son Ahab. We have a proof of the power of Omri in the fact that in Assyrian inscriptions the Kingdom of Israel and Samaria are called the "house of Omri".

The reign of Ahab, Omri's son, was distinguished, not only by foreign wars, but also by religious dissensions. Before he had become a king, Ethbaal of Tyre had been priest of Astarte, and his daughter, who was very pious, introduced the Phœnician cult of Baal into Israel. As for Ahab himself, there was perhaps no real intention on his part to abolish the worship of Jehovah. By adopting the policy of a religious tolerance practised by Solomon he may have hoped to gain over the numerous Canaanites dwelling in his kingdom. The result, however, was a fierce protest from the Prophets, who would acknowledge no other god beside Jehovah, the God of Israel.

Ahab, who had been victorious against Benhadad of Damascus in the battle of Aphek, finally concluded an alliance with his former enemy. Here, too, Ahab gave proof of political insight. A common danger was threatening the two kingdoms. Ashurnasir-pal II (884-860 B.C.), King of Assyria, having subdued the Aramæan kingdoms in Mesopotamia and on the middle Euphrates, had cast his eye on Syria. Shalmaneser III (860-826 B.C.)

was actually preparing for an expedition to the west. A coalition was therefore formed with a view to offering resistance to the kings of Assyria. Among the kings belonging to this coalition were Benhadad (Biridri) of Damascus, Ahab, King of Israel, and Ichrulini of Hamath. The kings on the coast of the Phœnician States also belonged to the coalition. Shalmaneser III defeated the allies in the battle of Karkar in 854.[1]

The Fall of Samaria

Ever since the battle of Karkar (854) Assyria had never given up the idea of subduing the westland, although some time elapsed before the plan was carried out. In the meantime the Kingdom of Israel was allowed to keep some sort of independence. Ahab's alliance with the Syrians soon ended, and the King of Israel was killed in battle in an effort to retake the city of Ramoth in Gilead. Ahab's death was a signal for the Moabites, who had been paying tribute to the Israelites for forty years, to shake off the yoke of Israel.

This is corroborated by the inscription on the Mesha stone, a stele erected at Dibon, which was discovered in 1868 and is now in the Louvre. In this inscription we read that Mesha, son of Nadab, had erected the stone to Chemosh.

"My father Nadab had reigned over Moab thirty years, and I reigned after my father. I have erected

[1] Lehmann-Haupt, l.c., 49.

this stone to Chemosh, the stone of deliverance, for he has delivered me from my enemies, he has avenged those that hate me. Omri was king of Israel and oppressed Moab for a long time because Chemosh was angry with his people. The son of Omri who succeeded him, said: I will also oppress Moab, but in my own day Chemosh said: I will cast my eyes on him and over his house and Israel shall perish for ever."

The dynasty of Omri came to an end with the revolt raised by Jehu. He slew all that remained of the house of Ahab "until he left him none remaining". Jehu was an energetic ruler, but ambitious and unscrupulous. He forcibly put down the Baal worship, not because he was anxious to restore the worship of the true God, Jehovah, but simply because it suited his purpose. He was even harbouring the idea of making himself king of a united Palestine and of re-establishing the Empire of David. This hope of the usurper was, however, frustrated, and even his own kingdom was greatly weakened in consequence of war against Syria. In the end Jehu had to come to terms and consent to pay tribute to Shalmaneser III, King of Assyria, to protect his kingdom from Syria. Israel's fortunes, however, somewhat improved under King Joash, a grandson of Jehu, who defeated the Syrians and recovered the towns which had been captured. The work of liberation was completed by Jeroboam II, the son of Joash, who reconquered the city of Cusham-Jerahmeel and also recovered the region of Maacath for Israel. An era of prosperity and peace was inaugurated, although dark clouds were already gathering on the horizon. The attitude of Assyria was becoming more and more threatening and the prophets Amos and Hosea were predicting the speedy fall of the northern kingdom.

The death of Jeroboam proved to be the beginning of the end of the northern kingdom. It fell a prey to anarchy and lawlessness, and revolutions and murders became the order of the day, succeeding each other with alarming rapidity. Zechariah, the son of Jeroboam, was assassinated by Shallum and the latter in his turn was murdered by Menahem. Menahem's son Pekahiah was assassinated by Pekah, son of Remaliah. From the annals of Tiglath-Pileser III we gather that this monarch was receiving tribute from Minikmi of Samirina, which may mean Menahem of Samaria. It is, however, possible that it was the north Arabian King of Meluhha who had at this time invaded Samaria and exacted tribute from Menahem.

The last king of Israel was Pekah, who was assassinated by Hoshea. The latter's authority extended only over a small portion of the kingdom, namely, that of Ephraim, and he was practically a vassal of the king of Assyria, to whom he paid tribute. The Assyrian king, however, was displeased because his vassal was not paying his tribute regularly. Either Hoshea's resources were insufficient or he may have relied on help from Egypt, to whose king he had appealed for assistance. Sabako, a powerful Ethiopian officer who had risen to a position of influence in Egypt and ascended the throne as the founder of the XXVth dynasty, was uneasy at the expansion of the Assyrian Empire. He therefore insisted on Hoshea's refusing to pay his annual tribute. Hoshea yielded to the pressure of Sabako and withheld the tribute. Thereupon Shalmaneser IV at once laid siege to Samaria. The siege was carried on by his successor, Sargon II, who captured Samaria and deported, in Oriental fashion, the population beyond the Euphrates to Assyria and Media.

The inhabitants whom Tiglath-Pileser, and after him Sargon, had transported were replaced by new colonies from different parts of the Assyrian Empire. The newcomers mixed and mingled with the old Canaanite and Israelite inhabitants, and in time formed a new race, that of the Samaritans. As for the exiles who had been carried away to foreign lands, they were speedily absorbed by the heathen populations among whom they had been placed and in the land to which they had been carried captive. They had lost not only their kingdom and their national independence, but also their separate national, religious and individual existence.

CHAPTER IX

ASSYRIANS, BABYLONIANS AND PERSIANS

The Southern Kingdom—Jehoshaphat, King of Judah—Jehoram and Athaliah—Joash—Invasion of the Aramæans—Azariah—The harbour of Elath—Material prosperity—Wealth and luxury—Pastoral life and mercantile pursuits—Social sins multiply—The Prophets—Enter Assyria—Assyria, the rival of Babylonia—Shalmaneser and Tiglath-Pileser—Assyria's Imperialistic policy—Ashur-nasir-pal and Ahab—Ashur-nasir-pal's boast—Shalmaneser III—His inscription—Ramman-nirari and Tiglath-Pileser III—The city of Nineveh—Shalmaneser IV—Egypt the evil genius of Palestine—The broken reed—Sabako—The siege of Samaria—Sargon—The turning-point for Judah—King Ahaz—The commercial port of Elath—A vassal of Assyria—Isaiah—Ahimit and Yaman—The peoples of Philistia, Judah, Edom and Moab speak treason—Merodach-Baladan—Sennacherib—The battle of Altaku—Tirhakah—The Old Testament and Herodotus—Esar-haddon—Hezekiah—Pharaoh Necho—Josiah—The Scythians—The decline of Nineveh—The independence of Babylon—Nabopolassar and Nebuchadrezzar—The fall of Jerusalem—The Babylonian captivity—Cyrus, King of Anshan—The overthrow of the Babylonian Empire—Zerubbabel—The state of Palestine—Danger of assimilation—The work of Ezra—Nehemiah—Politics and religion—The *Torah*, the constitution of the Jews

THE history of the Southern Kingdom is not so eventful as that of Israel. During the entire period of existence the petty Kingdom of Judah could rarely practise any independent policy. It was either dependent on the more powerful brother State or had to suffer from the depredations and raids of its stronger neighbours. Jehoshaphat (*c.* 874), King of Judah, concluded an alliance with Ahab, King of Israel, cemented by the marriage of his son Jehoram to Ahab's daughter, Athaliah, and for some time friendship existed between the two rival States. The queen introduced into Judah the heathenism and the profligacy of the house of Ahab. The Edomites revolted and the Philistines once more assumed the offensive. Philistines and Arabs even attacked Jerusalem. During the reign of Joash (*c.* 836) the Aramæans under Hazael, King of Syria, invaded the country and the king could avert the attack on Jerusalem only by paying an immense sum, emptying the treasures of the temple and the royal palace. Under the reign of Amaziah (*c.* 797–778) there was again a conflict with the Edomites, who were defeated.

Under Uzziah, or Azariah (*c.* 778–740), the kingdom recovered something of its former power. The king built the important harbour of Elath and new openings for commerce were discovered. Indeed, it was during the reign of this king that the Southern State reached the height of its prosperity. A chain of fortresses was erected against the Philistines and the king extended his power as far as the shores of the Red Sea. Wealth accumulated in the country, but it brought in its wake luxury and all the vices engendered by material prosperity. Both under the reign of Uzziah and of his son Jotham (*c.* 740–736) the Southern Kingdom was at peace with Israel, and the only occasional campaigns were those undertaken against the Ammonites and the nomadic hordes of the desert. Towards the middle of the eighth century B.C. both the kingdoms of Israel and Judah had reached a high state of prosperity. A change in the internal life had, however, in the meantime been effected. In consequence of the long wars and the military operations life in insecure unwalled villages became impossible and towns began to arise. Mercantile pursuits took the place of agriculture. Gone were the simple habits of a pastoral life, making room for those of town life and commercial communities with their concomitant moral dangers. Class distinctions made themselves felt and the difference between rich and poor was great. Both wealth on the one side and poverty on the other increased, and while the rich were living in abundance, the poor were groaning under the burden of poverty. Social sins multiplied. "The upper classes", to quote Professor G. A. Smith,[1] "were lifted away from feeling the real woes of the people."

It was against such a state of affairs, against the neglect of religion, against social inequality and social injustice, greed, corruption and oppression, that the prophets of the eighth century uplifted their voices. A social State based on iniquity, maintained the prophets, cannot last, for it is unjust. Amos, Micah and Isaiah inveighed against the social sins of their people.

In the eighth century B.C. the history of the country of Palestine was determined by Assyria. The Assyrians have been called the Romans of Asia, and to some extent this is true. They possessed not the Roman genius for either consolidating

[1] *The Book of the Twelve Prophets*, i. 33–34.

or civilizing the conquered provinces, but they were certainly the equals of the Romans in military skill.[1] It will be necessary, therefore, before proceeding with the history of the Southern Kingdom, to sketch as briefly as possible the rise of the power which, after having put an end to Israel, was also destined to deal the death-blow to Judah.

It was during the fifteenth century that Assyria had begun to found an empire on the Tigris and to rival Babylonia. Towards 1400 B.C. Assyria's power had grown to such an extent that she could venture to rival with Babylonia and to interfere with her schemes and conquests. Shalmaneser I, King of Assyria, who ruled about 1300 B.C., extended his dominions to the north as far as the modern Armenian city of Diarbekir. Tiglath-Pileser I lived in the days of the Hebrew Judges. In one of his inscriptions this king boasts that the gods had given into his hands success on the battlefield. "Countries, mountains and cities did I subdue, against sixty kings have I fought, as far as the mountains of Lebanon." For a little while, during a momentary decline of the Assyrian monarchy, the Hebrew and Aramæan kings had been allowed to develop their petty kingdoms. A moment, however, came when Assyria grew ambitious, and her imperialistic policy was fraught with danger for the petty States in the West, among them the two kingdoms of Judah and Israel, surrounded

[1] Cf. Driver, *Isaiah and His Times*, 6.

by foes on all sides. Henceforth Imperialism had become the policy of Assyria.

Ashur-nasir-pal (884–860) was a mighty king and a great warrior. He extended his Empire by his many conquests and sent terror into the heart of Ahab, King of Israel. Ashur-nasir-pal was a cruel monarch, and in one of his inscriptions he boasts of having impaled his enemies, immured them alive, put out their eyes and cut off their hands, ears and noses. He constructed a wonderful and magnificent palace in the town of Calah, which he had built. It was more particularly under Shalmaneser III, the son of Ashur-nasir-pal, that Palestine began to feel the effect of Assyria's imperialistic policy. Shalmaneser III (860–826) had defeated Ahab and the other allied kings at the battle of Karkar in 854. In one of his inscriptions he boasts: "Like a god of thunder I sent down a pouring rain, spread out their corpses, with which I stopped the course of the river Orontes." Ramman-nirari, a grandson of Shalmaneser II (811–782), conquered Damascus and received as tribute 2,300 talents of silver, 20 talents of gold, besides bronze, iron, costly tissues and ivory. He also became ruler of Babylonia.

In 745 Tiglath-Pileser III ascended the throne of Assyria and ruled until 727. He is called in the Bible by the name of Pul. Under this king Assyria had already grown to be a mighty empire which could pretend to world power. The beautiful country of Assyria in the days of Pul contained a number of cities, the oldest of which was Assur on the Tigris.

A little more to the north, opposite the modern Mosul, lay the famous capital of Nineveh, situated on the banks of the Choser, an affluent of the Tigris; to the south was Calah, where the palace of Ashur-nasir-pal was excavated about eighty-five years ago.

We have seen how Ahab, Joram and Jehu, Kings of Israel, Ben-Hadad and Hazael, Kings of Syria, had felt the effect of Assyria's imperialistic policy. Syria and the northern kingdom of the Hebrews were the first to bear the brunt of the attack of Assyria, while Judah managed to escape for a little while. The reasons of Judah's fate are not far to seek; they are due to the secluded position of the country. Assyria's imperialistic policy was directed principally against the Empire on the Nile, and for an Assyrian king with ambitious designs on Egypt, Samaria was much more important than Judæa and Jerusalem. Moreover, compared with the resources and material wealth and power of Damascus and of the Kingdom of Israel, Judah appeared almost insignificant.

Tiglath-Pileser died in 727, and was succeeded by his son, Shalmaneser IV. Availing itself of the opportunity offered by a change on the throne, the city of Tyre threw off the Assyrian yoke. Royal Tyre, built on a rocky island, was proud of its impregnable position. The King of Assyria laid siege to Tyre, but without effect. He thereupon plundered the cities on the coast and captured their fleets in the hope of subduing Tyre from the sea, but all his efforts proved vain. This failure of the Assyrian king gave new hope to his enemies in Samaria, whom Egypt was encouraging.

"Egypt", says Driver,[1] "was the evil genius of the peoples of Palestine; it encouraged them to revolt with promises of help, and then failed them when the hour of need arrived. Israel, the Philistines and Judah, all in turn paid the penalty of relying upon the same broken reed." In 725 a new dynasty, the XXVth, had been founded in Egypt by the Ethiopian Sabako (*So* of the Bible), and the interest of the Empire on the Nile in Syria and Palestine had revived. On the one hand, the petty principalities instinctively turned for support to their powerful neighbours, while, on the other, Sabako realized the fact that in pursuing their imperialistic policy the Assyrians would sooner or later invade Egypt if no barrier was in their way. It was therefore in the interests of Egypt to organize a proper resistance before it was too late. Sabako therefore sent his general, Seve, who concluded an alliance with Hoshea, King of Israel, and Hanno of Gaza. We have seen how Shalmaneser IV laid siege to Samaria. The King died during the siege and was succeeded by his son Sargon (722–705), who captured the town. The flower of the population, the proud sons of Ephraim, were dragged away as captives. Some of them were settled as

[1] *Authority and Archæology*, ed. by Hogarth, 103.

slaves, probably on the Chebar, an affluent of the Tigris, while others were dragged away westwards, beyond the Euphrates and the Tigris, into the mountains of Media. Ephraim was shattered. Sargon boasts of his victory in the following terms:

"The city of Samaria I besieged; I took; 27,280 of its inhabitants I carried away into captivity; fifty of their chariots I seized; the rest of their possessions I let my servants have; my officers I appointed over them; the tribute of the former king I laid upon them."[1]

An Assyrian governor was appointed in Samaria, but a new revolt soon followed. A Syrian prince named Ilubdi of Hamath on the Orontes organized the opposition of Syria and Samaria, together with Hanno of Gaza and Seve of Egypt. In 720 Sargon was back, defeated Ilubdi at Karkar and the Egyptians and Philistines at Raphia and killed the leaders of the revolt. The Pharaoh of Egypt and the Arabian Queen Samsie sent tribute. As for Judah, it had been able to hold out a little longer and to maintain its national independence. For some time the only real source of trouble for the kingdom under the rule of the Davidic dynasty had been that which came from Edom in the south. In the north, Samaria had all the time acted as a barrier against Syria, while in the east the country was separated from Moab and Ammon by the Dead Sea and the Arabah.[2] Egypt, too, had for

[1] See Schrader, 272, 274; *Records of the Past*, vii. 28.
[2] See MacCurdy, *History, Prophecy and the Monuments*, i. 318.

some time refrained from interfering in Judah's affairs.

The turning-point for Judah came under the reign of King Ahaz, who ascended the throne in 738. The kingdom had been attacked by the confederate armies of the Aramæans, Edom and Samaria. Elath, on the Red Sea, the only commercial port of Judah, had been taken and the enemy was marching upon Jerusalem. The heart of the royal household "quivered as the trees in the forest quiver before the wind".[1] Availing themselves of the favourable opportunity, the Philistines recovered several border towns. In this critical moment Ahaz appealed to the King of Assyria for help, offering to become his vassal.

"I am thy slave, and thy son," he wrote, recognizing the Assyrian conqueror as his liege lord. This appeal suited Tiglath-Pileser quite well, for it gave him an opportunity to attack the allies and to subdue them, although he offered but little help to Judah against Edom.

The policy of the country was directed at that time by the prophet Isaiah. He was the political counsellor of the king, the man behind the throne. Isaiah, like all the other prophets, was convinced that an independent political State was not the ultimate goal of Israel. The *raison d'être* of the people lay in religion and moral strength. To hold its own among the nations and kingdoms of the world, to play at politics on the arena of the world's

[1] Is. vii. 1, 2 Kings xvi. 3.

history, was and would always be a futile attempt on the part of a people destined to be guided by religious and moral principles alone. Israel's attempts to gain a place in the sun by means of statecraft or munitions of war were doomed to failure (Is. viii. 5-15). Isaiah, however, was not a mere dreamer, a religious enthusiast, but also a great statesman with clear political insight. He advised the king to adopt a policy of quietness and confidence (xxx. 15). Ahaz had been wrong to appeal to Assyria, but now that he had become the vassal of Assyria, the best thing for the petty State was to keep quiet and trust in God.

Ahaz died in 728 and was succeeded by Hezekiah, who was still a youth. Soon a new danger threatened the country. Gaza had been destroyed, but in 711 the Philistines of Ashdod, relying on the support of Egypt, rose up against Judah. Sargon sent his general-in-chief (Tartan) to Ashdod, where he deposed King Azuri and placed his brother Ahimit on the throne. The Philistines, however, soon expelled him and made Yaman, an enemy of Assyria, their king. Yaman now tried to win over to his policy Judah, Edom and Moab. Warned, however, by the prophet Isaiah, Hezekiah did not join the coalition. Sargon soon arrived on the scene, conquered Ashdod and Gath, carried off vast booty and great quantities of gold and silver and led away the majority of the inhabitants into captivity, making the district an Assyrian province. Yaman, who had fled to the Sinai desert, was given up to the Assyrian king by the nomadic Arabs.

"The peoples of Philistia, Judah, Edom and Moab, dwelling beside the sea, bringing tribute and presents to Asshur, my lord, were speaking treason. The people and their evil chiefs carried their presents to Pharaoh, a king who could not save them, and besought his alliance to fight against me."[1]

Sargon, however, was compelled to return home, for trouble had broken out in Assyria.

For twelve years Merodach-Baladan, the "Babylonian patriot",[2] had resisted Assyria, but now he threw off his allegiance. He now concluded an alliance with the powerful State of Elam and revolted against Sargon. The latter attacked the allies and devastated the Elamite provinces. Merodach escaped. Sargon carried off an immense booty and 90,580 men fell into his hands.[3]

Sargon captured the city of Dur-Yakir and re-established Assyrian dominion on the shores of the Persian Gulf.[4]

The Assyrian ruler was now at the zenith of power. Assur, Babylonia, Elam, the Armenian hill country, Syria, Palestine and Egypt obeyed his commands, and from distant Cyprus and the islands of the Persian Sea ambassadors appeared at his Court to pay homage to the "King of kings". The

---

[1] G. Smith, *Eponym Canon*, 130; *Assyrian Discoveries*, 291.
[2] Driver, l.c., 45.   [3] Lenormant, *Les Premières Civilisations*, ii. 203.
[4] *Records of the Past*, vii. 47.

defeat of Merodach had sobered Hezekiah, King of Judah, who had been inclined to adopt an anti-Assyrian and pro-Egyptian foreign policy. Indeed, Merodach-Baladan had even tried to secure an alliance with the King of Judah and sent an embassy to Jerusalem. Hezekiah had received the ambassadors with great pomp and effusiveness, displaying unto them all his treasures and wealth. Once more Isaiah had pointed out to the king the folly of a revolt against Assyria.

In 705 Sargon fell by the hand of an assassin. When the news of his death became known, Merodach-Baladan once more appeared on the scene and Babylon declared its independence. Sargon's successor, Sennacherib, was therefore busy for some time restoring his authority in Babylonia. This gave time to the small Syrian rulers, and to Hezekiah, King of Judah, to form a coalition with a view to throwing off the Assyrian yoke. The ruler of Judah, like the other kings, refused to pay tribute and sought the aid of Egypt. The Empire on the Nile began earnestly to fear the rising power of Assyria, and it was no longer content to support in secret the opponents of its rival. It was to Egypt's advantage to produce an open revolt, and therein it evidently succeeded. Hezekiah refused to pay the tribute which had been paid by his father Ahaz. The result was an invasion by Sennacherib. He conquered Phœnicia and arrived in the country of the Philistines. In Ashkelon he deprived Zedek of his crown and bestowed it upon Sarludari, captured and plundered the cities of Beth-Dagon, Joppa, Bene Berak and Azuru. Then he punished the Ekronites, who had deposed their king, Padi, because he had remained loyal to Assyria and had sent him bound in chains to Jerusalem. The Egyptians, summoned by the rebels, arrived in large numbers, but were beaten by Sennacherib at Altaku (Eltokeh of Joshua xix. 44). In 711 Edom and Moab had spoken treason while Ashdod was a centre of revolt, but now they were all courting the favour of Sennacherib.

The Assyrian conqueror took all the cities of Judah by force and prepared to march against Jerusalem. In this critical moment Hezekiah thought it wise to surrender. "He remained shut up in Jerusalem like a bird in a cage," we read in an Assyrian inscription. Sennacherib now turned his attention to Egypt and, marching down the maritime plain, reached the town of Lachish (Tell-el-Hesi). An Egyptian army was being formed at Pelusium, and Sennacherib guessed that Hezekiah had surrendered with a view to gaining time. Although the King of Judah had already paid a heavy tribute, the Assyrian did not hesitate to send part of his army to lay siege to Jerusalem. Having heard that an Ethiopian army under Tirhakah was advancing against him, Sennacherib redoubled his efforts to force the capital of Judah to surrender. Hezekiah was now in a critical position, but the prophet Isaiah reassured him that Jehovah would save His people. And lo! a terrible calamity befell the army of Sennacherib, which was destroyed by an "act of God". The narrative in the Old Testament states that a pestilence had destroyed the entire Assyrian army (encamped before the walls of Jerusalem, says Josephus) consisting of 185,000 men.

According to Herodotus, Egyptian priests maintained that the god Ptah, so as to reward the piety of Sethos, King of Egypt, had sent a multitude of rats into the Assyrian camp. In one night they gnawed all the strings of the bows and of the shields, so that the Assyrians could no longer fight. In reality the two narratives, that of the Bible and of the Egyptians related by Herodotus, maintain the same thing, ascribing the cause of the destruction of Sennacherib's army to the same cause. Both narratives point to an infectious disease. Rats are considered to be a symbol of destruction, particularly of the plague; such was the belief prevalent among the civilized nations of the Orient as well as among the Jews (1 Sam. vi. 6).[1]

Sennacherib hastily departed, although his departure was due, not only to the disaster which had befallen his army, but also to trouble which had suddenly arisen in his own empire. The information that had reached him compelled the Assyrian monarch to return to Nineveh. Belibus, whom Sennacherib had made King of Babylonia and whom he thought he could trust, had suddenly revolted. Sennacherib deposed the rebel and brought him and his family to Assyria. He had also to

[1] See Lehmann-Haupt, l.c., 67.

fight against Shuzub (Mushezib-Marduk), Prince of Bit-Jakin. For several years he fought against the Babylonians, Chaldæans and Elamites, and at last destroyed Babylon, and brought the principal god Marduk to Asshur, as a proof that Babylon had ceased to be an independent kingdom. Prince Esar-haddon was appointed governor of the province of Babylonia and resided at Borsippa, in the vicinity of the destroyed Babylon.[1]

Sennacherib died in 681 and was succeeded by his son, Esar-haddon (681–668). The latter's home policy, which differed from that of his father, does not interest us here, but in the West Esar-haddon continued the work of his father, Sennacherib. After his hasty departure Sennacherib had to fight the Arabs once or twice, but he had never again undertaken any expedition against Egypt, nor had he again troubled Palestine. Tirhakah of Ethiopia, who since 689 had been King of Egypt, now began to renew relations with the petty kings in Palestine. Immediately Esar-haddon directed an army against Egypt, and Palestine, too, had to suffer.

Hezekiah died in 686 and was succeeded by his son Manasseh (686–641). During his reign great events occurred in the world outside Palestine which affected the fate of the country. Esar-haddon rebuilt Babylon and appointed Merodach's son as Governor of Chaldæa. In 677 he renewed his campaign against Phœnicia, captured Sidon, led away the inhabitants and settled Assyrian colonists

---

[1] Lehmann-Haupt, l.c., 73.

in the city. In 671 he led a campaign against Tirhakah of Egypt. Passing Tyre, which he was unable to capture, he proceeded to the Sinaitic peninsula, which he reached in fifty-one days, subduing the hostile Arabs. Fifteen days later he was in Memphis. The old capital was stormed, sacked and destroyed. The treasures accumulated in the ancient city were carried off to Assyria. Esar-haddon was now master of Egypt and set up an Assyrian vassal king, Necho, as ruler of Sais and Memphis. The record of the Assyrian monarch's Egyptian campaigns is carved upon the rocks of the Nahr-el-Kelb, a short distance from Beyrout. The relief represents the King of Assyria in a long garment, sceptre in hand. As for Palestine, the petty kings were forced to renew their allegiance to the "King of kings". Twenty-two kings had to pay tribute to Esar-haddon and to send materials to Assyria for the construction of his gigantic palace at Nineveh.

Esar-haddon died while engaged on a second campaign against Egypt and was succeeded by Assurbanipal (Sardanapalus) (669–625). Assurbanipal was a great warrior and had to lead numerous expeditions against the vassal States, which were constantly trying to shake off the Assyrian yoke. Egypt once more revolted and Tirhakah returned, but in 663 Thebes, whither Tirhakah had to flee, fell. The Phœnicians were subdued. Soon Elam rose up against Assurbanipal, while his own brother in Babylon, in alliance with the Chaldæans, the

Aramæans, Arabs and Egyptians under Psammetichus, the son of Necho, revolted. Assurbanipal proved a match for all his enemies, whom he defeated. In Judah, Manasseh died in 641 and was succeeded by Amon, who reigned only two years. His son, Josiah, a youth of eight years, became king (639–608).

At this time, while Assyria was engaged in a life-and-death struggle with Babylonia and Elam, during the reign of Josiah, a new and terrible foe appeared on the scene and dealt the first blow to the mighty Empire of Assyria. Hordes of Scythians, descending from the Caucasus, suddenly began to traverse Western Asia. Ravaging the valley of the Euphrates, they appeared also in Palestine. They contented themselves, however, with pillaging the cities of the Philistines and, marching along the sea-coast, did not touch Judæa. The invasion, which affected the world-history of the time, nevertheless produced a deep impression in the petty kingdom of Judah, and the result was a religious reformation by Josiah.[1] Hilkiah, the high-priest, accidentally discovered the Book of the Law in the House of God, and a religious revival was inaugurated, although it proved only transitory and far from deep and permanent.

In the meantime the decline of Nineveh had begun and the doom of Assyria was approaching. Sinsariskum, the second successor of Assurbanipal, no doubt with a view to opposing the Scythian

---

[1] Smith, *The Twelve Prophets*, ii. 16.

hordes, had placed Nabopolassar, a Chaldæan, at the head of a mighty army, but the Chaldæan proved a dangerous rival. He availed himself of the excellent opportunity to free Babylon, as Merodach-Baladan had tried before him. In coalition with Kyaxares, King of the Medes, who had defeated the Scythians, he made an effort to crush the power of Assyria. At the same time Egypt, under Necho II, a son of Psammetichus, sent an army to wrest Syria and Palestine from Assyria. Necho II, who had ascended the throne of Egypt in 610, was anxious to annex to his own dominions the Assyrian Empire. King Josiah, however, who at the moment was not feeling the weight of Assyrian domination, was not inclined to become a vassal of Egypt. He decided to defend the independence of his kingdom, and marched with an army against the Egyptians. A battle took place at Megiddo, in the plain of Esdraelon, where Josiah was slain. The battle is alluded to by Herodotus.

The death of Josiah was a great blow to Judah. Palestine once more became an Egyptian province. Jehoahaz, a younger son of Josiah, was proclaimed king by the army, but Necho summoned him to Tiblah and carried him off as a prisoner to Egypt, where he died. In his place the Pharaoh appointed Jehoiakim as King of Judah (607–597). Necho II now conquered the whole of Syria and the north as far as the Euphrates. In the meantime the power of Assyria had been broken.

Nabopolassar had succeeded in asserting the independence of Babylon, and the siege of Nineveh, which began in 610, ended abruptly in 612. The Tigris, it is said, had overflowed its banks, devastated the walls of the city and thus enabled the besiegers to become masters of Nineveh. The overthrow and destruction of the Assyrian Empire was complete and the place of Assur was taken by Babylon.

Nabopolassar now entered upon the Assyrian heritage, but in the meantime other nations had seized what they could of the Assyrian possessions. Syria and Palestine had become tributary to Egypt. Nabopolassar did not remain idle. Once established on the throne, he set about reorganizing Western Asia and endeavoured to bring it under the sway of Babylon. The task fell upon his son Nebuchadrezzar, who had married the daughter of a Scythian king. He defeated the Egyptians in the battle of Carchemish in 604 B.C. and drove them back to their own land. The battle of Carchemish crushed the hopes of Egypt in Palestine, and the whole of Western Asia became subject to Babylon. When, after the death of Nabopolassar, Nebuchadrezzar returned to Babylon, where he assumed the crown (604–561), the Egyptians once more began to intrigue in Palestine, and the King of Judah, who had listened to the counsels of Egypt, was punished by the Babylonian. Jehoiakim was slain in 597, and his son, Jehoiachin or Coniah, succeeded him. Nebuchadrezzar laid siege to Jerusalem, and the king, with a number of the upper classes and the aristocracy, was carried off into captivity.

An uncle of Jehoiachin, Mattaniah, was appointed King over the remnant of the population and reigned under the name of Zedekiah (597–586). He had been allowed to reign over the petty kingdom by the grace of Babylonia, but his reign soon came to an end. He had concluded an alliance with Egypt, and, relying upon the support of the Pharaoh, Hophra (Apries, 588–569), refused to pay his tribute to Babylon. The doom of the Southern Kingdom was sealed. Once more Nebuchadrezzar came and sacked Jerusalem. The temple and the city were burnt, the bulk of the people carried off into captivity, while King Zedekiah was deprived of his sight and made a prisoner. The State of Judah had ceased to exist, and Palestine had become a Babylonian province.

Nebuchadrezzar was succeeded in 562 by his son, Evil-Merodach, but after two years the throne of Babylon was usurped by Nergal-Sharezer (Neriglissar, a son-in-law of Nebuchadrezzar). He died in 556, and Nabonidus, a favourite of the priesthood, was placed on the throne. During his reign a new power had arisen in the East. Already in the closing days of the Assyrian Empire the Persians had seized the larger part of Elam. The Persian kings acknowledged as their liege-lords the Scythian Kings of Ecbatana, but Cyrus, King of Anshan, defeated and dethroned Astyages in 549, seized Ecbatana and made himself King of Media. In 546 he was King of Persia, and in 539 attacked and overthrew the old Babylonian Empire. Although Cyrus had become the inheritor of the Assyro-Babylonian Empire, he was not yet in possession of his inheritance. Long fights were still required before he could become the real master of all the countries which his predecessors on the thrones of Assyria and Babylon had possessed. Every change of dynasty was a signal for the numerous tributary States to revolt and to shake off the foreign yoke, and every "King of kings" was compelled to reconquer the lands he had inherited. Soon, however, the great warrior had subdued the whole of Western Asia and had consequently become master of Palestine.

The old Semitic régime in Palestine had thus come to an end, and the Aryans now took the place of the Semites, who for nearly twenty centuries had been masters of the country. The world-empire had belonged to Egypt, Babylonia, Assyria and to New Babylonia, but now the turn of the Medo-Persians had come. The Hebrew prophets had watched the rising power of the Persian with growing excitement and thrills of joy. "Go up, O Elam; besiege, O Media" (Is. xxi. 2). They uttered a shout of joy at the news of Babylon's destruction: "Babylon is fallen, is fallen!" (Is. xxxi. 9).

The Persian conqueror, to a certain extent, realized the hopes of the exiles who sat and wept by the waters of Babylon. Cyrus issued his famous edict,¹ wherein he permitted the Hebrew exiles to return home and there rebuild their temple. The great king may have been moved by noble motives, but there was certainly method in his generosity. A Jewish population grateful to him, faithful and loyal, settled on the borders of Egypt, might prove useful in the case of war with the Empire on the Nile. Anyhow, the captives of Babylon were permitted to return home. Not many of them availed themselves of the permission. All the exiles hailed the national movement with joy, but the majority of them preferred to remain in Babylonia. The first expedition numbered only about 40,000 men, headed by Sheshbazzar, a prince of the house of David, probably an uncle of Zerubbabel, and the priest Joshua.

When the exiles returned home they were rather disappointed. They were permitted to return to Palestine and rebuild their "National Home", but they found the land of Palestine, nearly the whole of it, occupied by others, while bands of robbers and wild beasts were roaming over the remainder of the land, lying waste and desolate. The remnants of the Israelites had retired to Samaria, where they mixed with foreign blood and henceforth became known as the Samaritans.² The north was in the hands of the Phœnicians and Syrians. It became known as the district of the heathens, G'lil Ha-Goyim or Galilee. From the south the Edomites,

¹ See Note 9 in Appendix.
² See Note 10 in Appendix, on the Samaritans.

who were Northern Arabs, had pushed forward as far as Hebron, sacred to Jewish memory. Transjordania, called Peræa, was occupied by the Ammonites, who occasionally also crossed the Jordan, making inroads into the West. In the West the Philistines were masters of the maritime plain as far as the hill country of Judæa. In a word, Palestine was no longer the land of Israel, and the returned exiles were greatly disillusioned. Under Darius Hystaspes (520), work of building the temple was resumed, and the structure was completed in 515. Moral encouragement and money were sent by those who had remained behind, and who, although they themselves preferred to stay in Babylon, applauded the work of national reconstruction. In 458[1] Artaxerxes Longimanus encouraged the visit of Ezra the Scribe to Judæa. In the summer of 445 Nehemiah, a highly placed Babylonian Jew, a favourite cup-bearer of Artaxerxes, came to Palestine armed with the powers of a governor or high-commissioner. Ezra and Nehemiah brought some order into the old homeland. Nehemiah no doubt had deep attachments in Babylonia, and in 432 he returned there, but visited Jerusalem again the next year. He reorganized the temple worship and separated the Jews from the idolatrous aliens. Ezra and Nehemiah had definitely made the Israelites, or the Jews, as we shall now call them, the guardians of the Law

[1] For the question of the date of the Restoration, see Note 11 in Appendix.

of Moses, and from a political nation they became a religious community. Henceforth the bond of unity between the scattered members of the people of Israel was to be its religion, and the temple the visible symbol.

The restoration inaugurated in Judæa the reign of the high-priests. The Jewish State, after the return of the exiles from Babylonia, was not a *nomocracy* but a real theocracy. The highest authority was wielded by the high-priests, who united in their persons both the spiritual and the temporal power. The high-priests became virtually the kings of the land, and ruled until the triumph of the Hasmoneans, who once more established a monarchy. The high-priests were not better than lay kings. They plotted and conspired and cheated, and did not even hesitate to commit murders in order to pave their way to office.

The intellectual aristocracy of the Jews had been transferred to Babylonia, and it was there that the spiritual renaissance had taken place, a renaissance which saved the nation after the loss of the State. It was in Babylonia that the idea had dawned upon the exiles that Israel could exist without a State, without a king and without a territory. Torn away from their native land, but united by the common bond of faith, customs and hopes for the future, the exiles realized for the first time the whole depth of the world of ideas of their prophets. They now understood that the strength and future of the nation lay, not so much in a political State, in armies and military achievements, as in spiritual unity, in religion and morals. By the waters of the Euphrates the exiles sat and wept, but their national consciousness awoke in its intensity, and they became more united in exile than they had ever been in Palestine. The source of spiritual creation, the creation of permanent moral and intellectual values, was stronger and fresher in Babylonia than it had been in the Promised Land. The Jewish colony in Babylonia was therefore animated by a national-religious spirit, by a desire to create a spiritual centre in the old homeland, and it was in such a state of mind that the exiles returned to Palestine. Their chief aim was to live peacefully under Persian rule and to renew in the homeland their spiritual, intellectual and religious existence. But conditions in Palestine were for the moment very unfavourable. Surrounded by and living in close relations with the heathen populations occupying the country, mixed marriages were almost unavoidable, and the danger of complete assimilation was great. There was the danger of the returned exiles being merged among their heathen neighbours, of losing entirely their national characteristics and the religion of the Prophets. This would have really happened had not help come from the Diaspora, from Babylon. When the Jews in Babylonia heard how matters stood in Palestine they were alarmed and sent Ezra to save the situation. The great scribe succeeded in his efforts with the help of Nehemiah, who became the

Persian High Commissioner of Palestine. "Ezra", writes Herford, "had two main ideas, both of which he succeeded, to a great extent, in carrying into practice. One was to set up a barrier between Jew and Gentile, for the protection of the Jew living the life he ought to live in obedience to the will of God; and the other was to proclaim in the *Torah*, the Law, the revelation of the Divine Will given to Israel, and the consequent duty of every faithful Jew to conform to it."[1] In other words, a Jew who did not lead a religious life was no longer a Jew, the Jewish religion and the Jewish nation being identical. In order, therefore, to make it possible for the Jew to remain a Jew he had to be shielded from contact with the Gentile world. Had Ezra and Nehemiah not come to Palestine in the fifth century B.C. and laid the foundation of the national religion, consolidated the people and separated it from the surrounding heathen peoples, by putting a stop to the mixed marriages, the Jews in Palestine would have disappeared and left no name in the world's history. Unity, social reforms according to the Law of Moses, which became the charter and constitution of the Jewish commonwealth, a process of isolation and separation from the Gentiles, such was the work inaugurated and carried out by Ezra and Nehemiah. On the one hand, the *Torah* was proclaimed as the national constitution, and a solid foundation was laid for the spiritual peculiarity of the Jews, while, on the other, social reforms were

[1] R. T. Herford, *The Pharisees*, 1924, 19.

introduced with a view to putting an end to class-war and social injustice.[1]

"Restore, I pray you, to them even this day, their fields, their vineyards, their olive yards, and their houses, also the hundredth part of the money, and of the corn, the wine, and the oil that you exact of them. Then, said they, we will restore them and will do even as thou sayest" (Neh. v. 1–15). Ezra and Nehemiah thus introduced an administration of equal and impartial justice, the establishment of kindlier relations between rich and poor and a mitigation of abuses. Such was the work of Ezra and Nehemiah, and henceforth the real significance of the Jew was to lie in the preservation and development of the national faith and the peculiar culture of the People of the Book.

For two centuries Palestine formed part of a Persian satrapy and its political history, wrapt in darkness, was uneventful. As far, however, as the Jews of Palestine are concerned, it was a time of intense spiritual work, a time of transition or rather evolution—an evolution from the worldly national to a spiritual and religious conception. It was during this time that Aramaic, the language spoken by the inhabitants of Palestine, was substituted for Hebrew, even by the Jews. Aramaic became the vernacular of Palestine, the language of the Government and of business.[2]

[1] See A. S. Rappoport, *Labour, Social Reform and Democracy*.
[2] See W. Robertson Smith, *The Old Testament in the Jewish Church*, 35.

CHAPTER X

RELIGION AND POLITICS—THE HOUSES OF PTOLEMY AND SELEUCUS

Persian rule—Satraps—Satrapy of Abar-Nahara—Rebellion under Artaxerxes Ochus — The restoration — Cultural individuality—Advance of the Arabs—Battle of Issus—The Diadochi—Ptolemy Lagi—Seleucus—Palestine a Greek province—Paganism in Palestine—Hellenization of country—Battle of Raphia—Seleucus IV—Antiochus Epiphanes—Religious persecutions—The Pro-Egyptian Party—Introduction of Hellenism—War on Jewish religion—Religion and politics—The Hasmonæans—Judas Maccabæus—Diplomatic relations with Rome—The Pharisees—Nation and religion—The *Torah* as charter of religion—Pharisees and Prophets—Religious vitality—Joppa a Jewish port—John Hyrcanus—Aristobulus I—Alexander Jannæus—The Nabatæans—Transjordania—Hyrcanus II—Aristobulus II—Antipater—Appeal to Rome

POLITICALLY, the Persian period in Palestine was colourless and uneventful. It was, on the whole, a peaceful time for the country. The system of government of the Persian Empire was not at all oppressive. The Government in distant Susa was insistent only upon the recognition of the Persian suzerainty and the regularity of the tribute, which was, above all, a sign of acknowledging submission. The Persian Government rarely interfered in the affairs of the province, leaving the administrative power in the hands of the satraps, who were practically kings in the provinces. They could make their domination burdensome or light, as they pleased. For the most part, however, the Persian satraps took their responsibilities rather lightly, and rarely attempted to control the administrative affairs of the communities under their charge. The satrapy of Abar-Nahara (on the other side of the river) included the whole of Syria and Palestine, while Judæa was administrated by an under-satrap (or Pecha). In the first century of the Persian domination two Jews occupied the post of Pecha, Zerubbabel and Nehemiah, and there may have been others later on.

Jewish soldiers are said to have fought in the armies of their Persian master, and some may have been found among the Syrians who fought at Marathon, as we learn from Herodotus (vii. 89). Eusebius says that the Jews had taken part in a rebellion under Artaxerxes Ochus (359–338 B.C.), and a number of them seem to have been punished and transported to Hyrcania, on the shores of the Caspian Sea. The fact, however, of repressive measures on the part of the Persians is rather doubtful, as the Jews on the whole were found to be loyal to their Persian master when the Greeks invaded Palestine. If politically uneventful, the Persian period had, however, far-reaching consequences intellectually and spiritually as far as Judæa is concerned. The first century of the Persian domination was the period of restoration. The first restoration lasted from 537 to 516, and during that time the returned exiles had to face serious problems of living. They had to do pioneer work, to build houses and the temple, settle in Jerusalem and its districts and generally fight against the existing waste and desolation. Half a century later there was a second restoration (458–420), during which the Jewish colony was animated by a deeply national and religious spirit. It was during this period that the returned exiles became conscious of the spiritual individuality of Israel. The idea of the religious and ethical mission of the nation took root, and a theocracy was established. A nation evolved which henceforth was able to maintain its spiritual individuality; it became strong and self-conscious enough to withstand the onslaught of Greek culture and to ward off the dangers of assimilation.

It was also during the Persian period that the Arabs began to advance into the lands of Aramæan civilization. This we gather from the Prophets Ezekiel, Obadiah and Malachi. They advanced into the lands of the Edomites, of Moab and Ammon and in the south of the country of the Philistines. Geshem, the Arab, the friend and ally of Sanballat, lived near Jerusalem.[1] The prophecy of Zephaniah, "And the sea-coast shall be pastures, with cottages for shepherds and folds for flocks" (ii. 6), evidently refers to the Arabs.

In 333 the Empire of the Achæmenidæ was overthrown by the Macedonian conqueror after the battle of Issus, and victorious Hellenism conquered the Orient; Greek civilization and culture spread over Asia. The conquests of the great Macedonian involved a change of masters for Palestine. Alexander is said to have favoured the Jews and granted them

[1] See Wellhausen, *Israelitische und Jüdische Geschichte*, 183.

many privileges, but his fundamental idea, that of binding together his empire by a Greek civilization, had far-reaching consequences as far as Israel was concerned. The world-empire Alexander had founded fell to pieces after his death. It was portioned out among his generals and divided into three great States: Macedonia, Egypt and Syria. Palestine was included in the dominions of the satrap of Syria, and the small country once more became the apple of discord between two powerful kingdoms.

A fierce struggle was waged for many years between the various claimants called the Diadochi, and Palestine did not escape the general anarchy which ensued. The fight for the Phœnician coast and its hinterland became acute between the Powers on the Nile, the Euphrates and in Syria, the rulers trying to gain possession of the land of Israel. After the battle of Gaza in 312, Ptolemy Lagi became the ruler of Egypt, while Seleucus was the master of Babylonia-Syria. Once more Palestine became a buffer State between the two competing Powers of the Ptolemies and the Seleucidae. Both were anxious to possess the country which lay on the boundaries of their dominions. Seleucus had founded the Græco-Syrian kingdom and established his capital at Antioch, and for a time Palestine was the object of contention and in turn a vassal State dependent either upon Egypt or Syria.

It is a bewildering story—that of Palestine for

the next two centuries, a story of invasions and conquests, of usurpations, intrigues and bloodshed, of oppression and heroic struggles for liberty, of persecutions followed by splendid victories.

In 315 the war for the possession of Palestine broke out between Ptolemy Lagi and Antigonus, and henceforth the fluctuations were numerous, as is attested by the coinage of the period.[1] In 301, at the battle of Ipsus, Antigonus was killed, and the division of the Alexandrian Empire was finally settled. Seleucus received upper Asia and Mesopotamia, Macedonia fell to Cassander, while Ptolemy was confirmed in the possession of Egypt. As for Cœle-Syria and Palestine, Ptolemy claimed it and, although Seleucus protested against the injustice, he did not feel inclined to snatch it from his friend. The country thus remained in the possession of Egypt for another century, when, after the death of Ptolemy Philopator, it was conquered by Antiochus III.

Under the Ptolemies Palestine, on the whole, enjoyed a state of prosperity. The Jews were content as long as they were not being molested in the exercise of their religion. The Ptolemies left them in peace, and no forcible measures were undertaken against them. And yet the Hellenization of the country was being continued and the culture of Hellas was making rapid progress. Ever since the conquest of Alexander, Palestine had become a

---

[1] See Cooke, *North Semitic Inscriptions*, 351; Madden, *Coins of the Jews*.

Greek province, and numerous cities were peopled with the veterans of the Macedonian army.[1] Whether Palestine belonged to Egypt or formed part of Syria, the civilization of both the Ptolemies and the Seleucidae was Hellenic. Besides, Alexander had attracted a number of Jews to the newly founded city of Alexandria, and the relations existing between the Jews in the homeland and in the Egyptian Diaspora were instrumental in furthering Greek culture in Palestine.

It was part of the policy of the Ptolemies to promote intercourse between their Asiatic and Hellenic subjects, and Greek settlements were planted all over Palestine. Greeks and Macedonians became very numerous and influential in Western Asia. Many towns of Palestine became quite heathen, and paganism threatened to become a serious danger to the religion of Israel. It was no longer the paganism of the primitive inhabitants of Canaan which, during the age of the Judges and the periods of the Kings, had frequently turned away the nation from the worship of Jehovah; it was a new paganism, more dangerous because more refined, more elegant and more attractive.

Moreover, Ptolemy II, Philadelphus (285–247), was spreading Hellenism in Palestine by peaceful means, and had found many supporters among the Jewish upper classes and the aristocracy. While leaving the high-priest of Jerusalem undisturbed in his religious and even political supremacy, he

[1] See Derenbourg, *La Palestine*, 44.

succeeded in introducing Greek culture in the land. He built cities and erected temples, and paved the way for a *rapprochement* between his Greek and Asiatic subjects. The danger of assimilation was staring the Jews in the face, and had the Jewish aristocracy not been checked in its endeavours by a powerful opposition, its aims would ultimately have been realized. But the bulk of the Jewish people had remained faithful to their religion and to the Law of Moses upon which Ezra had based the constitution of the Jews.

At last the religious party, those who were anxious to save the national religion rather than the State, grew alarmed. They could well bear the loss of political independence, but when it became a question of the Jewish faith, of the ancestral religion and Jewish morality, they raised a vehement protest. Heathen influences were too great and penetrating, and the danger of relaxing the stringency of the law, which it had been their great aim to keep since the days of Ezra and Nehemiah, became acute. The problem once more arose how to save the nation, that is, the national religion, the theocracy, from heathen contamination. In such an emergency the Jews were capable of the highest sacrifices, and some of them imagined that religion would be safer under the rule of Syria than it was under that of the Ptolemies.

In the days of the Kings there had been two parties, a pro-Assyrian and a pro-Egyptian, and now the choice lay between Egypt and Syria.

When therefore in 221 war broke out between Ptolemy IV, Philopator, the successor of Ptolemy Euergetes, and Antiochus III (223–187), many Jews were in favour of the latter. In 217 Antiochus suffered a defeat at Raphia, and Palestine remained in the possession of Egypt, but for a short time only. Since his repulse at Raphia, Antiochus had not given up his hopes of wresting Palestine from the house of the Ptolemies. He could not rest as long as the valuable province, which was geographically united with his own territory, was still in the hands of the enemy. His chance came after the death of Ptolemy Philopator in 204, when a child of four, Ptolemy V, Epiphanes, ascended the Egyptian throne. The battle of Paneion, or Paneas, at the entry of the land, where the sources of the Jordan were marked by the precinct of a deity in whom the Greeks recognized Pan, in 198 B.C. resulted in a complete and decisive victory for Antiochus. It meant the substitution of the Seleucid for the Ptolemaic rule in Palestine.[1] The Jews of Jerusalem received Antiochus with open arms, while the Philistines held by the house of Ptolemy.

Egypt lost control of Palestine, and when Antiochus advanced into Judæa he was welcomed by a large portion of the Jews. He had delivered them from Egyptian spiritual bondage. They greeted the victor with enthusiasm and joy, little dreaming that dark days were in store for them, and that soon a more ruthless policy of Hellenization would be

---

[1] E. R. Bevan, *The House of Seleucus*, ii. 37.

inaugurated. Judæa was incorporated into the kingdom of the Seleucidæ and remained a province of Syria until the days of the Maccabees.

The Jews were at first kindly treated by their new ruler, and were granted the right to live in accordance with their own laws. The friendly legislation went even so far as to make it a crime to carry into Jerusalem such meats as the Jews were forbidden to eat. Seleucus IV is said to have borne all the costs of the sacrifices (2 Macc. iii. 3). Such a policy only helped to spread Hellenism in Judæa, the political sympathy being accompanied by a predilection for Greek culture. Had the Seleucidæ continued the same policy, they would have succeeded in realizing Alexander's dream more easily and brought about an assimilation of the Jews in Palestine, for Hellenism had indeed made great progress in the country. New towns bearing Greek names were founded, and the old cities of Gaza and Joppa were Hellenized. It was especially under Antiochus IV, Epiphanes (175–164), a brother of Seleucus IV (187–175), that the spread of Hellenism in the Promised Land of Israel made itself particularly felt. The process of Hellenizing went on even more rapidly, and it "was only a question of time before the Jews, like other dependent peoples, would become fused in a Hellenistic mould". But fortunately a strong countercurrent was also running which was destined to destroy the Hellenizing influence and to save the national faith of Israel.

Had the Hellenizing movement been allowed to run its course among the Jews, it is quite possible and even highly probable, that Judaism, and consequently the Jews, would have succumbed and disappeared, like many other nationalities. It was the king's own policy which swelled the counter-current and intensified the devotion of the Jews to their national faith and culture. The religious persecutions of Antiochus Epiphanes gave rise to the Maccabæan revolt. The king had been involved in a war with Egypt and had all but conquered the country, but he was suddenly ordered by Rome to return to Syria. It is quite possible that he now perceived the danger of having on the southern frontier of his kingdom an unassimilated nation like the Jews, who might at any time develop a strong pro-Egyptian party. For this reason he decided to consolidate his kingdom by the establishment of a common civilization. There was thus a political reason underlying the attempt at transformation undertaken by Antiochus. There was method in the apparent madness of the king called Epimanes, the Madman. Antiochus Epiphanes was keen enough to perceive that the weakness of his realm consisted in the fact that it lacked a national unity, and he was convinced that the principle of fusion and union lay in a uniform culture, and he decided to eradicate the differences of race, creed and tradition.

Coupled with these political reasons was also the king's ambition to realize the dream of Alexander the Great. Rome had circumscribed the activities of Antiochus as a conqueror, but it did not hinder him in his ambitions to be known as the champion of Hellenism—a Hellenism which extended to the sphere of social and private life as well as religious practice, to the manner of thought and speech. He wanted that "all should be one people, and that each should forsake his own laws" (1 Macc. i. 41).

Antiochus experienced no difficulty whatever in the case of the other inhabitants of Palestine, as they did not dream of opposing the introduction of Hellenism. "All the nations agreed according to the word of the king" (1 Macc. i. 42). Such was not the result of the king's Hellenizing frenzy in the case of the Jews. It is true that some of the Jews themselves were in favour of Hellenization, and had for some time already been trying to introduce Greek culture in Jerusalem. A deputation of the principal men of the Jews appeared at the Court of Antiochus soon after his accession, and craved permission to erect a gymnasium at Jerusalem and to turn the city into an Antioch. The new high-priest, Jason, was a great partisan of the Hellenizing movement. But the bulk of the nation were more than ever decided to repel the encroachments of heathenism. They hardened themselves in a more rigid exclusiveness and made the fence of the law still stronger. Political dependence was naught when compared to the religious belief which was to be Israel's distinctive heritage. Antiochus, now more than ever decided to eradicate the Jewish faith, adopted measures of coercion, prohibiting the practice of circumcision and the observance of the Sabbath. This was more than the Jews would bear. A formidable struggle was the result, a life-and-death struggle between Hellenism and Judaism.

When Antiochus declared war on the Jewish religion, the revolt broke out in all its fierceness. It was in the defence of its religion—and such has been its attitude all through history—that Israel gave full proof of its stern and sublime qualities, of its power of endurance and its obstinacy, its self-devotion and fidelity to an ideal. The fight for political freedom has never raised this people to such a pitch of self-sacrifice as did and does the fight for religion.

The rule of Antiochus Epiphanes in Palestine thus resulted in bitter and bloody wars, because the Jewish faith, the national religion and the nation were in danger of being wiped out entirely. That was more important to the Jews than the disappearance of their political State. It was a bitter life-and-death struggle of world-wide importance, not so much from the political point of view as from that of civilization and culture. The Jews were victorious in the end. History shows us that whenever the Jews are compelled to defend their national religion, the very existence of the nation, they triumph. The spirit, the power and strength of idealism and morality cannot be crushed by brute-force. It is quite different when it is a question of politics. Once the nation of the Jews begins to dabble in politics and to assert its political independence it is doomed to meet failure.

At the beginning the fight of the Jews against Antiochus was a religious and moral struggle, and the Jews therefore came out victorious. When, however, the Hasmonæans later on carried their heroic fight into the arena of politics, trying to establish an independent political State, they were beaten and fell a prey to the Romans. But we must not anticipate.

Antiochus inaugurated what meant to the adherents of the law a reign of terror. "All should be one people" was his motto, his aim being to establish in Palestine a community of Hellenized pagans. The ancestral faith of the Jews was forbidden. Sabbath and circumcision were to disappear, while the Temple of Jerusalem was dedicated to the worship of Jupiter Olympus. A sort of inquisition in the service of Hellas was instituted in Palestine. These persecutions only increased the devotion of the people to the God of their ancestors and to their national religion. Between desertion of their faith and death the Jews never did hesitate. The result was the rise and the heroic deeds of the Maccabees. The struggle of the latter originated in the defence of religion, of a theocratic constitution, but it ended in a fight for political independence, for a kingdom.

In 167 B.C., an attempt being made by Syrian officers to compel the Jews at Modin to sacrifice to heathen gods, Matthathias, a leading priest of the Hasmonæan family, was required to set an example. He refused, slew with his own hands the Jew who was about to comply with the request and killed the Syrian officer. This was the signal for a general rising, and under the leadership of Matthathias and after the death of his son Judas Maccabæus, the Hammer, a group of heroes collected, ready to fight to the bitter end in defence of their ancestral religion. In 162 the Syrian garrison was expelled from Acre.

Judas Maccabæus is said to have concluded an alliance with Rome (1 Macc. viii. 23–30), but this information is rather doubtful. Some scholars[1] deny the existence of any diplomatic relations between Judas Maccabæus and Rome, while others are of opinion that Judas actually did have friendly dealings with Rome.[2] He had entered into negotiations with the mighty republic with a view to securing its friendship. With regard to the treaty, as given in Maccabees, opinions again differ. Some hold it to be a genuine document, while others declare that it is a mere forgery.[3] In any case, with the conquest of Judas Maccabæus, the religious goal of the movement had been reached, but the stone brought into motion continued to roll on.

---

[1] Willrich, *Judaica*, 1900, 62–85; and also Wellhausen.
[2] See Schürer, *Geschichte des jüdischen Volkes*, i. 220, n. 32.
[3] See Schürer, l.c.; Niese, *Kritik*, 88; Bevan, *The House of Seleucus*, ii. 300.

RELIGION AND POLITICS

The Hasmonæan princes, relying upon their success, now began to dream of political independence, and concentrated their efforts upon the establishment of a political State. Jonathan, the younger brother of Judas, continued to fight against the power of the Seleucidæ, and Simon (142–135) finally established the Hasmonæan dynasty.

This political fight, however, did not please the Pharisees, to whom religion and national culture were dearer than the State. The Pharisees[1] have often been identified with the Scribes or Interpreters of the Law. This is not quite correct. Neither were all the Pharisees Interpreters of the Law nor were all the scholars Pharisees. It is evident that in a party which laid such stress upon the observation of the law, paying but little attention to worldly fortunes, scholarship and study played an important part (see Mark ii. 16, vii. 1),[2] but, apart from strictly religious ideas, the Pharisees were a non-political party.

The very name of Pharisees, from the Hebrew *Perishout* = separation, *Amixia*, shows that the Pharisees did not preach an absolute detachment from mundane things. They were only anxious for the nation to live its own religious and spiritual life and avoid as much as possible the contact with heathen nations. They were convinced that a State with a king and an army must ultimately lead to close relations with other nations.[3]

---

[1] See Note 12 in Appendix.
[2] Where the Pharisees and Scribes are constantly mentioned in the same connection. [3] Derenbourg, l.c., 16.

The Pharisees placed the national religion and the preservation of the nation above the State. They were ready to fight for religious autonomy and independence in order to keep Israel separated from the heathens, to make it *different* from the other nations. Quite opposed to this view was that of the political fighters. They wanted the State and political independence so as to be *like* unto the other nations. According to the Pharisees, one of the vital conditions of an integral conservation of the nation and of the national religion was the complete isolation of Israel, which alone could save pure monotheism and preserve the Jews from heathen contamination and assimilation. The Prophets had already laid stress upon the moral precepts of the Hebrew religion, and if they had also depicted the universal brotherhood of nations, this was only to come with the extinction of heathenism.

The Pharisees were therefore ready to fight and to go to war, not for political freedom, but for the law. They supported the Maccabees in their revolt against Antiochus Epiphanes when the latter forbade the free exercise of religion, but only as long as the law, as religion and Judaism, were in jeopardy. Once the religion was safe, they were prepared to make peace with the enemy. Politics for them were to be subservient to religion, never religion to politics. Religion and what is called patriotism or political independence were not necessarily inseparably united. On the contrary, without the basis of religion the Jewish State had no *raison d'être*. To the Pharisees religion was the essence while the State was only a means to an end. "The very fact that so many Jews, in spite of the loss of a national territory, have remained Jews nevertheless is a striking proof of the extent to which the Jewish religion has emancipated itself from dependence on the conditions of national political existence."[1] "To the Jews of the Diaspora, their Judaism is like a protecting sheath that secures their continued existence."[2] Even beyond the limits of Palestine the religion consolidated by Ezra wielded an immense power over the nation, which would otherwise not have survived the intercourse with and the various influences of the peoples of the land and, above all, the persecutions.

The Pharisees had, therefore, broken with the Hasmonæan family. For a time the danger threatened to the national religion by the introduction of Gentile ideas, the anxiety to defend and safeguard the Holy Law, had gathered the party under the banner of Judas Maccabæus. Since, however, the danger had disappeared, the Pharisees could only follow the Hasmonæans as long as they had the same aim in view, namely, religion and *not* politics. They were ready to give their support to a policy anxious to crush all foreign influence and to concentrate the moral strength and the force of vitality of the nation in the sole endeavour of saving the national faith and the national culture.

[1] Kuenen, *National Religions*, 1882, 171. [2] Ibid., 172.

The Maccabees owed their success to the unity of the people. As long as religion was in danger, all united for the defence of the *Torah*, Israel's charter of religion. But as soon as the political aims and ambitions of the Hasmonæan family became evident with the growth of their power, the Pharisees, to whom religion, national faith and culture were much more important than the Jewish State, broke with the Hasmonæan princes. In their opposition to the policy of the Hasmonæans, i.e. that of promoting the welfare of the nation by political methods, the Pharisees agreed with the older Prophets. The latter had already rebuked the Kings of Judah for intriguing with foreign Powers (Is. xxi.). The trial of strength between the religious and political conceptions of Jewish national life, inaugurated by the Prophets and strengthened by Ezra, has continued ever since, both in Palestine and in the Diaspora, while the "religious vitality of the Jewish nation has always remained unimpaired".[1] The political catastrophe of Israel was consummated in A.D. 70, and ever since politics, *without the fundamental basis of religion*, have never succeeded in saving the Jews as Jews and in hindering their assimilation and disappearance.

The Hasmonæan princes, however, intoxicated with their successes, had other views. They had lost that religious ardour and simplicity of heart which had helped them to re-establish the national cult. It was now no longer a religious but a royal dream

---

[1] T. Herford, *The Pharisees*, 45.

they were dreaming. When Antiochus Epiphanes had tried to make them accept the worship of Jupiter, they had stubbornly refused to be *like* the others, but now their ambition was to be, in some respects at least, *like other nations*. To occupy the office of high-priest no longer satisfied their ambition, for they wished to be masters of the country and to ascend the throne of David.

Antiochus IV had in the meantime died in the Far East, and the subsequent quarrels for the throne of the Seleucidæ enabled the Hasmonæans to shake off the foreign yoke and to found once more an independent State. The State of Syria, weakened and crippled by conflicts, favoured the establishment of a Jewish kingdom in Palestine under the Hasmonæan dynasty by Simon (142-135), the last surviving son of Matthathias. He made Joppa a Jewish port and captured Acre. Simon's son and successor, John Hyrcanus (135-104), was already strong enough to assert his independence against Syria under the successor of Antiochus VII, Sidetes, who had lost his life in an expedition against Parthia in 128.

John Hyrcanus extended the boundaries of his kingdom so that it attained the dimensions of the State founded by David, while Aristobulus I (104-103), his son and successor, was the first to assume the title of King. He continued his conquests in the north, annexed Galilee, and conquered the Arabs in the Lebanon and a portion of Ituræa, compelling the inhabitants to accept the Jewish faith. His brother and successor, Alexander Jannæus (104–78), still further extended his possessions, and took the important town of Gadara in Transjordania, but his conquests were stopped by the Nabatæans. The latter, a branch of the Arabs, considered the whole district of Transjordania as their natural possession. Alexander's widow, Salome-Alexandra, tried to extend still farther the boundaries of the newly founded kingdom, but after her death, owing to the conflict between her two sons, Hyrcanus II and Aristobulus II, the power of the Hasmonæan family declined. Antipater, an Idumæan by descent, Governor of Idumæa, supported Hyrcanus and gained for him the help of Aretas, King of the Nabatæans. The latter led an army into Judæa. The people, however, were divided, some of them supporting Aristobulus, the others being on the side of Hyrcanus. This crisis in Judæa took place at a moment when Rome was gradually extending her sway over Asia and annexing the possessions of the inheritors of Alexander's Empire. The rival Hasmonæan princes committed the error of appealing to the Romans, and the Romans "came, saw and conquered".

CHAPTER XI

PALESTINE IN THE TALONS OF ROME

The Romans—Pompey—The golden vine—Hyrcanus high-priest—The Roman protectorate—Hasmonæans and Idumæans—Scaurus—Gabinius—Division of Judæa—The Parthians—Antigonus—Herod and Antony—Palestine a Roman dependency—The Kingdom of Herod—Hatred of the Jews—The iron hand—The battle of Actium—Octavius—Native princes—Hordes of robbers—Ananel the high-priest—Alexandra and Cleopatra—Sebaste—The Temple of Herod—The sons of Herod—A deputation to the Emperor—Archelaus—Herod Antipas—Administrative districts—Herod Philip—The "fox"—The Decapolis—Greek cities—The Legate of Syria—The procurator—The *angariæ*—Agrippa I—The Birth of Christianity—The Redeemer—Judaism and paganism—The Romans and the Jews—The cruelties of the procurators—The war—Vespasian—Titus—The fall of Jerusalem

A NEW factor had thus appeared in Jewish politics: the Romans. They had been closing in upon Syria, and in 65 Pompey arrived and sent his general Scaurus to secure the country. Rome had already cast her eyes on Western Asia, and Roman Imperialism was soon to extend its sway over Palestine. When Pompey arrived himself at Damascus and the two Hasmonæan brothers appealed to him, the Roman was graciously pleased to settle their affairs. Aristobulus sent him as a present a golden vine worth 500 talents, but in the end Pompey decided in favour of Hyrcanus. Aristobulus was removed to Rome, while Hyrcanus retained the high-priesthood, but was deprived of his royal dignity.

After Assyria, Babylonia Persia, Egypt and

Syria, it was now mighty Rome which became mistress of Palestine. Rome, however, did not swoop down upon her victim immediately. Like a vulture, she first circled round her prey, even spreading out her wings as if to protect it. She first established a protectorate, but the victim instinctively felt that at the slightest movement or attempt to regain freedom and independence, the claws of the bird of prey would enter its flesh. The real Roman domination was to come later on, for the protectorate lasted about seventy years, from the moment when Pompey entered the Holy of Holies at Jerusalem (63 B.C.) until the day when procurators were appointed (in A.D. 6). During this period the Roman State passed a political crisis, changing from a republic to an empire (31 B.C.); but its imperialistic policy remained the same. For seventy years part of Palestine, Judæa at least, remained a semi-independent State. The central power at Rome, the Republican and afterwards the Imperial Government, first confirmed the princes of the house of the Hasmonæans and then the Idumæan rulers of the family of Antipater and Herod. But Rome was always watching, and at the slightest attempt on the part of the Palestinians to shake off the foreign yoke and to regain their freedom, the Roman legate of the province of Syria was ready to suppress the movement and to punish the rebels. Palestine had thus once more fallen under the control of a foreign master. Such has always been the fate of this peculiar country, which never could, and never probably will, enjoy political independence for any length of time.

Scaurus was left in Syria for two years in charge of the region between Egypt and the Euphrates with full prætorian power. Judæa was stripped of the territory won since the days of Simon, while the remainder was made subject to Scaurus. The cities of Hippos, Scythopolis, Gaza, Joppa, Dora and Stratho's Tower were all made free and remained strongly anti-Jewish, even when Augustus later on gave them back to Herod. Gabinius, the first proconsul of Syria (57–55), in order to weaken the country, divided Judæa into five districts: Jerusalem, Gadara, Amathus, Jericho and Sepphoris. This system of decentralization he had introduced in the whole of Syria with a view to destroying the monarchic constitution and replacing it by an aristocratic oligarchy. The autonomous municipalities, after the model of the Greek city-states were locally administered by an aristocratic council or senate.

Hyrcanus was nominally ethnarch of Judæa, but the real power lay in the hands of Antipater, the Idumæan, who was slowly paving the way for the fortunes of his own family. He never lost an opportunity of rendering valuable services to Rome. Cæsar made Antipater a Roman citizen and procurator of Judæa, and the Idumæan appointed his son Phasælus Governor of Jerusalem, while his younger son Herod was put in charge of Galilee.

The dethroned Hasmonæans had in the meantime

not given up the fight, and with the aid of the Parthians, Antigonus, the son of Aristobulus and nephew of Hyrcanus, tried to win back the throne. The Parthians overran the country, plundered Jerusalem and carried off Hyrcanus as a prisoner to Babylonia, while Antigonus was hailed king by the people. Herod fled to Alexandria and thence proceeded to Rome, where his friend Antony, with the consent of Augustus, conferred the crown of Judæa on him. Supported by Roman soldiers and provided with Roman gold, Herod set out for Palestine, where he succeeded in conquering the kingdom to which he had been appointed. Antigonus was taken prisoner and brought before Antony, who intended to lead the last Hasmonæan prince in triumph to Rome. Herod, however, persuaded his patron to put Antigonus to death, and the unhappy prince was beheaded at Antioch. It was the first time, writes Strabo, in which the Romans had executed such a sentence upon a king. The dynasty of the Hasmonæans had thus come to an end, and an Idumæan became King of the Jews.

"The Hasmonæan family", writes Josephus, "was a splendid one, both on account of the nobility of their stock and of the dignity of the high-priesthood, as also for the glorious actions their ancestors had performed for our nation, but these men lost the government by their discussions one with another, and it came to Herod, the son of Antipater, who was of no more than a vulgar family, and of no eminent extraction, but one that was subject to other kings."[1]

Since the return of the Jews from the Babylonian exile and the restoration, the supreme power had in turn been in the hands of either the high-priests or the king high-priest, but with Herod a temporal king once more became the ruler. Herod, however, was only a half-Jew. He had not been elected by the people but received his crown from the foreigner. Hated by both the people and the aristocracy, he was looked upon as a procurator appointed by Rome. The Government which Herod inaugurated lacked both the national and the theocratic basis. A warrior and a politician, Herod did not care for the spiritual ideals of the Jews and paid homage only to the physical strength and power of the Romans and to the external culture of Greece. But he was the right man to further the policy of Rome, and Rome recognized his capacities and even his genius. Nominally a Jewish State, Palestine, under Herod, was a Roman dependency ruled by an Idumæan, an Arab crowned on the Roman capitol.

The Idumæan was confirmed by Rome in the sovereignty of a wide and heterogeneous territory. His kingdom included, besides Batanæa, south of Damascus, Galilee and Peræa, and a number of Greek cities across the Jordan and south through Idumæa. All the privileges that an independent monarch could hold were granted to Herod, except that of issuing gold coins. But he held his territory only

[1] *Antiquities*, xiv. 16, 4.

for life, as the acknowledged beneficiary of Rome, and he had no right to dispose of his dominions. When we learn that Herod left a will distributing his possessions, this will carried no weight whatever, and Rome reserved the right to approve her vassal's will or annul it.

Herod made many efforts to conciliate his Jewish subjects, but in spite of the fact that he had many supporters, he remained unpopular. By many Jews he was regarded with hatred and bitter antagonism. Was it really his Idumæan descent that the Jews could not forgive him? He tried to prove his attachment to the law, and the Jews as a rule do not hate converts to their religion! It is more than probable that the hatred was provoked by Herod's cruelties and violence, but it may also have been due to the fact that Herod was the instrument of Rome, the *homme de paille* of the Imperialists on the banks of the Tiber. The Roman domination, the Jews were quick enough to realize, was the iron hand in the velvet glove. It represented a danger to the maintenance of their institutions. Rome would for a time allow them to cling to their ancestral institutions, but once their practices gave the slightest rise to a breach of the peace, then Rome would not hesitate mercilessly to suppress the reprehensible "superstitions". The Jews hated Herod because they feared and hated Rome.

For a short time Herod's career was in danger, namely, after the battle of Actium, when Octavius became master of Rome. The wily Idumæan, however, rushed to the help of Didius, the Governor of Syria, when the latter was attacked by a band of Antony's gladiators, and then went to meet the new master of the Roman Republic. Octavius saw the value of Herod as a servant of Rome, and not only re-established him in the kingdom, but also gave him back Jericho and added to his territory the cities of Gadara, Hippos, Samaria, Gaza, Anthedon, Joppa and Stratho's Tower.

As far as Rome was concerned, Herod was the right man in the right place. It was part of the policy of Rome, as of many Imperialist States since, to have the peace of a conquered region assured by means of a reliable native government rather than directly by Roman administration. The Roman rule, it was argued, would be more acceptable in Palestine if it came indirectly through the medium of a king who was a Jew, and to the Romans Herod was a Jew, although of Idumæan stock. The Jews might well call him "an Idumæan slave", but the Romans did not recognize the distinction between a Jew proper and an Idumæan. For the purposes of Roman Imperial policy, Herod was a trustworthy instrument. His Hellenic sympathies were well known, and he had proved his loyalty to his masters. Besides, constant turbulence was to be feared in the East, and a strong hand was needed to repel not only the hordes of plundering robbers, but also the Parthians. Such a strong man had been discovered in Herod, who fully justified Rome's trust in him. He kept order and paid special attention to the suppression of more or less organized brigandage which was often a disguised attempt at revolution. In a word, Herod fulfilled his engagement to the *populus Romanus*.

Once established on the throne, the king sent to death the members of the Sanhedrin and elevated to the high-priesthood a friend of his named Ananel. His mother-in-law, however, the Hasmonæan princess Alexandra, whose daughter Mariamne Herod had married, complained to Cleopatra, Queen of Egypt. Herod was compelled to cancel the appointment and to confer the office on the youthful Aristobulus, the brother of his wife, the proud and beautiful Hasmonæan princess. In his jealousy, however, Herod soon afterwards caused Aristobulus to be drowned.

Herod now improved the country by numerous buildings and by a number of fine towns. He built Gaba in Galilee, Heshbon in Peræa and Anthedon on the coast, calling it Agrippeum. Samaria was converted into a Roman city under the name of Sebaste. Herod's grandest structure, however, was the Temple of Jerusalem, which, with cautious regard to certain fears on the part of the Jews, he rebuilt on a magnificent scale.

Before his death Herod divided his kingdom among three of his sons. He left Judæa to Archelaus, with the title of king; Galilee and Peræa he gave to Herod Antipas, with the title of tetrarch; while the north-eastern districts he left to Philip, with the title of tetrarch.

This will had, however, to be confirmed by Augustus. The Jews sent deputations to the Emperor begging him to incorporate Judæa in the province of Syria, hoping that they might thus have liberty to live by their own laws. After some hesitation, Augustus ultimately confirmed Herod's will: Archelaus received Judæa, Samaria and Idumæa, but was granted only the title of ethnarch. If he governed well, the title of king would be bestowed upon him, later on. Herod Antipas received Galilee and Peræa, and Philip the regions of Gaulanitis, Auranitis, Trachonitis, Batanæa, Banis and Ituræa. Both received the title of tetrarch. Gaza, Gadara and Hippos were made subject directly to Syria. The reign of Archelaus was tyrannical and barbarous, and he was accused before Augustus of mismanaging his territory. He was summoned to Rome for trial and sentenced to banishment at Vienne in Gaul, where he probably died. A census of the taxable property of Judæa was now made, and Idumæa, Samaria and Judæa were put under the procurator Coponius.

Palestine now offered the following picture. In the borderlands, in Galilee, Peræa and in the districts of the Upper Jordan, ruled the sons of Herod as tetrarchs, while Judæa proper was being administered directly by the Roman procurator, who had his seat at Cæsarea on the coast, a town built by Herod I. The yoke of the foreign Power became heavier every day. By and by the procurators appointed by Rome began to mismanage the province under their charge and to interfere in the internal affairs. Palestine, exclusive of the Greek cities, was now divided into three administrative districts; the tetrarchies of Herod Antipas and Philip and the province of Judæa. While the latter province was now governed by a procurator, the two tetrarchies were independent.

Of the three brothers who succeeded Herod, Philip was the most respectable. He reigned peacefully and administered justice. After his death, his territory was added to Syria. Herod Antipas, who possessed some of his father's abilities, is called "fox" in the New Testament (Luke xiii. 32). He was accused of treason by Agrippa I, the brother of his wife Herodias, and Caligula deprived him of his possessions and banished him to Lyons.

Interspersed between Galilee, Peræa and the tetrarchy of Philip was the Decapolis, a confederation of ten Græco-Roman cities. Scythopolis, the capital, lay on the west of the Jordan, and each of the cities had a territory attached to it. Some of them were in the midst of the other political divisions but were not subject either to the tetrarch or to the procurator. Besides the Decapolis there were numerous towns west of the Jordan which were Greek and heathen, and even seething with anti-Jewish feeling. In a word, Judæa was Jewish, but the whole of Palestine was heathen and Greek.

Although Judæa did not form a part of Syria for administrative purposes, the legate of Syria possessed some power over the procurators.¹ The procurator was, above all, a fiscal agent, administering the taxes and the customs. The taxes collected were as a rule expended upon the province for improvements, roads, harbours, and public buildings, while the remainder was sent to the Imperial Treasury (the fiscus). The chief direct taxes were: the capitation or 1 per cent. of the wealth of the province; the *annona* or an annual contribution of grain and cattle for the Army, and the *angariæ* or *corvée*.² In addition to the taxes, there were also the customs, which were not collected by Roman officials but farmed out. They were sold to general farmers, who, in their turn, sold them out to various collectors, the publicans of the New Testament.³ Besides being a fiscal agent, the procurator had also military and judicial powers, and as a judge he wielded the power over life and death. While a number of cases were judged by the toparchical sanhedrins and the Great Sanhedrin, crimes involving capital punishment were in the hands of the Roman procurator.⁴

For a short time, however, the greatest part of Palestine was once more united under the sceptre of a prince of the house of Herod, Agrippa I, son of Aristobulus and grandson of Herod I. This prince had been educated at Rome, where he had

---

[1] See Marquardt, *Römische Staats-verwaltung*, i. 554.
[2] See *Revue des Etudes Juives*, xxxiv. 192; Marquardt, l.c., ii. 261.
[3] See Edersheim, *The Life and Times of Jesus the Messiah*, i. 515.
[4] See Shailer Mathews, *History of New Testament Times in Palestine*, 142.

gained the friendship of Caius, the future Emperor Caligula. On his accession to the throne, Caligula appointed his friend ruler over what had been the tetrarchy of Philip, with the title of king, and afterwards gave him also the tetrarchy of Herod Antipas (A.D. 39). The Emperor Claudius, who was obliged to Agrippa for his elevation to the empire, gave Agrippa all the territory that had once belonged to his grandfather Herod, together with the right to appoint the high-priests. After Agrippa's death, Claudius at first intended to make Agrippa II king in his father's place, but he was dissuaded from doing so, and the entire kingdom was administered by a procurator for a short time. Agrippa II received, however, the Kingdom of Chalcis, and in A.D. 53 the tetrarchy of Philip, to which Nero added portions of Peræa and Galilee, including the city of Tiberias. He died in A.D. 100, his tetrarchy continuing its political existence after the destruction of Jerusalem. Agrippa II, grandson of Herod, "the great King Agrippa, friend of Cæsar and the Romans", as he calls himself on his coins and inscriptions, was popular with the Jews. He secured his hold on the affection of his subjects by a complete adoption of Jewish customs. He is represented as a rigidly observing and pious Jew, and his respect and deference to the religious leaders of the people were quite unqualified. He seems to have been painfully conscious of the fact that he was only a stranger in Israel on account of his Idumæan descent. Whether Agrippa was really sincere in his piety and general conduct is another question. When we remember that he had been in his youth the boon companion of Caius and had associated with the rakes and voluptuaries at the Imperial Court, we have more than one reason to doubt his sincerity.

The Birth of Christianity [1]

While Judæa was bleeding in the clutches of Rome, an event occurred which was to have far-reaching consequences not only for the Jews but for humanity at large. On the soil of Palestine, in the midst of the Jews, Christianity came into being. The spiritual and intellectual life of the Jews during the Roman period was very complicated, and it contained germs of movements which were destined to revolutionize the world. It does not enter within the scope of the present book dealing with the history of the country of Palestine to discuss the origin of Christianity, and a few general remarks will suffice for our purpose. The idea of a Messiah, "the Anointed One", who was expected to come and deliver Israel, had long taken root in the hearts and minds of the people. The great prophets had foretold his coming, and Haggai and Zechariah promised his appearance if the temple were rebuilt. In the dark night of persecution the hope in the coming of the Messiah was being kept alive by the apocalyptic literature,[2] and the horrors of the

[1] For the origin of Christianity, see Note 13 in Appendix.
[2] See Note 14 in Appendix.

Syrian persecutions had strengthened this hope. The yearning for a Redeemer daily grew stronger. Opinions, however, with regard to the Messiah differed. The Zealots, fighting for the political freedom of the Jewish nation, for the Jewish State, imagined the Redeemer to be a prince of the house of David, who would crush the power of Rome and gain supremacy for the nation of Israel; while the peaceful Jews, the poorer classes, were expecting a Messiah who would establish a reign of justice and peace. Gradually, however, another idea took hold of the people, the idea of a mystic Messiah, a Redeemer who would save, not the nation, but the individual, by the strength of personal *faith* and individual regeneration.[1] Into the old belief in a Redeemer was thus introduced a new note, that of the human personality,[2] which minimized and even rendered superfluous the existence of the nation of Israel as a separate nation. During their long fight with Rome, it had become clear to many Jews that it was beyond their power to crush the mighty foe. Only the Messenger of God, the Messiah, the Superman, could save Israel. And now the question arose: Was the Redeemer to be a national Messiah, a prince of the house of David, who would save the nation as a whole, or a spiritual Redeemer who would redeem man the individual? The fighters for political and even religious independence still clung to the old conception, while those who were

[1] See Note 15 in Appendix.
[2] See A. S. Rappoport, *Labour, Social Reform and Democracy*.

mystically inclined or were growing tired of the political fights and struggles were attracted by the idea of a personal and individual, as opposed to a national, redemption. This redemption the Founder of Christianity and His immediate disciples were anxious to effect within the limits of Judaism itself, but the later exponents of Christianity decided to realize that potentiality of a universal religion which Judaism contained and upon which the Prophets had laid stress. And thus Christianity was born on the soil of Palestine, giving the small country another claim to fame. Had the Jews never produced the Prophets, nor given birth in their midst to Christianity, the whole history of Palestine would perhaps have been of little interest to us now. Races and nations have lived on the soil of Palestine and have died for ever, but Palestine has remained alive in our memory. This is due to the fact that two great religions were born on its soil.

The injustice and cruelties of the Roman procurators gradually goaded the Jews to rebellion, especially when it was a question of religion. Revolt and bloodshed became chronic and events converged towards the final catastrophe. The Jews, dissatisfied with the government of Albinius (A.D. 62–64), renowned for his greed and wickedness, insisted on his recall. Another procurator, Gessius Florus (64–66), was sent in his place. The new procurator, however, was so violent and his atrocities were so great that soon all Palestine was in a blaze.

The fight between the Jews and Rome had to break out ultimately. It was bound to come, it could not have ended otherwise. No compromise was possible between paganism and Judaism. They had so little in common, in cult, customs and beliefs. Besides, politically the motto of Rome was "might is Right", while the Jews maintained that "Right was might". The Jews despised the religious practices of the Romans; while to the pagans the religious life of the Jews appeared as a curious and strange phenomenon. As long as the Jewish State existed, Rome, accustomed to worship might and power, showed some respect for the Jewish religion, although it appeared to them so utterly strange. When, however, Judæa became a humble province of the Roman Empire, when Herod ascended the throne supported by Rome, and in order to curry favour with his masters more than once forgot the principles of the national faith which he was supposed to represent, then the attitude of Rome changed. For the Jews even in a state of dependency to exhibit the same contempt for the religion of their masters, was something which Rome could no longer understand nor tolerate. What had appeared hitherto as strange and incomprehensible was now revolting; what had appeared singular was now ridiculous. It sounded almost like a blasphemy to the Romans to proclaim the God of a defeated nation as the supreme divinity, as the only God. It was an anachronism in a century when a man was a god because he was powerful and when he

IN THE TALONS OF ROME

needed only to be powerful to become a god. A defeated people had no right to harbour such a pride, a pride based only on conscience and moral strength and not supported by material power.

It was, however, not so much the Judaism of the humble teachers in their schools and of the priests in their sanctuary that Rome would not tolerate; nay, there are proofs that the gentle teaching of the Pharisees made many converts in Roman society.[1]

To be just, it must be admitted that the central Government at Rome had shown marked respect for certain Jewish customs. The Romans could not comprehend the intense Jewish repugnance to images, but they were ready enough to grant concessions and be conciliatory. Thus no Roman coins for Judæa were issued which bore anything but the traditional symbols. Coins bearing the Emperor's effigy were carefully eliminated.[2] To the Romans the Jewish point of view was an irrational prejudice, but they were ready enough to respect it.[3] What the Romans detested, hated and despised was the religion and attitude of the upper classes, of the Herodians, who were Jews in Judæa and Romans in Rome; who had not the courage to be true to their own selves. Agrippa, after shedding tears in the Temple, went to Cæsarea, accompanied by his royal suite, to take part in Roman festivities and orgies. "All the absurdities and calumnies uttered and written against the Jews by so many Roman

---

[1] Renan, *Les Apôtres*, 306–308.   [2] See Madden, *Coins of the Jews*.
[3] See Note 16 in Appendix.

authors, from Cicero to Tacitus, are inspired by and due to the conduct of the Herodians and their followers."[1] To please the gods of Olympus they were too ready to forget the God of Sinai.

On the other hand, the Jews were dissatisfied with the rule of Rome's representatives, and friction arose between them and the colonial officers of the Imperial city on the banks of the Tiber. Insurrections spread over Palestine. Florus, the procurator, had to flee from Jerusalem, and Cestius, the Governor of Syria, was compelled to retire before the Jews. Such an insult proud Rome could never forgive. The pride of the Jews had to be broken; for the honour and also the interests of Rome were at stake. Vespasian arrived on the scene with a great army, reduced Galilee and prepared to lay siege to Jerusalem. In the midst of his preparations, however, he returned to Rome, where he was crowned Emperor, and the task of capturing Jerusalem fell upon his son Titus.

Josephus, who describes the fall of Jerusalem, was sent by Titus to persuade his countrymen to capitulate, but his persuasions proved futile. The Jews were decided to fight against Rome to the bitter end, and desperately they did fight.

It was a terrible fight, a life-and-death struggle between two Powers, the physical and material strength of Rome and the spiritual might of Israel, which was waged on the soil of Palestine. Both opponents, the sober realists of Rome and the

[1] Derenbourg, l.c., 222.

Jews, intoxicated with lofty idealism, were penetrated by a sense of their mission, that of conquering the world. Rome relied on physical strength, on might, while Judæa was inspired by truth, justice and religion. The Romans ignored idealism. "What is truth?" asked Pilate, while the Jews were ready to die rather than sacrifice their ideal. Rome wreaked terrible vengeance on her enemy. A million men lost their lives in Jerusalem alone, while countless numbers fell all over the country. The remainder were taken captive, sold as slaves or dragged to the quarries and mines of Egypt. Jewish prisoners were sold as slaves at ridiculous prices on the market-places or bled to death as gladiators in Roman circuses, torn by wild beasts. Seven hundred proud and valiant fighters surrounded the chariot of Titus when he passed under the triumphal arch on his entry into Rome.

The Jews, however, had to face a double fight, one with the external foe and the other in their own midst. In the turmoil of war with a mighty enemy, politics and religion were still dividing the nation. One party insisted on saving the State, the political independence, while the other cared most for the spiritual and religious inheritance. The Jewish religion, the legacy of Israel, was saved. Moreover, spiritually Israel triumphed over Rome. Judæa, as a political State, lay prostrate at the feet of the conqueror, but the God of the Jews, in the shape of Christianity, conquered Rome three centuries later. The history of Palestine had thus not been in vain, for it had produced immortal and permanent values: Judaism and its daughter-religion, Christianity. The latter, wiser, more adaptable, more conciliatory, conquered, thanks to St. Paul, the pagan world.

The Jewish nation expired politically, but it never died spiritually. The State ceased to exist, but the nation, the religious community, gathered new strength and vigour for life, growth and development. While thousands were bleeding for political independence and heroes were losing their lives in the turmoil of war, other heroes, the heroes of the spirit, were at work. The former lost the fight, the latter were successful. Foreseeing the cataclysm which threatened their political independence, they were carefully laying the foundations of a structure destined to survive the ruin of political independence.[1] Edomites, Philistines and Phœnicians and the other races inhabiting Palestine disappeared in the course of time, but the Jews continued to live. And why? Because the silent heroes who were fighting for the moral and religious existence of the Jews had succeeded in saving the law, the religion of Israel, which remained its appanage in captivity and in the Diaspora. Whether Rome was victorious, whether the Jewish State existed or not, the nation, thanks to its spiritual culture and its religion, was sure to live on.

[1] See Note 17 in Appendix.

PART III

PALESTINE, THE HOLY LAND OF CHRISTENDOM

CHAPTER XII

PALESTINE UNDER ROMAN AND BYZANTINE EMPERORS

(A.D. 70–634)

The inhabitants of Palestine—Religious interests—Mixed population—Nabatæans and Ituræans—Græco-Macedonian elements—Agriculture—The Edict of Milan—Constantine—Helena—Arius—The Council of Nicæa—Religious science—Bishop Macarius—The Holy Cross—Chosroes II—Heraclius—Persia and Byzantium—Native Syrians and Greeks—Siroes—Tiberias—Domitian—Hadrian—Persecution of the Jews—Bar Kochba—Jewish coins—Ælia Capitolina—Christian Jews—Jewish learning—Jamnia—Jochanan ben Zaccai—Antoninus Pius—The Patriarchate—The *Mishna*—Septimius Severus—Juda II—Græco-Roman influence—Julian the Apostate—Alypius—Justinian—Jews in Upper Galilee—The historian Theophanes—The Samaritans—Benjamin of Tiberias—The monks—The Fast of Heraclius

EVER since the destruction of the temple by Titus and the loss of their political independence by the Jews, Palestine can no longer be said to have had a history of her own. For centuries the country has never had a population united by a common bond and common interests. From A.D. 70 to our own days Palestine has not been inhabited by *one* nation bound to the soil and following a regular movement of development, of growth or decadence. It has been the theatre of important events, but the political history with which Palestine has been connected and which affected the destinies of her inhabitants has never been that of the country itself. The actors have always come from the outside, and Palestine itself, as a country, has never made this history, nor have its inhabitants ever had a common cause to defend. One might say that the idea of fatherland had become strange to them. Numerous races succeeded each other on the soil of Palestine, but they were strangers there. For the last nineteen centuries Palestine has been the Holy Land, and the interest men felt in the country was mostly one of religion, for two religions had evolved there. The conquest of Palestine by the Arabs is an episode in the history of Islam, just as the Crusades and the establishment of the Latin Kingdom at Jerusalem are episodes in the history of European nations. The political history of Palestine since 132 is therefore a series of events, the causes of which have to be sought elsewhere. As far as the country itself is concerned, it is the history of the Jews, of the Christians and of the Moslems living in Palestine, but not the history of the country or its people.

When the Romans took possession of Palestine the country was inhabited by a mixture of Semitic races: Aramæans, settled principally in Syria, outside Palestine, and in Phœnicia; Phœnicians; Samaritans, descendants of the Assyrian settlers who were brought to replace the conquered ten tribes, and Jews. The latter were most numerous in Judæa and Galilee, but they had large colonies all over Syria. To the east and the west were found a variety of Arab tribes, of which the Nabatæans, with their capital Petra, were the most important. The

Ituræans lived in Northern Palestine, while the Idumæans were settled in the south-west. Both Arabic and Aramaic were spoken among these tribes. The Ituræans and Galilæans may have included some Iranian element. In the south-west there were also the descendants of the Philistines, whose language had disappeared but whose old cities, such as Gaza and Ascalon, were still important. In addition to this mixture of races there was a Græco-Macedonian element in all the chief cities of Palestine. They were either old veterans or merchants who had come to seek their fortunes in the East. The state of Palestine under the Roman and later Byzantine Emperors will be dealt with in a subsequent chapter. For the present it will suffice to say that all through the period from A.D. 63 to 634 Palestine remained what it had been in the times of Christ, namely, a land of villages and peasants. It was, as we read in the Gospels, an agricultural land, and the character of the inhabitants was rustic. There were the wealthy owners of land, of large flocks of sheep and goats, and the tax-collectors. The common men, the poorer classes, consisted either of peasants toiling in the fields, in their gardens or vineyards, or of village-artisans, cobblers, carpenters, blacksmiths and so on. The period of Roman domination in Palestine was, on the whole, a period of peace and security and, to a certain extent, of prosperity. The country remained practically, under Roman rule, what it had been before, at least as far as the mass of the people were concerned. They lived in the old fashion, devoted to their fields and flocks and to their gods and their temples.[1]

Under Constantine the Great, however, a change was effected in the destinies and fate of Palestine. By the Edict of Milan in January 313, Christianity became a *religio licita* and the Church a recognized society. By this edict the civil and religious rights of which the Christians had been deprived were now restored to them. At Constantine's death Christianity became the religion of Court and Government. The result was that the Christian faith now spread rapidly. The freedom and dominance of the Church led to a revival of enthusiasm for the Holy Places and new churches were built at Jerusalem. Helena, the mother of Constantine, caused churches to be built at Bethlehem and on the Mount of Olives, and Constantine built the famous Church of the Holy Sepulchre (Anastasis).

A few years after the Edict of Milan, Arius spread his heresy, and when the Bishop of Jerusalem, St. Macarius, rose up against the new doctrine he met many adversaries in Palestine. The theories of Arius, based as they were on the speculations of Philo, Plotinus and the Alexandrian sophists, appealed, however, to the Oriental clergy. Palestinian ecclesiastics were all in favour of Arianism.[2] The Council of Nicæa, however, decided in favour

---

[1] See M. Rostovzeff, *The Social and Economic History of the Roman Empire*, 1926, 249–253.
[2] See Note 18 in Appendix.

of orthodoxy and Macarius was thanked by the Council for his firm stand for orthodoxy.

From the time of Constantine, too, dates also the advancement of the See of Jerusalem. By the Council of Nicæa the unique dignity of the Holy City was recognized without, however, interfering with its canonical dependence on Cæsarea, the metropolis. In other words, the suffragan Bishop of Jerusalem had precedence over his metropolitan. At the Council of Chalcedon, Jerusalem was ultimately made a Patriarchate.

The Orient, and Palestine in particular, also became the centre of religious science. It was there that during the fourth and fifth centuries the various theological schools flourished. The great doctors of the Greek Church—St. Athanasius, St. Basil, St. Gregory of Nazianzus, St. John Chrysostom—were Orientals. The great dogmatic controversies, proofs of the intensity of religious life, were initiated. It was also during the fourth century that Christian art was developed in the Orient, in Syria and Palestine. From the beginning of this century we meet in the Orient and particularly in Palestine the principal types of religious edifices which Christendom was to adopt later on—the various forms of basilicas.[1] Palestine became the land of saints and anchorets, of monks and monasteries, of nuns and convents, of basilicas and relics.

[1] See L. Bréhier, *Les Basiliques Chrétiennes*, 1906; De Vogüé, *Syrie Centrale*, 1865–1876.

Helena, the mother of Constantine the Great, went as a pilgrim to Jerusalem and was seized by a desire to find the actual wooden cross on which Christ had been crucified. She succeeded in inspiring Bishop Macarius with her religious ardour and caused Mount Calvary to be excavated. Three crosses were discovered and the pious lady was faced by a difficult problem: which of the three crosses was the Holy Cross? The question was ultimately solved by holding the three crosses in turn over the face of a lady who was sick unto death. By the efficacy of its shadow the true cross healed the patient. The true cross was then divided into two parts, one of which was sent to Constantine, while the second part was put in a silver case, of which the Bishop of Jerusalem kept the key, and deposited in the Church of Resurrection. The Holy Cross became the most precious relic of Christendom, a material instrument of redemption, apart from its intrinsic value.

At the beginning of the seventh century Jerusalem, the Holy City, was not only the centre of the Christian religion but one of the richest and most prosperous towns in the East. Palestine was enjoying an era of peace and prosperity. This prosperity, however, was already being threatened. For over a century the kings of Persia had been dreaming of the pillage of Jerusalem. It was a constant cause of annoyance to them to see the commerce and the wealth of the world flowing into a foreign city. War broke out between Persia and the Byzantine or Later Roman Empire. At the head of a powerful army Chosroes II invaded the Byzantine dominions. The Persian monarch passed the Euphrates and occupied the Syrian cities of Hierapolis, Chalcis and Aleppo, and soon encompassed the walls of Antioch. The loss of this city (in 611) was followed by the capture of Cæsarea and Damascus. Soon Galilee and the region beyond the Jordan were in the enemy's hands.

In 614 the Persians had conquered the country of Palestine. They plundered Jerusalem, burned the Church of the Holy Sepulchre and carried off the Holy Cross, with the Patriarch Zacharias, to Persia. The Christians in Jerusalem were massacred and the Jews were afterwards accused of having helped the Persians to destroy and burn the churches. "It must be confessed", writes Finlay, "that the desire of the Jews of availing themselves of the misfortunes of the Roman Empire, and of the dissensions of the Christian Church, was the natural consequence of the oppression to which the Jews had long been subjected, but it not unnaturally tended to increase the hatred with which they were viewed, and added to their persecutions."

It appears, however, that even the Christians in Palestine preferred the rule of Persia to that of Byzantium, although Syria was not strong enough herself to shake off the Byzantine yoke. The different races which peopled the country then, as in the present day, were extremely divided, and the separation by religion, language, manners and interests made it quite impossible for the inhabitants to unite in opposition to the Imperial Government. The native Syrians who showed some strength of national character were divided by their religious opinions; they were either Monophysites or Nestorians. As for the Greeks, the descendants of the colonists who had prospered under the Seleucidæ and increased by the influx of Greeks engaged in the service of Church and State, all the other classes of the population were opposed to them. The Greeks had become almost aliens to the country and were therefore incapable of offering any resistance to a foreign Power without the support of the Imperial armies.[1]

The Persians remained masters of Palestine for fourteen years, until they were driven out by Heraclius. A revolution had in the meantime broken out in Persia. Chosroes II was seized and murdered by his rebellious son Siroes, and on April 3, 629, his ambassador arrived at the camp of Heraclius. A treaty of peace was concluded between the Persian monarch and the Emperor, and the Persians vacated the Holy Land. The Holy Cross, which the Persians had carried off from Jerusalem, was restored to Heraclius with the seals of the case which contained it unbroken. The Emperor entered Palestine in triumph. In September 629 Christianity once more triumphed in the Holy Land and the Cross was replanted on Calvary. But the religious policy of the Emperor Heraclius

---

[1] See Finlay, *Greece Under the Romans*, 320.

had embittered the majority of the inhabitants of the country, and Heraclius did not succeed in satisfying any Christian party. His persecutions of the Monophysites made the latter his bitter enemies, while the Arabs on the frontiers were growing restive. A new enemy had already arisen who was to destroy for ever the Byzantine power in Palestine and in the whole East. The armies of Islam were approaching.

The Jews of Palestine from A.D. 70 to 634

After the fall of Jerusalem in A.D. 70 the majority of the surviving Jews drifted away to the larger towns of Northern Syria, while a veteran Roman settlement was planted at Emmaus, not far from the captured capital. Jerusalem was left in ruins. A military governor was appointed for Palestine, which was definitely separated from Syria.

The national aspirations of the Jews had been crushed, but the national hopes still remained alive. The temple was no more, but the *Torah* still existed and its bond was strengthened. In spite of oppression the Jews of Palestine were able to maintain their hearth of learning and intellectual activity, of study and thought. During the first three centuries of the Christian Era the great teachers of Judaism, the sages and rabbis, were nearly all Palestinian Jews.

The centre of Palestinian Judaism was shifted from Jerusalem to the north, and gathered new strength in the friendly valleys of Galilee and on the western bank of the blue Sea of Tiberias. No revolts took place under the Flavian Emperors, although the rule of Rome was heavy, especially under the avaricious Domitian. This Emperor still distrusted the Jews, suspecting their Messianic dreams. All the Jews who boasted of Davidic descent were to be exterminated, but only a couple of poor artisans, supposed relations of Jesus of Nazareth, were arrested and soon set free. When, during the last years of the reign of Trajan, the Jews of the Diaspora, in Egypt, Cyprus and Mesopotamia, rose up in arms against Rome, the Jews of Palestine took no part in the revolt. Under Hadrian, however, in 132, a new generation had grown up which mustered courage enough to revolt when once more an attempt was made to obliterate the Jewish religion. Hadrian is said not to have harboured any hostile intentions against the Jews in particular. A lover of art and a great builder, he was anxious to further the Greek renaissance in the Roman Empire. On the site of destroyed Jerusalem he decided to build a new city, Ælia Capitolina, and a heathen temple dedicated to Jupiter was to be erected on the spot where once the Temple of Jehovah had stood. The Emperor, moreover, issued a decree against castration, and considering circumcision as a mutilation of the body, he forbade it. Circumcision was being practised by various other nations in the East, but no religion was so hard hit as Judaism. Among the

Jews the custom of circumcision was not a religious act to which some men voluntarily submitted; it was one of the fundamental obligatory laws of religion. To the Jews, therefore, Hadrian's decree came as a deliberate attack upon their ancestral faith. They had paid the *fiscus Judaicus*,[1] but a heathen temple on the sacred Mount of Zion and the suppression of the rite of circumcision were religious questions, and the Jews refused to obey.

Like one man the Jews rose up, to the amazement of the Romans, who never suspected that there was still so much vigour in the defeated nation. Once more the Jews were ready to fight mighty Rome.

All were united in the defence of religion, but the dreamers of political independence again saw in the war an opportunity to rebuild the Jewish State. They rallied to the standard unfurled by a courageous leader, a certain Simon, who proclaimed himself as the Messiah. The rabbis, ready enough to die in the defence of religion, looked perhaps askance at a fight carried into the arena of politics, but one of the most celebrated of them, the famous Rabbi Akiba, greeted Simon as the Messiah, Bar-Kochba, the "son of the star". The courageous leader displayed considerable military skill and was successful in the beginning. The Governor of Jerusalem, Annius Rufus, proved unequal to the task and his troops were unable to suppress the sudden outbreak. The Jewish fighters, who had

[1] See Note 19 in Appendix.

once more dared to declare war to the mighty Roman Empire, gathered in all strong places: in fortresses, caves and subterranean passages. Within a short time Bar-Kochba was master of the country. A new day seemed to have dawned for Israel. The Messiah issued coins with the proud inscription of "Simon, the Prince of Judah". He captured Jerusalem, which he held for two years. On his coins the Messiah now wrote: "For the freedom of Jerusalem." It was not easy for the surprised Romans to suppress the movement. The revolt had spread to other countries of the Empire and, as Dio Cassius writes, the whole world was in a state of unrest. Troops after troops did the Emperor send, and the Legate of Syria, Publicius Marcellus, rushed to the assistance of his colleague, Annius Rufus, the Governor of Palestine. It was all of no avail until Hadrian sent his ablest general, Julius Severus, whom he recalled from Britain. It was a difficult guerrilla warfare which the experienced soldier had to face, and the fight lasted three years and a half.

Once peace was restored Hadrian tried to efface all memory of ancient Jerusalem. He issued a decree forbidding the Jews to return to Jerusalem on penalty of death. Guards were stationed to prevent them from even approaching the city. Even the very name of Jerusalem disappeared. A new city, called Ælia Capitolina, was founded on its ruins. Peopled as a Roman colony, the city was adorned with the usual public buildings, pagan temples, baths and theatres. Roman freedmen and Syrian Greeks were the chief inhabitants of Ælia Capitolina. The Christians who were allowed to settle there were converted Gentiles, while the Christian Jews or the Jewish Christians dared not approach the place. In the eyes of the Roman authorities they were Jews.[1] Hadrian did everything to give Ælia Capitolina the character of a Roman colony and of a pagan city. On Mount Zion a temple dedicated to Jupiter was erected, and statues of heathen gods defiled the Holy of Holies.[2] The Roman Governor, Annius Rufus, ordered the foundations of the temple to be torn up, and the plough was drawn over the site, a mark that it was devoted to perpetual desolation.[3] Eusebius[4] says that the Christians, too—that is, the Jewish Christians—were not spared. The site of the Holy Sepulchre was covered over with earth and a temple dedicated to Venus was erected on the sacred spot. The Jews of Palestine remained in a state of unrest. Hadrian, with a view to obliterating finally their nationality, which depended on their religion, decided to follow the example of Antiochus Epiphanes and suppress the Jewish cult. The reading of the law and the observance of the Sabbath were forbidden.

No persecutions, however, could daunt Jewish intellectual and religious activity, and Jewish learning flourished in the ancestral country. Rab-

---

[1] See Eusebius, *Eccles. Hist.*, iv. 6.
[2] *Dio Cassius*, lxix. 22.
[3] See *Babyl. Talmud*, tractate *Taanith*, 4.
[4] In his *Life of Constantine*, iii. 26.

binic lore developed, and Palestinian Jewry exercised a spiritual supremacy over their co-religionists in the Diaspora. Palestine was still the spiritual and cultural centre of the Jews. After the destruction of Jerusalem by Titus, Jochanan ben Zaccai and his disciples had founded a centre of learning at Jamnia, or Jabne. Among Jochanan's famous disciples and contemporaries may be mentioned Josua ben Halafta, Simon ben Jochai and Meïr. Gamaliel II, a descendant of the house of Hillel, assumed the title of Prince (*Nasi*), which Origines translates by *Ethnarch*, and through him the academy of Jabne gained a wide renown. As Judæa, however, had become entirely heathen, the centre of intellectual activity was shifted to the hills of Galilee. It was the time when the Jews had to suffer from the persecutions of Hadrian. Better days, however, dawned for the Jews under Antoninus Pius, who revoked some of the hard laws issued against the Jews. He allowed the practice of circumcision, although the Jews were still excluded from Jerusalem. The Patriarchate was established, and the first to assume the title of Patriarch was Juda I, the compiler of the *Mishna*.[1] He became the spiritual and temporal head of Palestinian Jewry and was acknowledged as such by the Roman authorities. In the Galilean town of Sepphoris, Juda I led the life of a noble Roman official and stood in daily relations with the Roman dignitaries, who treated him as their equal.

[1] See Note 20 in Appendix.

A change had now taken place in the life of the Palestinian Jews. The rabbis and spiritual leaders were no longer working men and artisans, as in former days, but wealthy and enterprising merchants. Juda I was succeeded in the Patriarchate by his son Gamaliel. He lived under the reign of Emperor Septimius Severus, who granted the Jews the rights of Roman citizens. Septimius had married a Syrian woman, Julia Domna, and henceforth Syrian women exercised a powerful influence at Rome. Their sons became Roman Emperors and their rule was rather advantageous for the inhabitants of Palestine, whether Jews or Christians. The splendid temples and theatres, the roads and aqueducts, testify even to-day of the activity of these Emperors. Alexander Severus (222–235) favoured both Christians and Jews, and in his *Lararium* the images of Christ and Abraham figured by the side of that of Orpheus. Jewish learning in Palestine flourished under the reign of this Emperor. The Patriarch Juda II transferred his seat from Sepphoris to Tiberias, a town constructed by Herod Antipas. Juda II was a Romanized Jew, dressing like a Roman. In his days the synagogues in Galilee were built after Roman models. Altogether, Græco-Roman influences are noticeable among the Palestinian Jews of the third century. A famous rabbi, Jochanan bar Napacha, who taught at Tiberias, permitted the study of the Greek language, while Rabbi Abbahu, who lived at Cæsarea, led the life of a noble Roman. Not only himself, but even his daughters, mastered the Greek language.

Gradually, however, the centre of Jewish learning had shifted from Palestine to Babylonia, to Sura and Pumbadita. The Patriarch himself was still recognized by the Roman State as *illustris* and *clarissimus*, but he was no longer the recognized head of Jewry in the Diaspora, and the Palestinian academies were being abandoned. The Patriarchate of Tiberias soon became only a dignity of local importance.

Soon new dangers threatened the Jews of Palestine. With the triumphs of Christianity under Constantine, fresh persecutions began. Gone were the days of tolerance which had enabled the Jews to live in peace and to develop their intellectual activity. Hitherto the Jewish faith, like all the other religions in the Roman Empire, had enjoyed to a certain extent the protection of the State, but now Judaism became a *nefaria secta*. The Christian Church, now powerful, resorted to violence. Constantine, however, was tolerant in comparison to his successors, and especially to his son Constantius, under whose reign the persecution of the Jews began in grim earnest. The academy of Tiberias was dissolved and the majority of the rabbis wandered out to Babylonia, where, under the rule of the Sassanidæ, they found a second home.

The miserable position of the Jews in Palestine continued now for centuries until the conquest of the country by the Arabs. A fleeting ray of sunshine fell upon the Jews of Palestine during the reign of Julian the Apostate, who ascended the throne in 361. This Romantic on the Imperial throne favoured the Jews, not because he had any preference for the Jewish religion, but out of hatred against the Christian Church. He went, however, so far as to permit the Jews to rebuild Jerusalem and the temple. A certain Alypius, a former Governor of Britain, was sent to Palestine to supervise the work. But the enterprise never went ahead. The Jews themselves had lost all hope and courage. Jovian and Valens were still favourable, to a certain extent, but under Theodosius the attitude of the Church was again very hostile to the Jews. Theodosius deprived the Jews of the right to occupy any official position or dignity. He forbade the Jews to build new synagogues, and in 415 he abolished the Patriarchate. Gamaliel V, the last holder of the office, was himself favoured at the Imperial Court, and received not only the honorary diploma (*codicillus honorarius*), but also the dignity of the *prefectura*. As a personal favour he was allowed to retain his office of Patriarch for life, but after his death, in 425, the Patriarchate came to an end.

Under the Byzantine Emperors the number of Jews in Palestine became almost insignificant. They were to be found only in Tiberias and in a few hill-towns in Upper Galilee. At the beginning of the seventh century there were a few Jews in Cæsarea, Neapolis (Sichem) and Nazareth. Under the Byzantine Emperors the position of the Jews in

Palestine went from bad to worse. Thus the historian Malabas relates that when, under Leo the Isaurian, the Jews were massacred at Antioch and their corpses were burned, the Emperor exclaimed: "Why did they burn only the dead Jews and not the living too?" Under Justinian I (527–565) the sufferings of the Jews in Palestine increased. The reign of this Emperor is distinguished by numerous persecutions excited by the Christian clergy. To orthodox bigotry must be attributed the religious persecutions not only of the Samaritans and the Jews but also of the Arians, Nestorians, Eutychians and other heretics, as well as of Platonic philosophers and Manichæans. Justinian enacted various laws with a view to enforcing unity of opinion in religion and to punishing any difference of belief from that of the established Church. He disqualified the Jews from giving witness against Christians and forbade the celebration of the Passover. He allowed the Jews to occupy the dignity of the *decurionat*, because the office involved considerable expense, and he added: "They shall bear their yoke with sighs and be considered as unworthy of any dignity or honour." Justinian also insisted that the Jews should use Greek and Latin translations of the Holy Scriptures in their synagogues.

No wonder therefore that Jews hated the Byzantine Government, and it would not have been surprising if they had participated in the armed rising of the Samaritans against the Government. The

UNDER ROMANS AND BYZANTINES

assertion of the historian Theophanes, however, that the Jews had actually participated in the rising is devoid of any foundation. The Samaritans had, in fact, taken to arms, and Justin II passed a law giving them the choice between conversion and extermination.

It was only at the beginning of the seventh century that the Jews of Palestine revolted against Byzantium. When Chosroes II invaded Palestine, the Jews of Tiberias and of the Galilean hills, of Nazareth and its environs, gathered under the leadership of the rich and influential Benjamin of Tiberias and joined the Persians. For fourteen years they remained under Persian rule, but when, in 629, Palestine was reconquered by Heraclius, the Jews had to pay dearly for their pro-Persian policy.

Heraclius seems to have been inclined to forgive the Jews, and at Tiberias, where Benjamin gave hospitality to the Emperor and his army, Heraclius assured the Jews of complete amnesty. This generosity, however, did not please the Christian monks. When the Emperor entered Jerusalem, the Patriarch Sophronius and the monks insisted on the extermination of all the Jews in Palestine. Such an act, they maintained, would be pleasing to God, and as for the Emperor's breach of faith, they were ready to take upon themselves the responsibility for the sin which the Emperor would thus commit. In fact, the Patriarch instituted a special week of fasting in expiation for the Emperor's breach of faith. It was called the "Fast of Heraclius", and was still observed by the Coptic Christians in the tenth century. The Jews, too, instituted a fast-day commemorating the persecutions of Heraclius. In 628 Heraclius renewed the laws of Hadrian and Constantine, forbidding the Jews to enter Jerusalem under the penalty of death. Thus the hope of the Palestinian Jews of shaking off the Byzantine yoke was shattered.

CHAPTER XIII

PALESTINE UNDER THE MOSLEMS
(A.D. 634–1096)

The invasion of the Moslems—A victory of Islam—Edomites and Nabatæans—Greek inscriptions—The penetration of Bedouins—Vassal States—Mar'al Kais—The Ghassanidae—Mohammed—Liberty of conscience—Abu-Bekr—Instructions to the Army—Justice and toleration—Arabs settled in Palestine—Arabs in pay of Byzantium—Oppressions of Jews and Christians—The fiscal screw—The spirit of unity—Capture of Damascus—Indifference of inhabitants—"Farewell, Syria"—The Patriarch Sophronius—The Caliph Omar—The Mosque of Omar—The Al Masjid-al-Aksa—Mohammed's night journey—The winged steed Al Burak—The five Junds—Property in Palestine—The Omaiyads—Mu'awiya—Abd-al-Malik—The Dome of the Rock—Hisham—Damascus and Bagdad—The Abbasids—The Fatimids — Nicephorus Phocas — Biamrillah — Persecutions—The Seljuks—Tutush and Malkshah—Sufferings of Christian pilgrims

TOWARDS the close of the first half of the seventh century Palestine, which, as we have seen, had in turn been in the possession of Israelites, Assyrians, Babylonians, Persians, Greeks and Romans, once more changed masters. The great wave of Islam swept over Syria and Palestine, and the land was wrested from the dominion of Byzantium. The invaders came down the well-known caravan route leading from Mecca and Medina to Damascus. The territories which first came under the power of Islam were the countries east of the Jordan and the Dead Sea. After the capture of Damascus the Moslems overran Galilee, the lowlands of the Jordan and Southern Palestine. It was a victory of Islam, but the invaders, the Arabs, were not strangers to the country nor new-comers. When the Romans established their sway over Palestine a number of Arabs were already settled in the country, for in the sixth century B.C. they had penetrated into the old home of the Edomites. They were the precursors of the Nabatæans, who established a flourishing kingdom in the fourth century B.C. These Bedouins gradually passed from the nomadic to a settled life and acquired Aramæan culture and civilization, so that the Moslem Arabs later on applied the designation of Nabatæans to the Aramaic-speaking agriculturists. The bulk of the population, however, retained the Arabic speech. The Greek inscriptions discovered in Transjordania show that in Roman times the majority consisted of Arabs, the settled population being continually increased by wandering tribes from the desert.

The Roman power was unable to keep the Bedouins away. When St. Jerome complains that the environs of Bethlehem "are an inconsolable wilderness full of barbarians", he evidently means the Bedouins.[1] Now, long before Mohammed, Arabia had been in a state of unrest, and there was a slow infiltration of Arabian tribes into the adjoining civilized lands in Roman territory. Here they met with the descendants of earlier Semitic immigrants, the Aramæans, who were already long acclimatized there. Rome suffered greatly from this constant unrest in her border provinces and organized the Syrian Arabs under the leadership of

[1] See Migne, *Patrologia Latina*, xxii. 1104.

native princes. In the fourth century A.D. vassal States of semi-Bedouins were created on the borders of the country, one of these States being that of Mar'al-Kais Ibn'Amr, King of the Arabs, whose funerary inscription at Nemara, east of the Hauran, has been discovered. From the biographies of the Saints we also learn that the real power in the land was in the hands of Arab chieftains, who were in the service of the Empire as *pylarches*, but who in reality were a danger rather than a help to the Empire. Very important was the dynasty of the Ghassanidæ of the house of Gafna,[1] but unfortunately a short-sighted policy permitted the ruin of this State.

Now such a state of affairs greatly facilitated the conquests of Islam, while the circumstances of the age in which Mohammed lived were favourable to his career. It was a period both of intellectual decline amongst the governing classes throughout the civilized world and of dissatisfaction with the existing order of things among the inhabitants of many countries in the East. In Arabia Mohammed found a nation in search of knowledge and power, and feeling that a better religion than paganism was needed. Unity, Mohammed realized, was a principle which would ensure universal assent, and he seized on this principle of unity by proclaiming that "There is but one God". He embodied this idea of unity in the whole frame of Arabic society, in the religious, civil, judicial and military administration.

[1] See Nöldeke, *Die Ghassanischen Fürsten*, 1887.

Mohammed, moreover, declared that liberty of conscience would be granted to all those who put themselves under the protection of Islam, a declaration which could not fail to appeal to many nations in the East at an age when they were suffering from the introduction of a State religion. Thus while Chosroes, the King of Persia, was persecuting the Christians in his realm and Heraclius was tormenting the Jews and heretics within the bounds of his dominions, the Moslems promised freedom of religion.[1] To the inhabitants of Palestine, therefore, Islam appeared as a protection against religious persecution, and they were ready enough to exchange the Byzantine yoke which was weighing heavily on them for the rule of the Moslems. For a long time Islam kept its promises.

The tone adopted by the Caliph Abu-Bekr in his instructions to the Syrian Army was also calculated to attract the attention of and to please the people who were groaning under the oppression of the Byzantine Government. "Ye men," said Abu-Bekr, "ten things I command you to observe. Be just, the unjust never prosper; be valiant, die rather than yield. Do not steal. Keep your word—even to your enemies. Be merciful, slay neither old men, children, nor women. Destroy neither fruit trees, grain, nor cattle. Kill neither sheep, oxen nor camels, except for your sustenance. Molest not those who live retired from the world, so that they may continue to fulfil their vows. Compel the rest

[1] See Ockley, *History of the Saracens*.

of mankind to become Moslems or pay us a tribute. If they refuse these terms, slay them." It must be admitted that for the early Middle Ages such a proclamation, which was generally obeyed by the Moslem troops, was mild. It breathed a spirit of justice and toleration. Neither the emperors of Byzantium nor the bishops of the Church had ever expressed such sentiments in the name of Him who had preached a religion of love. Such a document as the proclamation of Abu-Bekr must have produced a deep impression on the minds not only of the Jews but also of the Christians in Syria and Palestine. The former were suffering from oppression, while the latter were being persecuted by the State Church for their various religious opinions. Both were feeling the yoke of the officials and of heavy taxation. No wonder that Islam appeared to them as the deliverer from the bondage of Byzantium.

It was, moreover, natural that when the Moslems began to invade Syria and Palestine the Arab elements already settled in the country should endeavour to unite with their kin who were advancing under a new banner, that of religion. Islam, it must be borne in mind, was not essentially a religious movement; it was an expansion of the Arabs to which religion only supplied unity. It was brigandage under the cloak of religion. The brigands, it is true, had assumed the rôle of apostles, but the impelling forces were conquest, avarice and hunger, much more than religion. "The conquest of the Moslems was a migratory movement, set on foot long before Islam had given it a new watchword, a party cry and an organization,"[1] and this movement was encouraged rather than checked by the Arabian tribes in the borderlands of Syria. Some of these tribes were in the pay of the Byzantines, but Heraclius, who was in great financial difficulties, suspended their yearly subsidies, and "as Byzantium withdrew the subsidies from them, they made an alliance with the Moslems to recoup themselves by plundering raids".[2] As for the other Semitic elements in Syria and Palestine, they hated the rule of Byzantium, and the numerous Christian Arab tribes and the Aramæans welcomed the Moslems both as blood relations and deliverers.

Not only the Arabs, however, who were living in Syria, but also the other inhabitants, the Christians and the Jews, were ready enough and even pleased to submit to the new masters. A rigid observance of justice had characterized the earlier acts of the new conquerors, and the inhabitants of the country hoped that they would be less oppressed by the Mohammedans than they had been by the Emperor of Byzantium. The Jews knew that they could not be worse off under the Crescent than they had been under the Cross; while the religious dissensions rendered the Christians hostile to the Byzantine Government and to the Emperor, whom

---

[1] See C. H. Becker, *The Expansion of the Saracens*, Cambridge Mediæval History, ii. 332.
[2] Ibid., 340.

they considered a heretic. Even the Patriarch Sophronius, when Jerusalem capitulated, thought more of his bishopric than he did of the country.[1] Monophysites and Jews were being persecuted, while the Emperor's heavy and enormous debts compelled him to "put on the fiscal screw" to its utmost tension. Islam, on the other hand, permitted complete religious liberty, for primarily there was no great impulse on the part of the Moslems towards religious proselytism, and the tribute demanded was not heavy. All these circumstances were, therefore, in favour of Islam and against Byzantium.

The hostilities between the followers of Islam and the troops of Heraclius broke out in 629, but Heraclius did not yet realize the danger, and the incursions of the Saracens caused but little alarm in his mind. While he was bearing the Holy Cross on his shoulders up Mount Calvary, he little expected that soon the Crescent would be planted in the Holy City. While he was persecuting his subjects, driving the Jews out of Jerusalem, he overlooked the danger of Islam, which his subjects in the Holy Land might consider as a deliverer. Mohammed himself did not live to realize his plans, but his successor, Abu-Bekr, the first Caliph, the chief of the true believers, continued the work begun by the Prophet. In 633 the Mohammedans invaded Syria and their progress was rapid, in spite of the efforts and the military skill of Heraclius. The Arabs were animated by a new spirit, a spirit of unity,

[1] See Finlay, l.c., 358.

while there was a lack of patriotism in the armies of the Emperor.

Abu-Bekr delegated the command of the army destined to invade Syria to Abu 'Ubaidah, one of the companions of the Prophet, but the soldiers demanded the superior military genius of Khâlid, the "Sword of God". Heraclius sent his forces under the command of his general, Werdan, but the Byzantines were defeated. The troops of Abu-Bekr then laid siege to Bostra, a strong frontier town of Syria, which surrendered in 634 in consequence of the treachery of the governor. In the same year the armies of Heraclius were beaten at Ajnadain, in the south of Palestine, and at the bloody decisive battle on the banks of the River Yarmuk. The Saracens gained possession of Damascus by capitulation and guaranteed to the inhabitants their full municipal privileges. They allowed them to use their local mint, while the Christians were left in possession of fifteen churches. Damascus itself was surrounded by Arabs who materially aided the armies of Islam, but all the other Syrian towns, too, were indifferent to the cause of their rulers and were thinking only of their wealth. They were, therefore, ready to make a separate truce with the Arabs, and on the first occasion the inhabitants sought to make an arrangement with the invader so as to insure their town from plunder.

The following account of the capitulation of Damascus is given by Arab historians: Khâlid Ibn Walid, the victor of the battle of Yarmuk, had scaled the walls of the city by means of rope-ladders and opened one of the gates, whereupon the Damascenes, afraid of plunder and alarmed for their wealth, surrendered to the generals who were besieging the other gates. Damascus was, therefore, considered by the victor half as a conquered city and half as one which had voluntarily surrendered. Thanks, to a great extent, to the indifference of the native population and to the help rendered to the Arabs by their kin, they soon possessed Syria as far as Aleppo.

Heraclius now gave up the hope of reconquering Syria and left for Constantinople, carrying with him the Holy Cross, which he had recovered from the Persians. He thought it necessary to remove it now to Europe for greater safety. Before leaving he is supposed to have exclaimed: "Farewell, Syria; thou belongest now to the enemy."

The Moslems now laid siege to Jerusalem, and after four months the city was forced to surrender. The Patriarch Sophronius sued for peace, but demanded that the Articles of Security should be ratified by the authority and the presence of the Caliph himself. Omar, therefore, came in person to receive the capitulation of the city.

To the inhabitants of Jerusalem, accustomed to the pomp and the gold-bedecked garments of the Byzantine Emperors, the appearance of the Caliph was a wonderful spectacle. The successor of the Prophet, arrayed in a poor mantle of camel-hair, rode into Jerusalem on a camel which carried all his baggage and the provision of dates which he required for the journey. The contrast between this rustic simplicity of the conqueror and the extravagance usually displayed, not only by the Emperors of Byzantium, but also by their provincial representatives, was striking. It could not fail to produce a favourable impression on a population embittered against a Government which had proved so oppressive and rapacious.

Thus Palestine became a Moslem possession about seven hundred years after Pompey had established there a Roman protectorate.

When Jerusalem capitulated, Omar caused a mosque to be built on what was considered to be the ancient site of the Temple of David. Tradition reports that the Caliph verified the position of the site by the rediscovery of the Rock concealed under a dung-hill, which had accumulated there during the time of the Byzantine rule. A description of the Rock had been given to Omar by the Prophet, who pretended to have made his prayer-prostrations at Jerusalem on the occasion of his Night Journey.

The Arab annalists make no mention of the structure raised by Omar, but there is no reason to doubt the fact, which is mentioned by the Byzantine historian Theophanes.[1] Before the settlement of the Caliphate in the family of the Omaiyads, the mosques were built of wood or sun-dried bricks, and the structure therefore erected by Omar, of wood or other perishable material, could not have

---

[1] See L'Estrange, *Palestine Under the Moslems*, 91.

lasted long, so that little must have remained of it in 690, when Abd-al-Malik erected the magnificent stone mosque known as the Mosque of Omar. As for the great mosque of Jerusalem, Al Masjid-al-Aksa, it derives its name from the traditional Night Journey of Mohammed to which allusion is made in the words of the Koran xvii. 1: " I declare the glory of Him who transported His servant by night from the Masjid-al-Haram (the mosque at Mecca) to the Masjid-al-Aksa (the Further Mosque) at Jerusalem." Mohammed is said to have mounted the winged steed called Al-Burak and to have been carried, with the Angel Gabriel as escort, from Mecca to Jerusalem.

During his presence in Jerusalem, Omar also regulated the State administration of the country. Syria was divided into provinces, each of which was termed a *Jund*, i.e. a troop of soldiers, or a military district in which a special body of troops lay in garrison. The five Junds were: the Jund of Damascus, the Jund of Hims, the Jund of Kinnasrin, the Jund of Al-Urdunn, and the Jund of Filastin. These divisions corresponded almost entirely with the old Roman and Byzantine provinces, such as the Arabs found in existence at the time of the conquest: Palestina Prima, Palestina Secunda and Palestina Tertia; Phœnicia Prima, Phœnicia Secunda; Syria Prima and Syria Secunda.

Palestina Prima, with Cæsarea as its capital, and comprising Judæa and Samaria, became the Arab Jund of Filastin.

Palestina Secunda, with Scythopolis (Beth Shean, Baisân) for its capital, comprising the two Galilees, and the western part of Peræa became the Jund of Al-Urdunn (the Jordan), with Tiberias for the new capital.

Palestina Tertia, or Salutaris, including Idumæa and Arabia Petræa, was absorbed into the Damascus Jund, and partly was counted in Filastin.

Jerusalem (Al-Kuds) became the Holy City of the Moslems, just as it was the Holy City of the Jews and the Christians, although politically it never was the Moslem capital of the province of Palestine. But the Holy City, containing within its precincts the Mosque-al-Aksa, the Rock and other Holy Places, was only held second in point of sanctity to the twin holy cities of the Hedjaz, Mecca and Medina, in the eyes of all true believers. Jerusalem, the Moslems also believed, was to be the great gathering on the Last Judgment Day.[1]

The position of the inhabitants of Palestine, from the administrative point of view, changed but little under the rule of Islam. The Moslems distinguished between conquered places and those which had voluntarily surrendered. In the latter case the property remained in the possession of the original owners, who had to pay a tribute, while in the former case the land theoretically belonged to the conqueror. In reality, however, the owners were allowed to keep their property on payment of a tax. A large portion of land fell nevertheless into

[1] See L'Estrange, l.c., 84.

the hands of the conquerors, the property having been abandoned by the owners, who preferred emigration to foreign rule. Such emigrants were mostly the Greeks, who constituted the urban population, and their houses were taken possession of by the Arabs. With regard to religion, the Arab rule, at least at the beginning, was tolerant, and the inhabitants were not hindered in the exercise of their respective religions. Churches and synagogues were spared. Jews and Christians were, of course, not considered as full citizens, but for the Jews and the Christians who did not belong to the Greek Church, Islam meant an era of toleration.

The Omaiyads

In 656 the Caliph Othman fell by the hand of an assassin and Ali, the son-in-law of Mohammed, succeeded him. With the assassination of Ali in 661, the rightful succession of the vicegerents of the Prophet ceased and the energetic and intelligent Mu'awiya established the rule of the Omaiyads. "In 660", we read in a Syrian fragment, "many Arabs assembled at Jerusalem and proclaimed Mu'awiya king, whereupon he went to Golgotha and prayed, and then to Gethsemane, where he again prayed." It is evident that with the beginning of his rule Mu'awiya was already harbouring the idea of making Jerusalem the religious centre of Islam in the place of Mecca. In any case, the new

Caliph transferred the political capital of Islam from Medina to Damascus.

In 672 Mu'awiya conceived the ambitious project of conquering the entire Byzantine or Later Roman Empire and prepared a great naval expedition. The army set sail under the command of Abd er-Rahman and some of the ships anchored at Smyrna, the rest off the coast of Cilicia. About April the troops sailed into the Hellespont, but the Greeks were ready to receive the enemy and constructed a number of fire-ships and boats provided with tubes for squirting fire. The result was that the Saracens returned.

While Mu'awiya had thus failed in his ambitious desire, he was faced by another trouble in Palestine. Here bands of freebooters leading an outlaw life had penetrated as far as the Mount Lebanon. They harassed the unbelievers and assisted the cause of Christendom. These freebooters are known by the name of Mardaites.[1] Increasing in number and power, the rebels soon dominated Palestine "from the Black Mountain to Jerusalem". The presence of these Christians soon became a serious danger to the Saracens, and Mu'awiya declared himself ready to make peace with the Greek Emperor. A treaty was concluded to the effect that the peace was to last thirty years.

Mu'awiya, a gifted and efficient monarch, just and tolerant, was followed by his son Yezid (680–683), and in 685 Abd-al-Malik became Caliph,

[1] See J. B. Bury, *History of the Later Roman Empire*, ii. 312.

and his rule was important for Palestine. As the admission to the Kaaba in Mecca was at that time refused to the Omaiyads, the Caliph, for political reasons, commanded his followers to undertake the yearly pilgrimage to Jerusalem instead of Mecca. In order to render the city more attractive to the faithful, the Caliph built the famous Dome of the Rock. There is a cufic inscription in the interior of the building which gives the year 691 (72 of the Hegira) as the date of the erection of the Dome, although it names as its builder the Abbasid Caliph El-Mâmûn, who reigned from 813 to 833. From the different colour of this part of the inscription it is, however, evident that the name of El-Mâmûn was substituted at a later period for that of Abd-al-Malik.

The following account of the erection of the Dome of the Rock is given by Arab historians: In A.D. 684, in the reign of Abd-al-Malik, the ninth successor of Mohammed, and the fifth Caliph of the house of Omaya, attention was once more turned to the city of David. The Moslem Empire had been distracted by factions and party quarrels. The inhabitants of Mecca and Medina had risen against the authority of the Caliphs and proclaimed Abdallah Ibn Zubair as their spiritual and temporal head. In vain had the Caliphs Yezid and Mu'awiya II attempted to suppress the insurrection; the usurper had contrived to make his authority acknowledged throughout Arabia and the African provinces, and had established the seat of government at Mecca itself. Abd-al-Malik trembled for his rule; year after year crowds of pilgrims would visit the Kaaba and Ibn Zubair's religious and political influence would become disseminated throughout the whole of Islam. In order, therefore, to weaken his rivals' prestige, Abd-al-Malik conceived the plan of diverting the Moslems' minds from the pilgrimage to Mecca and inducing them to make the pilgrimage to Jerusalem, to the Rock, in place of the Black Stone in the Kaaba at Mecca.

Abd-al-Malik's plan, however, to make Jerusalem take the place of Mecca was no longer necessary when, in 692, Mecca fell into his hands. Under his rule Palestine enjoyed a state of prosperity. The Caliph made an attempt to establish a new system of administration and introduced the first Arabic coinage. Numerous Christians now embraced Islam, and in order not to diminish the revenues of the State the new converts to Islam were, nevertheless, obliged to pay their tribute. Under Abd-al-Malik many stately buildings, besides the Dome of the Rock, were erected, such as the Omaiyad Church at Damascus. Poetry flourished at the Court of Damascus, and Arabian science began to make its appearance.

Abd-al-Malik's successor, Al-Walid I (705–715) ameliorated the state of the streets in the cities of Syria and Palestine and is said to have erected many buildings. From the description of St. Willibald[1] it is evident that under Al-Walid buffaloes were introduced into Palestine.

---
[1] Tobler and Molinier, *Itinera Hierosolymitana*, i. 261.

The first Omaiyads had occasionally sought recreation in Palestinian villas and castles, but the Caliph Sulaimân (717–720) transferred his Court to the very heart of Palestine. It was this Caliph who, in 716, founded the town of Ramleh, which became his residence. The tradition that the town occupies the site of the Arimathæa of the New Testament is, of course, a fabrication, as Ramleh signifies in Arabic sand.

Under Abd-al-Malik and more so under the Caliph Hisham (724–743) the principle of taxation and the fiscal system were altered. Hitherto the tribute had been paid only by non-Moslems and ceased in the event of conversion, while now it was changed into a ground tax to be levied on all property owners, irrespective of creed.

The Abbasid Caliphs

Now for several centuries Islam had been not only a spiritual and religious but also a political bond. Mohammed's position, both secular and religious, was inherited by his successors, the Caliphs. Gradually, however, disputes began to arise and opened the way to a schism. The legitimate line of the successors of Mohammed was being disputed. In 750 a reaction against the Omaiyads set in, and the powerful family of the Abbasids of Meccan origin secured the upper hand by the cruel assassination of the Omaiyads. The seat of government was transferred from Damascus to Bagdad, and the central point of the Empire was removed to the banks of the Euphrates and Tigris. Once more Palestine, as in the days of Babylonian domination, was ruled from Mesopotamia. The Holy Land belonged to the Abbasid Caliphs, but they never really were sovereigns of the country. Palestine became the scene of party struggles and political rivalries, of dissensions and plottings, of intrigues and murders. Under Haroun-al-Rashid (786–809) a taste for scientific knowledge was developed among the Arabs, and schools were founded in Syria, especially in Damascus. The constant dissensions, however, undermined the power of the Caliphate and secondary dynasties arose.

At the beginning of the tenth century a rival Caliphate, that of the Fatimids, claiming descent from Fatima, the daughter of the Prophet, was established. While the Hamdanites took possession of Northern Syria, the Fatimids, rulers of Egypt, held supreme power at Damascus.

The constant fight between the Moslems had in the meantime never ceased. In 950, availing themselves of the dissensions and quarrels among the Moslems themselves, the Byzantine armies, under Nicephorus Phocas and Tzimiscus, penetrated into Palestine and devastated the country. In twenty-two days Phocas is said to have plundered and burned twenty-two towns. He killed the inhabitants, burned down houses and devastated fields and gardens, cut down fruit-trees, and sold men, women and children into slavery. The Holy Land may be said to have been turned into a wilderness by Christian hands.

Towards the end of the tenth century the Fatimids became masters of Palestine. In 990 Biamrillah, the eleven-year-old son of the Fatimid Caliph Abu-Tamin Ma'add, ascended the throne. He assumed a hostile attitude to Islam and declared himself to be an incarnation of Ali. He persecuted both Jews and Christians, gave orders to demolish churches and synagogues, and left the "infidels" the choice between expulsion and conversion. This persecution, however, did not last long and the churches were soon rebuilt, while the Jews and Christians who had been compelled to embrace Islam were permitted to return to their old faith.

The Seljuks

The power of the Fatimids gradually diminished, and Palestine once more fell into the hands of a new master. The Seljuks, chief of the nomadic Turkish tribes who had been recognized in Bagdad as temporal rulers, began to make conquests in Western Asia. In 1071 their Sultan, Assiz, took possession of Jerusalem, but when he attacked Egypt he was defeated and the Egyptians advanced into Syria, and only the arrival of Tutush, the brother of the powerful Seljuk Sultan Malekshah (1072–1092), compelled them to retreat. Thus the Seljuks were repulsed from Egypt, but they conquered the whole of Syria and Palestine, where they reigned for twenty years (1076–1096). After the death of Malekshah the empire of the Seljuks was divided, one branch establishing itself at Damascus and the other at Aleppo.

The victory of the Seljuks was a fatal blow to Oriental Christians, Latin pilgrims and Jews alike. On the whole the Caliphs had proved tolerant and granted both Christians and Jews safety of person and property. They rarely interfered with their respective religious exercises. For over four centuries the Holy Land had enjoyed comparative peace, but now everything was changed. The regular government of the Caliphs was replaced by the iron yoke of barbarians. Religion and property were no longer safe. The Seljuks, nominally Moslems, began to oppress Christians and Jews. Divine worship in the Church of Resurrection was often disturbed by rude and savage masters. Great were the sufferings of the pilgrims to the Holy Land, and their pathetic tales when brought to the West aroused general indignation.

The news of the persecutions of Christian pilgrims which "roused the martial nations of Europe" and made them rally to the standard of the Cross was one of the causes which brought about the Crusades.

CHAPTER XIV

PILGRIMAGES TO THE HOLY LAND

Pilgrimages—Constantine—St. Helena—The Holy Cross—A cheque upon the Treasury—A splinter from the True Cross—St. Jerome and women pilgrims — Paula — Melania — St. Augustine — Piety, adventure and mercantile pursuits—Relics a source of revenue—Religion and business—Expiations for sins—Frotmond—Seigneurs troubling the public peace—A country which "devours its inhabitants"—Superstitious and educated pilgrims—The Bordeaux pilgrim—The Saracens—Bishop Arculf—The Church of the Holy Sepulchre—Willibald—Haroun-al-Rashid—Charlemagne—The Republic of Amalfi—An elephant and the keys of Jerusalem—Bernard the Wise—Pope Sylvester II—The Seljuks—Heavy taxes—Poor and wealthy pilgrims—Jewish pilgrims—The Wall of Lamentations—The ninth day of Ab—Byzantine sentinels—Visits to the Holy Land—Rabbi Zeira—The air of Palestine—The Resurrection of the Dead—Judah Halevy—Maimonides—The Karaïtes—The land of longing and yearning

FROM the very first centuries of the Christian Era the country which had been the theatre of the life and death of the Saviour became for pious Christians an object of particular veneration. The Holy City of the Jews was now also the Holy City of Christendom, for the old prejudice against deicidal Palestine, the country which had rejected and sent to death the Saviour had soon been overcome. In vain had the Emperor Hadrian erected a statue of Jupiter on the spot of the Resurrection and a statue of Venus on Calvary. All his profanations had no effect upon the zeal of the early Christians, whom piety urged to visit the Holy Land.[1] The custom of making pilgrimages

[1] See Fleury, *Histoire Ecclésiastique*, 1840, i. 123–124.

to the Holy Land was therefore practised from the very earliest ages of the Church, and the ardour increased among the faithful under the reign of Constantine. Now the Christians began to flock to Jerusalem and to other places of the Holy Land from all the provinces of the Empire to worship Christ upon His own tomb. No longer in dread of persecutions, the Christians could give themselves up to the fervour of their devotions; they were protected by the Roman eagle ornamented with the Cross. They came in thousands from the forests of Germany and the depths of Gaul, from the banks of the Rhône and the Dordogne to the shores of the Jordan, in whose waters they renewed their baptism.

St. Helena, the mother of Constantine, accomplished a pious pilgrimage to Jerusalem, where she discovered the Holy Cross, and her son replaced the temple of Venus, built by Hadrian, by his famous Church of the Holy Sepulchre.

Already, some twenty years before Helena, Antoninus the Martyr and John the Presbyter went from Piacenza in North Italy on a pilgrimage in 303,[1] but pilgrimages before the conversion of Constantine were few. The fashion spread apace only in the fourth century. The Church of Rome recognized a pilgrimage to the Holy Land as an act of piety which merited a considerable indulgence and which in those days was a sort of cheque upon the Treasury of the next world. The example

[1] See C. R. Beazley, *The Dawn of Modern Geography*, 1897, 54.

set by Helena and the building erected by Constantine, coupled with the discovery of the Holy Cross, greatly stimulated pilgrimages to the Holy Land. Pious Christians were anxious to fetch water from the Jordan, earth from the Sepulchre or a splinter from the true Cross. Under Julian the Apostate (361–363) the movement suffered some check, but it was soon again in full swing.

A new impetus was given by St. Jerome, who exercised a powerful influence over Christendom and managed to draw devotees to the Holy Land and to his own cell at Bethlehem. He insisted on Christians going to Palestine not only for a visit, but to live there. In St. Jerome's age, therefore, women became prominent among the pilgrims to the Holy Land. Paula and her daughter Eustochium and other ladies went to Palestine and stayed there in cells and convents constructed at their own expense. Melania, who gained the name of Thecla, founded a convent in which she lived, with fifty other women, for twenty-seven years.[1]

It appears that in the fourth century the pilgrimages to the Holy Land had become so frequent that they led to many abuses. St. Augustine and St. Gregory of Nazianzus pointed out the moral dangers of pilgrimages. The latter dwelt on the wickedness of the cities in the East through which the pilgrims had to pass. Women, he thought, would in particular meet on their route with

---

[1] See Vincent de Beauvais, *Speculum Historiale*, xvii. 89; xviii. 99; xix. 35; see also Migne, *Patrologia Latina*, xxii. 493.

frequent opportunities for sinning. Jesus Christ and the Holy Ghost were not in one place more than in another. Even St. Jerome (A.D. 393) said that after all innumerable crowds of saints and doctors enjoyed eternal life without ever having seen Jerusalem![1]

The stream of pilgrims to the Holy Land continued during and after the Crusades, when the country was in the hands of the Sultan of Egypt or of the Ottoman Turks. It continued when the spirit of the Crusaders had died out and the Reformation of the sixteenth century had wrought such a change in the Christian Church. In course of time, instead of monks and soldiers, Europe began to send merchants, scholars and consuls to the Holy Land, but the pious pilgrims are still continuing to flock to the Sacred Places.

The majority of the early pilgrims were animated by a sincere desire to visit the Holy Places where Christ had lived and died, but there were many among them whose purposes were of a more worldly nature. Adventure, ambition, mercantile pursuits were to a great extent responsible for such pilgrimages. Bishops and Abbots went to the Holy Land in search of holy relics which constituted a source of income to them, while merchants from the Mediterranean coasts came to visit the annual fair established at Jerusalem by the descendants of Omar.[2]

[1] See Smith, *Dictionary of Christian Antiquities*, s.v. ii. 1642.
[2] See Jacques de Vitry, *Historia Orientalis*, 68, 111.

Not all the pilgrimages undertaken to the Holy Land were, however, voluntary; some of them were imposed by the Church as a penance in expiation for some sin committed. Thus in 855 a noble Breton of the name of Frotmond had committed some deed of blood and was condemned by the Church to a penance. A chain was riveted round his body and his arms, and covered only with a coarse garment, his head sprinkled with ashes, he was ordered to visit barefoot the Holy Places. He and his brethren went to Syria and stayed for some time at Jerusalem, where he practised all sorts of austerities. He returned to Rome, but having failed to obtain pardon of Pope Benedict II he set out again with his brethren on their wanderings. They passed the sea to Jerusalem, went to Cana, in Galilee, and then to the Red Sea. They suffered all kinds of outrages from infidels, but nevertheless wandered on until they came to Mount Sinai, where they remained for three years, and then returned to Italy and thence to France.[1]

Sometimes the ecclesiastical authorities commanded a Christian to undertake a pilgrimage to the Holy Land for political reasons. They were anxious to get rid for a time either of persons troubling the public peace or of noblemen and seigneurs who were constantly quarrelling with their bishops. The knights who infringed the law of "Trêve de Dieu" were ordered to undertake a

[1] Mabillon, *Acta* SS. ord. S. Ben. saec., iv. 219.

pilgrimage to Jerusalem. It was a method employed which reminds us of that of both the Tsarist and Communist Governments in Russia, who used to send (or are still sending) the adversaries of their respective régimes to distant Siberia in the hope that they would never return. Palestine in those days, to use the expression of an English chronicler, had the privilege of "devouring its inhabitants". Few, indeed, returned from a pilgrimate to the Holy Land, and even when the exile had survived the fatigues and hardships of the journey he usually succumbed on his return home or died soon after his arrival.

While the majority of the pilgrims were pious but ignorant and superstitious, some of them were men of experience and education, and their subsequent narratives rendered valuable services to the knowledge of the Holy Land.

One of these earliest pilgrims, whose narrative has come down to us, was the famous Bordeaux pilgrim who visited the Holy Land in 333, two years before the consecration of the Church of the Holy Sepulchre, built by Constantine. The Bordeaux traveller's narrative is known as the *Itinerarium a Bardigala Hierusalem usque*. On leaving Bordeaux, this pious Christian passed by Arles and other towns, crossed the Alps into Italy, which country he traversed until he reached Constantinople. Crossing the Bosphorus, he continued his route through Asia Minor to Syria and Palestine. Towards the end of the fourth century

St. Paula, accompanied by her daughter, left Rome for Syria, and landed at Sidon, where she visited the Tower of Elijah. After visiting Cæsarea she arrived in Jerusalem. Here the Governor of Palestine prepared to receive her with due honours, but she preferred to take up her abode in a small cell. She visited all the Holy Places, then went to Egypt to see the hermits of the desert. Returning to Bethlehem, she built cells and hospitals for pilgrims, and there she lived in retirement until her death. Although the downfall of the Roman Empire and the Frankish conquest of Gaul interrupted the relations which had so long existed between Gaul and the Orient, we learn from Gregory of Tours how people in the West were interested in all that concerned Palestine. During the sixth century pious pilgrims flocked to Palestine from Europe, especially from the British Isles, for in those distant days already the Britons seem to have been great travellers.

It was in the sixth century, or perhaps early in the seventh, that the Italian, St. Antonio, visited the Holy Land. Soon after this period—that is, after 736, when Omar obtained possession of Jerusalem—the circumstances of the pilgrims who arrived in the Holy Land changed. The capitulation of Omar allowed the Christians to visit the Holy Land and to use their churches on payment of a tribute, but they were not permitted to build new churches, yet the Saracens encouraged pilgrimages. They were clever enough to realize that they could reap considerable advantages from such visits. For two or three centuries, therefore, after the conquest of Palestine by the Arabs, pious pilgrims continued to flock to the Holy Land. They were, of course, exposed on their long journeys to hardships and privations and even to insults and oppression, according to political circumstances, but the taxation imposed upon them for visiting the Holy Places was not greater than it had been before.

Towards the year 700, most probably in the latter part of the seventh century, the French bishop Arculf went on a pilgrimage to the Holy Land and his narrative was taken down from dictation by Adamnan, Abbot of Iona and successor of St. Columba. Arculf's pilgrim record has become more widely known than any other through the abstract and paraphrase made by Bede.

Bishop Arculf's description of the Church of the Holy Sepulchre is interesting. "The Church of the Holy Sepulchre is very large and round, encompassed with three walls, with a broad space between each, and containing three altars of wonderful workmanship, in the middle wall at three different points: on the south, the north and the west. It is supported by twelve stone columns of extraordinary magnitude; and it has eight doors or entrances through the three opposite walls, four fronting the north-east and four the south-east. In the middle space of the inner circle is a round grotto cut in the solid rock, the interior of which is large enough to allow nine men to pray standing, and the roof of which is about a foot and a half higher than a man of ordinary stature. The entrance is from the east side, and the whole of the exterior is covered with choice marble to the very top of the roof, which is adorned with gold, and supports a large golden cross. Within, on the north side, is the tomb of Our Lord, hewn out of the same rock, seven feet in length, and rising three palms above the floor. This tomb is broad enough to hold one man lying on his back, and has a raised division in the stone to separate his legs. The entrance is on the south side, and there are twelve lamps burning day and night, according to the number of the twelve apostles: four within at the foot, and the other eight above on the right-hand side. Internally, the stone of the rock remains in its original state, and still exhibits the marks of the workman's tools; its colour is not uniform, but appears to be a mixture of white and red. The stone that was laid at the entrance of the monument is now broken into two, the lesser portion standing as a square altar before the entrance, while the greater forms another square altar in the east part of the same church, covered with linen cloths. To the right of the round church (which is called the Anastasis, or Resurrection) adjoins the square of the Virgin Mary, and to the east of this another large church is built on the spot called Golgotha. Adjoining the Church of Golgotha, to the east, is the basilica or church erected with so much magnificence by the

Emperor Constantine, and called the Martyrdom."[1]

One of the most remarkable Anglo-Saxon pilgrims who followed Bishop Arculf's example was Willibald, a native of the Kingdom of Wessex. With two sons and a daughter he went on a pilgrimage to Jerusalem in about 722. Towards that epoch hostilities commenced between the Caliph Yezid II and the Greeks, but they did not put a stop to pilgrimages from the West. The travellers, however, were compelled to pass by way of Egypt. Peace was restored during the reigns of Haroun-al-Rashid (786–809) and Charlemagne, the great monarch of the West, who entertained close relations with Asia. On the whole, the conquest of Jerusalem by the Arabs had rather stimulated than suppressed the pilgrimages to the Holy Land. Crowds of pilgrims from the East and the West continued to visit the Holy Sepulchre, more especially at the festival of Easter. Latins and Greeks, Nestorians and Jacobites, Copts, Abyssinians, Armenians and Georgians, Normans and Franks undertook long and perilous journeys to Jerusalem. Charlemagne protected the pilgrims, while in the interests of commerce the Republic of Amalfi transported them to the coast of the Holy Land. The friendship which existed between the Christian monarch and the Caliph gave rise to the tradition that Charlemagne himself had visited the Holy Land. It has even been suggested that Haroun-al-Rashid had

[1] See Thomas Wright, *Early Travels in Palestine*, 1848, 2–3.

the intention of ceding Palestine to the Christian Emperor. To Aix-la-Chapelle, the residence of the Frankish monarch, the Caliph sent an elephant and the keys of Jerusalem. Charlemagne is also said to have collected a library in Jerusalem and to have built there a hostelry for the benefit of Christian travellers. In any case, Palestine was now opened to the Christian pilgrims on much more liberal terms, and pilgrimages became much more frequent during the latter part of the eighth and in the ninth centuries. Bernard the Wise, a Breton monk of the monastery of St. Michel, went to the Holy Land in 867. He is the first traveller to mention the miracle of the holy fire, and lodged at Jerusalem in the hostel founded by Charlemagne. Before the end of the ninth century new wars broke out between the Greeks and the Saracens; the whole of Judæa was taken from the Moslems by the Emperor John Tzimiscus, and the Holy Places were naturally thrown open to Christians. Tzimiscus died in 976 and Palestine was seized by the Fatimid Caliphs of Egypt. They, too, saw their advantage in the pilgrimages and were not slow in deriving a benefit from both religion and trade. An annual fair was instituted on Mount Calvary, and the convent and hospital of St. John of Jerusalem was founded by Italian merchants. With a view to developing commercial relations with the Franks, the Fatimid Caliphs encouraged pilgrimages and on the whole treated the Christians with leniency. During the reign, however, of Hakem, the third Fatimid Caliph, a cruel despot, the Christians had to suffer terribly. They were oppressed and massacred, their churches were taken from them, profaned and destroyed. During these persecutions the pilgrimages nevertheless continued, and one of the most celebrated pilgrims at this period was the famous Gerbert, who became Pope under the name of Sylvester II. He published a letter in 986, in which he called upon the Christian world to come to the aid of the Holy City. Many pilgrims now, particularly from France and Italy, began to proceed to the Holy Land in armed bodies in the hope of wreaking vengeance on the infidels. The result was that Hakem increased his persecutions and in 1008 demolished the Church of the Holy Sepulchre. The news both threw Europe into consternation and increased the eagerness for pilgrimages. In spite of perils and insults, crowds flocked to Jerusalem.

In the meantime Palestine had once more changed masters. The Seljuks conquered the Holy Land from the Fatimids, and massacred both Christians and Saracens; mosques and churches were pillaged and the fate of the pilgrims became deplorable. A heavy tax had to be paid before the pilgrim was permitted to enter the gates of Jerusalem. And yet, from all corners of Europe there came those pilgrims, eager to lay their foreheads on the stone of the Holy Sepulchre.

There their sins would be forgiven and they

would find not only pardon but also consolation and peace. They came either overland, trudging thousands of miles over deserts and mountains, through savage and inhospitable lands, or they preferred the sea journey, on which they endured not less miseries. But what were all these hardships compared to the hope which animated their breasts, that of kneeling on the Spot where the Saviour died and came to life again! Here all their guilt would be washed away and eternal bliss would await them in the world to come. But, alas! the goal was not so easily to be reached. At the gates of the Holy City the poor pilgrims had to sit and weep, waiting for permission to pass the gate. When Palestine was in the hands of the Seljuk Turks the governor exacted a gold piece from every pilgrim. Few, however, had even a silver coin, and only when rich and generous pilgrims came along they paid the toll for the poor too. But even when the pilgrims had been lucky enough to gain admission into the Holy City new outrages awaited them there. Everything that the pious Christians held most sacred was being defiled by unbelievers and trodden underfoot. This deplorable state of the Christian pilgrims was one of the causes which led to the Crusades.

Jewish Pilgrims

The Jews, too, frequently undertook pilgrimages to the Holy Land. They went there to weep and mourn and pray for the restoration of Zion, although for centuries they were not permitted to enter the City of Jerusalem. In spite of the constant persecutions, the fond attachment of the Jews, as we gather from Jewish writings, to the very air and soil of the Holy Land never abated. Hadrian had forbidden them to enter Jerusalem under the penalty of death. It is doubtful whether this edict was rescinded in 138, when Antoninus Pius revoked the other severe laws of his predecessor directed against the practice of the Jewish religion, but the Christian Church Fathers state that the law was in force uninterruptedly since the time of Hadrian. On the other hand we hear that after the Church Council of Nicæa (325) Constantine renewed the edict of Hadrian barring Jerusalem to the Jews, and this would tend to prove that the edict had not been in force for nearly fifteen years of Constantine's reign. Anyhow, from Constantine's time onwards (with the exception of the two years of Julian's reign) the Holy City was forbidden territory to the Jews. Christianity had triumphed and the daughter-religion had supplanted the mother-faith in its old homeland. The result was that the Jews were prohibited from residing in Jerusalem, and only once a year, on the ninth of the month of Ab, were the exiles permitted to approach the temple in ruins, there to recite the Lamentations. Byzantine sentinels would come along and demand bribes for the permission granted to the Jews to tarry and weep a little longer at the sacred spot. Jerome describes the procession of the mourners on this day. A sad crowd: decrepit women and old men in rags, tears streaming down their cheeks, would approach the city, anxious to pray and weep at the Wall of Lamentations. But, alas, even in their prayers and lamentations the mourners were often interrupted, as the Byzantine soldiers soon came along to ask for money from these people if they wished to prolong their prayers and wailing. In spite, however, of the humiliations which the hostile and heartless mob was heaping upon the mourners at these annual visits, the pilgrims came in crowds, hailing from Judæa, but mostly from Galilee, which contained a greater number of Jews than the southern part of the country. The pilgrims came also from other countries, for all over the lands of the Diaspora it was considered a religious duty by the Jews to visit the Holy Land. "The great wise men", we read in the Talmud, "were wont to kiss the borders of the Holy Land, to embrace its ruins, and to roll themselves in its dust." Rabbi Zeira waded through the waters of the Jordan, and his impatience to tread on the sacred soil was so great that he did not waste his time in removing his clothes.[1] Unable to enter Jerusalem on the territory around the Holy City, the Jewish pilgrims from Babylon and the East or from the Western countries went as far as Tiberias, or stopped at Gaza or at Soar, by the Dead Sea, where they could at least obtain a glimpse

[1] *Talmud Jerushalmi, Shebuot,* iv. 9.

of the hills constituting the Holy City of Jerusalem. But for the Jews it was not sufficient to have paid a visit to the Holy Land. Their visits were usually coupled with a desire to live and be buried there.

In their daily prayers the Jews in the Diaspora turned their faces to Jerusalem, the city of David, and to Mount Zion, where the Messiah was expected one day to establish his reign of justice and universal peace. For Israel, downtrodden and oppressed, scattered all over the world, Palestine was the Land of longing and yearning, the Home lost but once to be regained. For the moment the exiles were not permitted to live in peace in their ancestral home, they were debarred even from weeping at the Wall of Lamentations, but they could at least die in Palestine and be buried there. "The air of Palestine", say the rabbis, "makes a man wise"; "he who walks four cubits in the land of Israel is sure of being a son of the life to come"; "the sins of all those are forgiven who inhabit the land of Israel." But even those who are buried there are esteemed blessed. "He who dies out of the Holy Land dies a double death." "He who is buried in the Holy Land is reconciled with his God, as though he were buried under the altar." "The dead buried in the Holy Land come first to life in the days of the Messiah." To be buried therefore on the slopes of the Mount of Olives and in the Valley of Kidron was the dream of pious Jews. There the trumpet-call of the Messiah was expected to resound and the dead would arise at once and witness the glory of the New Jerusalem. Among the noted pilgrims to the Holy Land before the Crusades we may mention Judah Halevy, who in 1140 came to kiss the stones of his ancestral home and, as legend relates, perished there. Maimonides visited Palestine in 1165, and when Saladin conquered the country in 1187 many Jewish pilgrims came from Egypt and Babylonia to weep at the graves of the Patriarchs at Hebron. Later on the Karaïtes showed great devotion to the Holy Land and a company of pilgrims journeyed to Jerusalem in the tenth century. Thus Palestine had become the Holy Land, the land of longing and yearning for both Christians and Jews.

CHAPTER XV

THE CROSS AND THE CRESCENT

(A.D. 1096–1517)

The Crusades—Fanaticism—Popular indignation—Ambition and business considerations—The Norman Knights—The Republics of Pisa, Genoa and Venice—An ideal pretext—Godfrey of Bouillon—Penitence and prayers—Massacre and riot—A vassal of the Church—Feudal jurisprudence—An unwritten Creed—A mixture of races—Peace and prosperity—A *creatio ex nihilo*—Clericalism and militarism—A foreign civilization—Disadvantages of feudalism—A powerful enemy—Saladin—A leper, a child, a woman and a coward—"We shall all die of thirst"—Renaud of Châtillon—A cup of iced sherbet—Frederic II—The Carizmian Turks—General Beibars—Holagu—Kotuz—"Reign thou in his place"—The Abbasid Caliph—*Finità la tragedia*—Desolation and ruin—Six *mamlakas*—Yellow and blue turbans—The Bahrite and Burjite dynasties—Berkuck—Bertrand de la Brocquière—Jakmac—Mamelukes and Osmanlis—Selim I, the Grim—The Jews of Palestine

The Crusades

It has often been asserted that the Crusades were the result of a religious enthusiasm which had suddenly taken hold of European Christianity or, as some maintain, of fanaticism and religious mania. In reality, however, there were many causes which brought about the Crusades. The news of the cruelties of the Seljuks had, no doubt, roused popular indignation in Europe, but popular indignation never produces wars or brings about peace if those in power see no advantage to themselves in either peace or war, as the case may be. The policy of the Popes, the ambition of Norman knights and business considerations were some of the many causes of the Crusades.

The sufferings of Christian pilgrims had certainly increased under the rule of the Seljuks and the complaints had become more numerous, but in spite of all the romance attributed to the first Crusades the moving force was of a social and political character. Neither the Arabs, when they conquered Palestine, nor the Christian knights who came to deliver the Holy Sepulchre, were animated solely by religious thoughts. It was primarily a question of conquest for both, and the difference between the conquests of Islam and those of the Crusaders lies only in the fact that the Arabs had much more in common with the Syrian Christians, who were Orientals, than did the Frankish knights. Whereas the victory of Islam meant a change of masters for the *land*, the result of the victories of the Crusaders was a change of the *population*. It resulted in the establishment of a Frankish, Western kingdom in an Oriental country.

As far as the military leaders were concerned, the first Crusade was really an enterprise for the conquest and partition of Syria. The Norman knights were anxious to carve out for themselves principalities or kingdoms in the East, for which they had but little chance at home, and they were the first to answer the appeal of Pope Urbain. On the other hand, the Republics of Pisa, Genoa and Venice were seeking outlets for their commerce, and the shores of the Mediterranean being in alien hands was a sore point to them. The delivery of the Holy Sepulchre furnished only an ideal pretext, *tout comme chez nous*.

It does not enter within the scope of the present work to treat in detail the history of the Crusades, and we shall only briefly relate the events as far as they affected Palestine and the inhabitants of the country.

In June 1099 twenty thousand Latins approached Jerusalem, and the famous Tancred gazed upon the Holy City from the Mount of Olives. The siege of Jerusalem lasted forty days, and the Holy City, the centre of faith dear to Jews, Christians and Moslems, was captured. On a Friday, at three in the afternoon, the day and hour of the Passion (July 15, 1099), Godfrey of Bouillon at last stood victorious on the walls of the Holy City. Four hundred and sixty years had elapsed since Omar had wrested Jerusalem from Christendom, and Christianity triumphed once more. The Holy Sepulchre was free, and humbly, barefoot and bareheaded, the victors ascended the Hill of Calvary to weep tears of joy and penitence at the spot where Christ is said to have suffered. But, alas, the victors had forgotten His teaching and His religion of Love. Their contrition and their prayers were preceded by bloody sacrifices and by massacres which lasted seven days. For seven days the victorious Crusaders indulged in riot and carnage, forgetting the teaching of the Prince of Peace, of the gentle prophet of Nazareth. Seven thousand Moslems were put to the sword without distinction of age or sex, while the Jews, Rabbinites, Karaïtes and Samaritans were driven into the synagogue and perished in the flames.

The conquerors now proceeded with the business of distributing the spoils. Edessa was a Burgundian princedom, Antioch was Norman and Tripoli Provençal.

The Latin Kingdom

A Christian kingdom was established at Jerusalem, and Godfrey of Bouillon, the blameless knight and humble Christian, was chosen king. He refused to wear a crown where his Master had suffered for the sins of humanity, but he was persuaded in the end to take upon himself the responsibility of protector of the Holy Sepulchre. He was to be known as duke and vassal of the Church. The Latin kingdom established in the Holy Land was based on the feudal system and was divided in fiefs ruled by knights and seigneurs, the chief vassals being the Count of Edessa, the Prince of Antioch, the Count of Tripoli and the Prince of Galilee. The authority of the King of Jerusalem was limited by a body of feudatories, whose power was represented by the High Court, composed of vassals and rear-vassals. This Court was alone empowered to make laws or assizes. The King of Jerusalem was sometimes quite powerless against such vassals as Renaud de Châtillon, who became Lord of Montreal in 1174. The power of the king was further limited by the Church. A Latin Church was established in Palestine, and the patriarch, elected by the clergy, was confirmed by the Pope. He was independent of the king and exercised great authority in the country. The orders of religious knighthood, the Hospitallers of St. John (1113), the Templars, founded in 1128, and the Teutonic Knights, created in 1143, were independent of both the king and the patriarch. They owed spiritual allegiance to the Pope, but in temporal matters they were quite independent of both Church and State. Each of the three orders owned numerous fiefs and castles in Palestine and they even enjoyed the right to conclude treaties with the Moslems. Thus the royal authority in the Latin kingdom was rather restricted.

The Assizes of Jerusalem

It has been generally maintained that Godfrey of Bouillon drew up a code of law, a monument of feudal jurisprudence based on statutes and customs of Europe, for the guidance of the tribunals of Palestine. This document, regulating the laws of the new kingdom, was contained in the Assizes of Jerusalem and is supposed to have been lost when Saladin captured the city. In reality, however, no written document ever existed. The kings of the Latin kingdom merely dispensed justice in the Holy Land in accordance with customary law, which was gradually built up. The unwritten code was then set down in writing by John d'Ibelin, Count of Jaffa, about the middle of the thirteenth century.[1]

It was a strange mixture of races which inhabited Palestine and Syria during the period of the Latin kingdom. First of all there were the native elements: the Moslem peasants and wandering Arabs; the fellahin, Moslem by name but not of pure Arab race, descendants of Hittites, Amorites and Nabatæans, who spoke mostly Aramæan; the wandering Arabs or Bedouins in the deserts to the east; and, lastly, the Jews and the Samaritans. Then there were the Syrian Greeks, who had little Indo-European blood in their veins. They were of Arab race but Greek by religion. The population, further, included the elements from almost all parts of Europe: Normans, Italians, Franks, Germans, Hungarians, Bretons, Scots, English, Bohemians, Bulgarians, Georgians, and Greeks, besides Egyptians and Indians. The languages spoken in the country were: Greek, Syriac and an Arabic dialect of an Aramæan character, Norman-French and, naturally, mediæval Latin, the language of the Church and the Law.[2]

It must be admitted that the economic prosperity which the Latin kingdom attained in the twelfth

---

[1] See G. Dodu, *Histoire des Institutions monarchiques dans le royaume Latin de Jerusalem*, 1894; Röhricht, *Geschichte des Königreich's Jerusalem 1100–1291*, 1898; J. G. C. Anderson, *The Student's Gibbon*, ii. 227, note.

[2] See Conder, *The Latin Kingdom*, 66.

century was high. Peace and prosperity were in any case greater in the Holy Land than in European lands in those days.¹ It has even been maintained by some historians that the native peasantry preferred the Christian rule to that of the Turkish and Egyptian tyrants. Industries peculiar to Syria —the manufacture of silk and cotton materials, dye-works and glass-factories—were developed and stimulated commerce. The ships going to the West were laden with costly merchandise brought from the interior of Asia, while the Western ships brought to Palestine European products.²

And yet, the Latin kingdom in Jerusalem could not exist for any length of time. It was a Frankish State created on Oriental soil, a Western State in the spirit of Christian mediæval knighthood, a *creatio ex nihilo* which had no connection whatever with the past of either the country or its inhabitants. The characteristic traits of the Latin kingdom were clericalism and militarism, and its efforts tended to implant in the East a foreign growth and a new civilization. This is clearly manifested by the still existing constructions raised in the Holy Land during the period of the Crusades—the numerous churches and castles. It is Western mediæval civilization which speaks to us from these monuments. For this civilization, however, the East had neither understanding nor sympathy. The Orientals, Jews and

¹ See Conder, l.c., 119.
² See Rey, *Les colonies franques de Syrie aux* $12^{\grave{e}me}$ *et* $13^{\grave{e}me}$ *siècles*, Paris, 1883.

Syrian Christians, who had much in common with the Moslems, felt themselves to be the possessors of an older civilization, and they were little inclined to adopt foreign goods. Moreover, the young Christian kingdom lacked all the conditions which could have furthered its growth and development. It had no firm foundations, nor did it possess the moral and material support of a Great Power. For its revenues it depended not upon the country itself but upon the pilgrims from the West who annually flocked to the Holy Land. It lived on charity. Besides, the Christian knights began to intermarry with the native Syrians and acquire their vices. The barons quarrelled among themselves, having only their separate interests in view, and not those of the State.

Based on the feudal system, the Latin kingdom had all the disadvantages of feudalism. There was no unity in the kingdom. It could therefore exist only for a short time thanks to the strife in the Moslem world, but it had to reckon with the possibility of a union between its Eastern and Southern neighbours. Once a powerful foe arose, the Latin kingdom was doomed to disappear, and soon such a foe did arise in the person of the mighty Sultan Saladin. Noureddin, the master of Mesopotamia and Northern Syria, put an end to the dynasty of the Burides at Damascus in 1154, and aspired to reign also in Egypt under the name of the Abbasid Caliphs. He attacked Egypt in 1164, and by his command the Fatimids were deposed and the Caliph Mostadi of Bagdad was acknowledged as the true Commander of the Faithful.

On the death of his uncle, Shiracout, Saladin, the son of Ayoub, became Vizier, and thanks to his genius he soon became all-powerful. While Noureddin lived, Saladin professed himself his humble servant, but after the death of the Sultan in 1174 he made himself master of Egypt, and his usurpation was sanctified by the Caliph of Bagdad. Not content with the possession of Egypt, Saladin decided to conquer also Palestine.

The kingdom of Jerusalem, which during its short existence had been supported by the rivalry and discord of Saracens and Turks, was thus threatened by a powerful enemy, and the guardians of the Holy Sepulchre were too weak to fight against him. After the two first Baldwins, a brother and a cousin of Godfrey of Bouillon, the sceptre devolved to Melisenda, a daughter of the second Baldwin, and her husband, Fulk of Anjou, the father of the English Plantagenets. Their two sons, Baldwin III and Amaury, waged a war against the Saracens, but Baldwin IV, a son of Amaury, was a leper and unable to rule. His natural heiress was Sybilla, his sister, the mother of Baldwin V, after whose death Sybilla crowned her second husband, Guy of Lusignan. "Such", writes Gibbon, "were the guardians of the Holy City: a leper, a child, a woman and a coward."

After a number of border attacks, Saladin finally

assembled an army at Damascus, and crossing the Jordan south of the Sea of Galilee laid siege to Tiberias. Within the city were the Countess of Tripoli and her sons, and she appealed to Guy, King of Jerusalem, for help. Raymond, Count of Tripoli, notwithstanding the fact that his wife and children were within the walls of Tiberias, tried to dissuade the King from marching to the relief of the city. "We shall all die of thirst before we get there," he insisted. Unfortunately, the Master of the Templars, who hated Raymond, persuaded the King not to listen to the sound advice. A fierce battle was therefore fought at the Horns of Hattin, and the Christians, exhausted by heat and suffering agonies for lack of water, were defeated. Thirty thousand Crusaders are said to have fallen, and the last survivors surrendered to Saladin. Among the captives brought before the Sultan were King Guy and Amaury, his brother, Humphrey of Toron, Master of the Temple, and Renaud of Châtillon, Master of the Hospital. Saladin offered a cup of iced sherbet to King Guy, but when the latter gave it to Renaud of Châtillon the Sultan observed: "It is thou, not I, who hast given him to drink." Food was given to all except Renaud, whom Saladin reproached with cruelty and insolence. Indeed, Renaud of Châtillon, the Master of the Hospital, had seized a caravan of Moslem pilgrims coming from Mecca and taken them prisoners. When Renaud refused to accept the Koran the Sultan swiftly raised his scimitar and cut off his head,

Saladin now laid siege to Jerusalem and on October 1, 1187, the city capitulated on certain terms.

Thus the Moslems were once more in possession of the Holy Sepulchre, and Christendom in Europe was full of consternation. A new Crusade was preached and was undertaken by the Emperor of Germany and the Kings of England and France. The Crusaders failed in their endeavour to capture Jerusalem, but a truce was agreed to and a treaty was concluded between the Moslems and the Christians. The Crusaders received free access to Jerusalem, and Ludd and Ramleh were to be considered common ground. The Latin kingdom, which still continued to exist, consisted now of a small strip of land with Acre as capital. New Crusades were preached and undertaken, but none of them changed the fate of the Holy Land.

In 1228 Frederic II, although excommunicated by Pope Innocent III, accomplished a crusade without bloodshed. Entering Jerusalem in triumph, he took the crown with his own hands from the altar of the Holy Sepulchre. He obtained from the Sultan the restitution of Jerusalem, Bethlehem, Nazareth, Tyre and Sidon, and the Christians could once more worship at the Holy Sepulchre. This state, however, was soon terminated by the invasion of the savage hordes of the Carizmian Turks in 1240. Like an avalanche they fell upon Syria and the Holy Land. Jerusalem was destroyed and seven thousand Christians were slain.

The women were carried off into captivity. The Ayoubite Sultan of Egypt, so called from Ayoub, the father of Saladin, formed an alliance with these barbarians against his Syrian uncle, Ismael, between whom and the Crusaders a union prevailed. He sent his Mameluke general, Beibars, against the combined armies of the Franks and the Moslems, who were defeated near Joppa. The whole of Syria and the Holy Land thus once more fell under Egyptian sway.

The Mamelukes

In 1250 a new time of trial was at hand for the Holy Land. It was at that time that the Mongols under Holagu appeared. They laid siege to Bagdad, took the city and gave it up to all the horrors of war. The Caliphate of the Abbasids was put an end to and the last Caliph lost his life. The Mongols then invaded Syria, and ravaged the country with unheard-of barbarity. Kotuz, the Sultan of Egypt, gathered an army and advanced to Akka, where he found the Crusaders bound to the Mongols by a promise of neutrality. In a fiercely contested battle, Kotuz and his general, Beibars, defeated the Mongols, whose general, Ketbogha, was slain. The Christians and the Jews who had saluted the Mongols as deliverers from Islam were mercilessly massacred. Kotuz and Beibars drove the enemy out of Syria and the former governors were appointed throughout the country. Kotuz, however, did not enjoy his victory for long. He was assassinated by Beibars, who was saluted Sultan and entered Cairo with the acclamations of the people. Abulfeda relates that when, all blood-stained, Beibars appeared before the atabeg or lieutenant of the prince and announced the death of the Sultan, the atabeg asked him who had killed Kotuz. "It was I", said Beibars. "In that case", replied the atabeg, "reign thou in his place."

Beibars, who inaugurated the long line of Bahrite Mameluke sultans, reigned from 1260 to 1277. He gradually brought the whole of Syria and the Holy Land under his sway. In order to strengthen his dynasty both against the jealousies of his former comrades and the attacks of the partisans of the Fatimid dynasty, he decided to re-establish the Caliphate of the Abbasids. He installed as Caliph a member of the family who had escaped from the massacre of Holagu at Bagdad, and the new Caliph, in his turn, conferred on Beibars the sovereign title.

Macrizy relates that Beibars, accompanied by his Court and the emirs of his army, went out to meet the Caliph at Fostat. The principal inhabitants of Cairo and Fostat followed the procession, the Jews carrying the Law and the Christians the Gospels.[1] In 1268 Antioch was taken by Beibars, and in 1291 St. John of Acre, which, after the loss of Jerusalem, had become the metropolis of the Latin kingdom, was stormed. The churches and

[1] See Quatremère, *Histoire des Sultans Mamlouks*, Paris, 1837, I. i. 147.

fortifications were demolished, although the pilgrims were still allowed to worship at the Holy Sepulchre. Palestine now definitely remained in the possession of the Moslems.

The tragedy had thus come to an end. The Latins had been unable to establish a permanent rule in the Holy Land, because they could not adapt themselves to the East. The results of their presence in the country were only desolation and ruin, the consequences of the constant fights against Islam. As for Palestine itself and the whole of Syria, the country was not strong enough to play an independent rôle, and it became a dependency of Egypt. During the reign of the Mamelukes Syria was divided into six *mamlakas* or principalities, and Palestine itself into three: *Dimashk, Safed* and *Al-Kerak*.

The Mameluke Sultans of the Bahrite dynasty remained in possession of Palestine until 1382, when they were overthrown. The Christians were at first allowed to enter the Church of the Holy Sepulchre on paying a tribute, but in 1305, under the reign of Nasir (1293–1341), restrictions were issued against both Jews and Christians, who were debarred from public offices and employment. The intolerant rules which had been allowed to fall into abeyance were sternly enforced. In order to distinguish Jews and Christians from Moslems, the Jews had to wear a yellow turban, the Christians a blue one. The churches and synagogues built since the rise of Islam were to be demolished.[1]

[1] See W. Muir, *The Mameluke Dynasty of Egypt*, 60–61.

In 1363 an attempt was made to recover what had been lost by the Latins when the King of Cyprus made a truce with Egypt, which gained him half the rights of trade in Tyre, Acre, Beirut, Jerusalem and Damascus. Christian churches were rebuilt in Nazareth and Bethlehem as over the Holy Sepulchre.

The Bahrite or Turkish dynasty of the Mamelukes came to an end in 1384, and Berkuck-Al-Zôhair inaugurated the Burjite or Circassian rule, which lasted until 1517. This Sultan introduced many reforms in Palestine, and the new governor whom he sent to the Holy Land abolished all the illegal taxes which had been introduced by previous governors.[1] Berkuck was succeeded by his son Faraj (1399–1412), and during his reign Palestine was thrown into terror by the invasion of the Mongols under Timur or Timurlane. The Mongols conquered Aleppo, Emessa and Damascus, but did not touch the Holy Land.

For over a century no event of any importance occurred in the Holy Land. The Christians, we are told, were exposed to tyrannical laws and oppression, the Moslems, still remembering the Crusades, being suspicious of the Christians in Europe; and the Oriental Christians alone were tolerated in the Holy Land. The traveller Bertrand de la Brocquière, who came to the Holy Land in 1432,[2] says that he found in Jerusalem

[1] See Munk, *La Palestine*, 643, quoted from an Arabic MS. in the *Bibliothèque Nationale*.   [2] See *Early Travels*, 287.

only two French monks (Cordeliers), who were subjected to cruel treatment, while the Christian merchants were habitually locked up overnight in their bazaars. The Jews were better treated. In 1452, under the reign of Jakmac (1438-1452), the Christians were again persecuted in the Holy Land, and churches and convents were demolished.

The Mameluke Sultans, who relied on the strength of their sword, were able to hold Syria and Palestine for over three centuries because Syria and Palestine, the constant battlefields of the world, now as before, had no combined or independent policy. Those slaves on the throne of Egypt were cruel and treacherous, but there are not wanting among them instances of just and upright, even benevolent and honourable, rulers. They often checked in Palestine the oppression prevailing against Christians and Jews, and they left behind them beautiful constructions and monuments. They also paid attention to the amelioration of the land. In the meantime, however, the Osmanlis had gradually been rising to power, and in the end the Mamelukes were not strong enough to resist the onslaught of the new invader.

The Osmanli family was founded in 1288 by Othman, a Carizmian vassal of the Sultan of Iconium. They established themselves at Broussa, and even before Timur appeared began to threaten Constantinople, but the Tartar onset delayed the conquest of the city by the Osmanli Turks. In 1453, however, the Osmanlis captured Constantinople.

The Emperor Constantine Palæologus was defeated by Mohammed II and the Byzantine Empire was overthrown. Half a century later the Turks sought to conquer Egypt, Syria and Palestine, and Selim I, the Grim, made war on the Mamelukes, who were defeated in Northern Syria. In 1516 Selim advanced to Gaza, and in 1517 he entered Cairo as victor. In the same year he became master of the Holy Land, which henceforth, for four centuries (1517–1917), had once more to feel "the evils of a foreign tyranny".

The Jews in Palestine after the Moslem Conquest (634–1517)

After the conquest of the Holy Land by the Moslems, the position of the Jews there greatly improved and their intellectual activity increased. The Jewish Academy of Tiberias, which had existed there all through the centuries of Byzantine dominion, was transferred to Jerusalem. It became the spiritual centre not only of the Jews in the Holy Land but also of the Jewries in Syria and Egypt. When, under the Omaiyad Caliphs, Arabic civilization began to flourish, the Jews, too, took part in this intellectual activity. The literary productions of Palestinian scholarship were the *Masorah*, or the fixation of the Hebrew Text of the Old Testament,[1] and the Tiberian punctuation.[2] The study of the Arabic language induced the Palestinian Jews to

[1] See Note 21 in Appendix.   [2] See Note 22 in Appendix.

study also their own sacred tongue, Hebrew, and liturgical poetry flourished. It was in Palestine where the best *Piyyutim*, or liturgical poems, were composed. Jose Hayatom, Jannai, and probably Eliezer Hakalir, were Palestinian Jews. The Jews also distinguished themselves in other branches of science. In 683 we find a Jewish physician at Bosra, and it was a Jew who engraved the new coins for the Caliph Abd-al-Malik. Rabbinic Judaism flourished until Anan, the founder of the Karaïte sect, came to Jerusalem, where he built a synagogue and gathered adherents.

Under the Fatimid Caliph Al-Aziz (975–996), a Christian, named Isa ben Nestorius, became vizier. He favoured his co-religionists, but appointed as his chief deputy at Damascus a Jew, Manasseh Ibn Hazra, who did for the Jews in Syria and Palestine what the vizier Isa did for the Christians in Egypt, so that Christians and Jews ruled the State. The Moslems protested, and both Isa and Manasseh were arrested. Isa was soon restored to his dignity, but what happened to Manasseh is not clear, although the Arabian authors maintain that he was crucified.[1] In any case, Manasseh's management of affairs in Syria was beneficial to the Jews of Palestine. Under the Caliph El-Hakim both the Jews and Christians were persecuted, but as far as the Jews were concerned their sufferings were

---

[1] See *Abhandlungen der Göttinger Königl. Gesellschaft der Wissenschaften*, xxvii. *ab*. ii. 64–66; see also J. Mann, *The Jews in Egypt and Palestine under the Fatimid Caliphs*, i. 19.

soon followed by much greater misery when the Crusaders conquered Jerusalem.

The terrible massacres of the Jews in Europe, in France and Germany, were a prelude to the cruelty with which the Crusaders treated the Jews in their ancestral home. It is astonishing that any Jews at all remained in the Holy Land during the Crusades. We gather some information with regard to the position of the Jews in the Holy Land in the eleventh century from the *Travels of Benjamin of Tudela* (1160–1173). In the whole of Palestine the traveller found only 1,100 Jews, 200 of them dwelling in Jerusalem, 300 at Toron de los Caballeros (the ancient Shunem)[1] and 50 at Tiberias. There were 12 Jews at Bethlehem and one at Jaffa, all dyers by profession. At Damascus, which the Crusaders had not been able to capture and which belonged to the kingdom of Noureddin, there were three times as many Jews as in the whole of Palestine. When Pethahiah of Ratisbon visited the Holy Land (1175–1190) he found only *one* Jew at Jerusalem.

The time of the Crusades was a period of decadence for the Jews of Palestine, and their position improved only when the Crescent once more triumphed over the Cross. When Saladin captured Jerusalem in 1187, he permitted the Jews to enter the city once more, and under the mild reign of the son of Ayoub several Jews attained a high degree of prosperity. At that time the sufferings

[1] Joshua xix. 18.

of the Jews in Europe were great, and many of them found a haven of refuge in the dominions of Saladin. The number of Jewish immigrants from the West to Palestine increased. In 1211 about three hundred Rabbis from France and England arrived in the Holy Land, where they met with a friendly reception at the hands of Abadil, the brother of Saladin.

In 1259 Rabbi Jechiel, the head of the French Tossafist school, left Paris and settled at Acre. German Jews, in whose hearts the old Messianic hope had revived, wandered out to the Holy Land from Mayence, Worms, Spires and Oppenheim. In the thirteenth century we hear once more of an Exilarch, or a Prince of Captivity, who had his seat at Damascus and who was the acknowledged head of all the Jews in Palestine.

In 1267 the famous Nachmanides arrived in the Holy Land, where he exercised a tremendous influence over the development of Palestinian Jewry. Nachmanides found Jerusalem in a state of desolation and set about reorganizing the Jewish communities in the Holy Land. He built synagogues and brought about a revival of Jewish intellectual activity.

In the fourteenth century, when, with the fall of Acre in 1291, the power of the Crusaders had been completely crushed, the immigration of the Jews from the West to Palestine increased and has never since ceased. It was the time of terrible persecutions of Jews in England under Edward I (1290) and in France under Philippe le Bel (1306).

Israel once more became the homeless wanderer, the Ahasverus of Christian legend, and the flight to the East, and to Palestine in particular, began. From Christian lands the Jews escaped to find a refuge in the lands of Islam and in their ancient home. The number of Jews in the Holy Land greatly increased. There were large communities at Jerusalem, Hebron, Safed and Ramleh. There were to be found in the Holy Land not only Jewish artisans, dyers, weavers, glass-blowers and merchants, but also physicians, mathematicians and astrologers. Some of them were agriculturists, and in the southern parts of the country Jewish shepherds, by the side of Moslems, tended their flocks. The intellectual activity, too, of the Palestinian Jews revived, although it was particularly the Kabbala or Jewish mysticism which flourished in the Holy Land. Palestine once more became the centre of religious speculation and the goal of mystic and Messianic dreams.

In 1492, almost on the very day on which Christopher Columbus, supported by Jewish financiers and scientists, set out on his voyage of discovery, the Jews were expelled from Spain. In Portugal, where Manoel was rather favourably disposed towards the Jews, the King had to yield to the bigotry of the Queen, a daughter of Ferdinand the Catholic and Isabella. On December 20, 1496, the Jews were, therefore, expelled from Portugal. Deprived of their native homes, the exiles sought a refuge in Navarre, Italy and Africa, but the majority of them wandered out to the dominions of the Turks, where they found a haven of refuge. The exiles also flocked to the Holy Land, which was still in the possession of the Egyptian Mamelukes. In 1495 the Jewish community of Jerusalem numbered 200 families instead of 70 in 1488. In 1521 it increased to 1,500 families. Towards the end of the fifteenth century, Obadia di Bartinero came to Jerusalem, where he remained twenty years and reorganized the Jewish communities in the Holy Land. In 1517 Selim I, the Grim, conquered Palestine and a new era began for the Jews in their old Homeland.

CHAPTER XVI

FOUR CENTURIES OF TURKISH RULE
(A.D. 1517–1917)

The Ottoman Turks—The Pashalik of Falestin—A rotten régime—Heavy taxation—The Golden Age—Sultans Selim I and Suleiman II—Revenue and taxation—Inroads of Bedouins—An emir of the Druses—The ambitious chief—The master of Galilee—Reforms and discontent—Petty tyrants—A powerful sheikh—Peace and security in Tiberias—Treaties of alliance—The tyranny of the pasha—Brutal despotism—Napoleon in Egypt—Visions of a World-Empire—The ambitious Bashibazouk—A dictator of Egypt—From the Nile to the Jordan—Revolutions and fights for freedom—The conquest of Palestine—Hopes and disillusions—Heavy taxation—Sympathy and hostility—A regenerator of the East—An unarmed Crusade—Churches and monasteries—Russian pilgrims—An asylum for the exiles—Jewish communities—A dreamer of dreams—Mysticism and Kabbala—Persecutions and oppressions—Messianic hopes—False Messiahs—The tragedy of Jewry—Jehuda Hassid—Disappointments—Ritual murder—European Consulates—A peaceful reconquest of Palestine

The Holy Land under Ottoman Rule

For four centuries, from 1517 to 1917, Syria and Palestine remained under the sway of the Ottoman Turks. The entire province of Syria, including Palestine, was divided into five pashaliks, and Palestine proper consisted of the pashalik Falestin and parts of the pashaliks of Damascus and Acre. At the beginning of the twentieth century, and until the occupation of the country by Great Britain, Palestine was included partly in the autonomous Sanjaq (Liwa, Mutesarriflik) of Jerusalem, partly in the vilayet of Beirut. It consisted of thirteen quazas, each administered by a qaimaquan responsible to the Mutesarrif. The total area of Palestine, according to Turkish divisions, was 13,724 square miles. The rule of the Sultans was based on military power, but as soon as the central Government at Constantinople no longer had at its disposal the necessary armies, the decadence of the Turkish Empire began. During these four centuries, in Palestine as in the whole Ottoman Empire, the Turkish régime was one of heavy taxation, of negligent and unjust administration, of an entire absence of suitable measures for the development of commerce and industry or calculated to assure the safety and prosperity of the inhabitants. It must, however, be admitted that for at least half a century, during the so-called Golden Age of the Ottoman Empire, Palestine enjoyed an era of some prosperity. The change of administration introduced in the country after the rotten rule of the Mamelukes appeared as a blessing to the land. During the reigns of the victorious Sultans, Selim I and Suleiman II, the Porte had not yet commenced to exploit the provinces of Syria and Palestine. A few years, however, after the death of Sultan Suleiman II in 1566, the sad Turkish rule began which lasted until 1856 and with some ameliorations until 1917. It was the rule of the pashas, who quarrelled among themselves or with the native governors and princes. The only interest the Government of Constantinople had in the provinces was that of revenue derived from taxation.

The inhabitants, Christians and Jews alike, were never safe from sudden outbreaks of religious and racial hatred, or from the cruelties and acts of violence on the part of the provincial officials. Nor could they rely on the help of the Government against the devastating inroads of the Bedouins dwelling in the desert.

Under Sultan Murad IV, Turkey nearly lost the whole of Syria. The danger came from one of the native chiefs, the famous Emir Fakr-ed-Din, who ruled at Beirut from 1595–1634, and extended his sway over the Southern Lebanon and Upper Galilee. Appointed chief of the Druses, he at first endeavoured to gain the confidence of the Porte by the warmest professions of fidelity. He made war against the Arabs, who were infesting the plain of Baalbec and the neighbourhoods of Tyre and Acre, and delivered the inhabitants from these hostile incursions.

The powerful emir had, however, ambitious designs and neglected no opportunity to become independent and to shake off the Turkish yoke. The natural enemies of the Turks were then the Venetians, and the city of Beirut offered a desirable point of communication with them as well as with other foreign nations. Availing themselves of the misconduct of the aga, Fakr-ed-Din expelled the latter and offered the Ottoman Government the payment of a larger tribute. He took the same course with regard to Sidon, Baalbec and Tyre, and in 1613 found himself at last master of the country as far as Ajalon and Safed. The Pashas of Damascus and of Tripoli were unable to stop the encroachments of the native chief, and their intrigues at Constantinople proved of no avail. At last the Porte took alarm at the progress of the Druses and an expedition was sent to crush them. Fakr-ed-Din fled to Italy, where he remained nine years at the Court of the Medicis at Florence. In the meantime his son Ali had managed to repulse the Turks and to keep things in order. When Fakr-ed-Din returned home, he tried to introduce Western innovations in his dominions.

His reforms and the favour he showed to Christians provoked the discontent of his Mohammedan subjects, and Sultan Murad availed himself of the hatred of the Moslems against Fakr-ed-Din and ordered the Pasha of Damascus to attack the emir. The latter's son Ali was defeated at Safed and Beirut was captured, while the emir himself was brought to Constantinople, where he was strangled in 1631. Thus the hope of the Christians—who for a long time cherished the memory of the emir—for better days was frustrated.

During the second half of the eighteenth century, Palestine once more attracted the attention of Europe. In this province, as in all the other parts of the vast Ottoman Empire, the pashas were now invested with unlimited and absolute power, while the agas and sheikhs, subservient to the pashas, in their turn oppressed the districts under their jurisdiction. The Porte tolerated all these petty tyrants, allowing them to grow rich at the expense of the inhabitants. One of these sheikhs who has become famous was Omar-es-Zahir, known as Daher or Taher.

The career and story of Daher is one of the many instances of the petty revolutions which were continually taking place in Syria and Palestine, as in the whole of the Turkish Empire. Daher, the son of Omar, was an Arab chief of the tribe of Beni-Ziadneh, born in 1685 or 1686. His family is said to have been one of the most powerful among the Bedouins who frequent the Valley of the Jordan and the environs of Lake Tiberias. After the death of his father, Daher shared the government with an uncle and two brothers, and his principal village was Safed. To this he soon added Tiberias, which he seized from the Pasha of Damascus. In 1742 the sheikh was besieged in Tiberias—which he had fortified—by another pasha and owed his delivery only to the sudden death of his enemy. Daher was now left undisturbed, as far as the Ottoman Government was concerned. Involved in disputes with his uncle and brother, he put them to death and could now pursue his ambitious plans. In 1749 he seized Acre from a subordinate of the Pasha of Sidon and established himself there. He restored the defences of the city under pretence of building for himself a house and some towers on the coast. Turning his attention to the internal government of his dominions, he improved the conditions of the country with a view to rendering it more productive. By threats and promises, by force of arms or presents, he succeeded in subduing the Arab tribes and restored peace and security to the country. By his good government Daher attracted a population which, exposed as it was to constant alarm and fear of being oppressed and despoiled, was glad to take refuge under his protection. Europeans, finding here a market for their goods, formed establishments at Acre. Daher further renewed his treaties of alliance with the chief tribes of the desert and with the Metawileh, who had for some time given trouble to the Pashas of Damascus and of Sidon.

The astute sheikh was now practically master of Galilee, and the Porte grew alarmed. The apprehensions were strengthened by the sheikh's demand in 1768 to be invested permanently with the government of his dominions, for himself and his heirs, under the title and style of "Sheikh of Acre, Prince of Princes, Governor of Nazareth, Tiberias and Safed, and Sheikh of all Galilee". The Porte had yielded in many things to the inducements of fear and money, but this request provoked the animosity and jealousy of the Divan. Osman, who enjoyed the confidence of the Porte, was made Pasha of Damascus in 1760, and in 1765 Jerusalem and the greater part of Palestine were added to his dominions. His two sons were nominated Pashas of Tripoli and Sidon. The new pasha prepared to strike a blow at Daher, but was beaten by the latter's son Ali. Osman's tyranny, on the other hand, also served Daher's interests. The pasha's severities and atrocities at Ramleh and Gaza (in 1769) excited universal discontent, and all over Palestine the population longed for a foreign protector, to follow the example of Egypt.

It was at this time that the famous Mameluke Ali Bey had turned his thoughts to the conquest of Syria. Ali Bey found an ally in Daher, who had also obtained the help of Russian ships. Ali's general, Mohammed Bey, entered Palestine at the head of 500 Mamelukes and a decisive encounter took place on June 6, 1770. The troops of the pasha were beaten, but for some reason or another Mohammed Ali returned to Egypt, and Daher was left alone to fight the enemy. Ali Bey died in 1773, and the following year peace was concluded between Turkey and Russia. These circumstances and the quarrels of Daher with his own sons contributed to his final defeat and death in 1775.

After the death of Daher, Djezzar Pasha (the Butcher) was appointed his successor at Acre. A man of brutal disposition, and in many respects exhibiting a striking contrast to the enlightened policy of the Arab sheikh by his rapacity and oppression, he converted the fine plain of Acre into a wilderness little better than a marsh. He laid a tax on wine, grain and other articles of consumption, and his measures were fatal to agriculture and commerce. Djezzar became the most powerful ruler in Syria, uniting in his hand the pashaliks of Acre (which he fortified), Gaza,

Tripoli and Damascus. He was, in fact, absolute master of the whole of Syria, and his pashalik included the whole coastline of Palestine and Galilee. The Porte began to fear his power, which was more formidable than that of Daher had ever been. Had they been able, the Government would have dispossessed him more than once, but the Ottoman Government had grown weak, and many provinces were in open revolt against the power of the Sultan. Thus Djezzar had ruled for twenty years over the greatest part of Syria and Palestine when Napoleon invaded Syria.[1]

In 1798 Napoleon, who was dreaming of an empire in the East rivalling that of Alexander the Great, conceived the plan of invading Egypt, and, with the permission of the Directory, he embarked at Toulon in May 1798. The Ottoman Porte, not deceived by his excuse that he was fighting the Mamelukes, declared war against the French, and the Turkish armies were organized in Syria. As a defensive measure, Napoleon decided to invade Syria before the organization of the enemy was complete and to take possession of the coast of Palestine. Napoleon, as he indeed declares in his Memoirs, may have had hopes of conquering the whole of Syria; he may have had visions of an invasion of India by way of Mesopotamia or of a victorious return to France by way of Asia Minor and Constantinople.

[1] See Volney, *Voyage en Syrie*, tome 2, xxv.; Josiah Conder, *A Popular Description of Syria and Asia Minor*, i. 6 ff.

The French advance commenced in February 1799. Gaza, Esdud and Ramleh were taken, and siege was laid to Jaffa, which was captured in March. Acre was the next objective, and a siege was laid to this city. The siege of Acre, the defence of which was bravely conducted by Djezzar, proved impossible, and on May 20th Napoleon, despairing of taking the town, returned to Egypt. "Had Acre fallen," he is supposed to have said later on, "I would have changed the face of the world." After the retreat of the French, Djezzar, who had displayed a rare personal valour during the siege of Acre, regained his personal ascendancy in Syria; but quarrels arose between him and the grand vizier and his favourite, Abu Marra. Djezzar died in 1804 and the authority in Palestine was seized by Ismael Pasha, who was soon replaced by Suleiman Pasha.

In the meantime a new danger was threatening the Sultan in Syria and Palestine. With the Turkish armies which came to Egypt at the time of Napoleon's invasion, was an Albanian Bashibazouk, or volunteer, by name of Mohammed Ali. He became the head of the Albanian element and, playing his hand with skill and audacity, proclaimed himself Pasha of Egypt in 1805. He got rid of the Mamelukes in 1811 by entrapping them to the citadel and having them massacred. Mohammed Ali was now virtually dictator of Egypt, but his ambitions went farther.

In the nineteenth century the process of dissolution of the Ottoman Empire had made rapid progress. Ali Pasha of Macedonia had openly revolted against Sultan Mahmud II, while Alexander Ypsilanti made an attempt to conquer Moldavia. His brother placed himself at the head of the Greek movement for freedom, and in 1822 Greece proclaimed her independence. Too weak to put down the Greek insurrection single-handed, Sultan Mahmud got help from the Pasha of Egypt. After the conquest of Missolonghi in 1826 a war of annihilation was carried on by the Turks, and the European Powers—England, France and Russia— demanded the emancipation of Greece. The Turks refused, but after the naval victory of Navarino, in which the Turkish fleet was destroyed (1827), the Sultan was compelled to yield. The freedom of Greece was now proclaimed and Otto, son of Ludwig of Bavaria, became hereditary king.

This weakness of the Ottoman Empire Mohammed Ali, the powerful Pasha of Egypt, and his son Ibrahim, decided to exploit for their own purposes. They turned their attention to Syria and Palestine, which they resolved to wrest from the Sultan of Turkey. Circumstances in the country seemed favourable for a conquest by a daring enemy, for the control of the Turks in Syria and Palestine was rather weak and the Government of Constantinople was unable to crush the movement to shake off the Turkish yoke, which made itself felt in the Lebanon. Beshir, the Emir of the Druses, who was ruling in the Lebanon since 1789, had made himself independent after the death of the Pasha Djezzar in 1804.

In 1831 an Egyptian army, under Ibrahim Pasha, invaded Palestine. The expedition was supposed to be directed only against Abdallah, Pasha of Acre since 1820, with whom Mohammed Ali had a quarrel. Egyptian peasants had fled from the tyranny of Mohammed Ali for protection to the dominions of the Pasha of Acre, and Mohammed Ali demanded their extradition. When his request was refused he sent an army of 30,000 men to invade Syria. Gaza, Jaffa and Haifa were taken, and on November 27th the Egyptian troops laid siege to Acre. The Sultan considered the invasion of Syria by the ruler of Egypt as a challenge to his authority and sent a force under Osman Pasha against the rebel, but the Turkish troops were defeated and Acre was taken on May 27, 1832.

Syria and Palestine fell into the power of Mohammed Ali. Once more, as in the days of the Pharaohs, the country on the banks of the Jordan became a dependency of the Power on the Nile, but this time the Egyptian rule in the Holy Land lasted only eight years. On the one hand, the European Powers had taken umbrage at the success of the Viceroy of Egypt, while on the other hand the whole of Syria soon revolted against the tyranny of the new ruler. The inhabitants who had supported the Egyptians against the Turks in 1832 gradually changed their sympathy owing to the unwise government of the pasha, whose administration proved to be worse than had been that of the Ottomans. Mohammed Ali increased taxation and imposed a rigorous conscription. Europe was singing the praises of the enlightened ruler, the regenerator of the East, but in reality Mohammed Ali was only following his barbarian instincts, while arraying himself in the cloak of European civilization. He was crushing the inhabitants of the Holy Land under a heavy yoke. Even his religious tolerance and protection were only a make-believe in order to hoodwink European public opinion. The antipathy and hostility of the Syrian and Palestinian population to the Viceroy of Egypt induced them to give help to the Sultan when the struggle was once more renewed in 1839. At first Mohammed Ali was successful. On the 25th of June a battle was fought at Nezib, when whole Turkish regiments, with their officers, bought by Ibrahim Pasha, went over to the Egyptians. The Turkish forces were routed and the Ottoman fleet was treacherously delivered into the Viceroy's hands. The European Powers now intervened. A fleet representing the Allies attacked the Syrian coast, and Mohammed Ali was finally compelled to acquiesce to the terms of a treaty signed in London on July 15, 1840. Syria was restored to the Sultan, while Mohammed Ali and his successors were to remain hereditary rulers of Egypt under the nominal suzerainty of the Porte.

From this time onwards the European nations began to take an increased interest in Palestinian affairs, and ever since their intervention in the country there was a constant competition among the Great Powers, who were trying to establish their respective influences in the Holy Land. A veritable crusade of unarmed ecclesiastics swept over the country; churches, monasteries, schools, hospitals and missions were built everywhere. In addition to Europeans, North American Protestants penetrated into Palestine, establishing their headquarters in Beirut. In 1841 England, jointly with Prussia, established an evangelical episcopate in Jerusalem, representing mostly English interests, so that Prussia soon retired. France, not to be outbidden, sent a consul to Jerusalem and made herself the protector of the Roman Church in the Holy Land. In 1847 the Latin Patriarchate was renewed, while the interests of the Greek Church were furthered by Russia. The dispute concerning the Holy Places at Bethlehem and Jerusalem furnished Russia with a pretext for the Crimean War, and after its conclusion Russia, too, like England and France, began to build churches and hospitals in Palestine and to establish missionary institutions there. During the last decades of the nineteenth century and the beginning of the twentieth nearly 20,000 Russian pilgrims visited the Holy Land annually. From the middle of the nineteenth century Austria and Prussia also had their consuls in Jerusalem. Germany, too, took a great interest in the Holy Land, especially after the visit of the Emperor William II in 1898.

The Jews of Palestine from 1517 to 1917

In spite of the rotten régime of the Ottoman Empire, the Jews, for a time at least, were better off in Palestine than in most of the European countries. The Turks are less religious than the Europeans and the Semites and therefore less fanatical. Towards the end of the fifteenth and the beginning of the sixteenth centuries Palestine, like the whole Ottomon Empire, became the asylum of the Jews expelled from Spain and Portugal or fleeing from persecutions and vexations in other European Christian lands. During the Golden Age of the Ottoman Empire numerous Jews had found a haven of rest in the lands of the Crescent. The Jews of Palestine derived an advantage from the fact that they could entertain constant communications with their brethren in the Empire. Materially and intellectually the Jewish communities in Palestine found an opportunity to develop themselves freely, and it seemed indeed as if the Holy Land was once more to become the spiritual centre of Judaism. Isaac Hacohen Shuleil, the last Nagid of the Egyptian Jews, came to Palestine, where he built new houses of learning and supported the poor. In Safed a Jewish community, more numerous than that of Jerusalem, was formed, thanks to the efforts of Jacob Berab, a famous Talmudical scholar who had fled from Spain and settled in Palestine in 1533. Jacob Berab failed to realize his idea of making Safed the seat of a new Sanhedrin, but the town counted among its inhabitants the most celebrated rabbis of the age, such as Joseph Karo, the famous compiler of the *Shulkhan Arukh*.

The flourishing state of the Jews in the Ottoman Empire was, to a certain extent, due to the influence of the Duke of Naxos. Joao Migues, a nephew of the graceful and noble Grazia Mendesa, a Marrano who had openly returned to his ancestral faith at Constantinople, and acquired considerable influence at the Court of Suleiman II. The Sultan made him a gift of a strip of land on the Lake of Tiberias, authorizing him to rebuild the ancient town and to settle only Jews there. Suleiman's successor, Selim II, raised Joao Migues (Joseph Nasi, as he was called by the Jews) to the dignity of Duke of Naxos, and as such he conquered the island of Cyprus for the Turks. The Sultan commanded the Pasha of Syria to further the building of Tiberias, and the Arab fellahin were compelled to help. They did it very reluctantly, for they harboured a superstitious belief that once Tiberias was rebuilt, Judaism would be victorious and Islam would disappear. Joseph Nasi resolved to make Tiberias a factory town and to develop there the silk industry destined to compete with that of Venice on the world market. The Duke of Naxos even dreamed of establishing a small Jewish State on the banks of Lake Tiberias, but his dreams were never realized.

The importance, however, of Palestine in the sixteenth century, as far as the Jews were concerned, lay not in its economic development but in the religious life of the inhabitants. Mysticism and Kabbala[1] were the characteristic traits of a new religious revival, and Safed became the centre of this movement. Here we find Joseph Molcho, who subsequently suffered the martyr's death at Mantua in 1532. The Kabbala reigned supreme in Palestine and two Palestinian Jews were its apostles. They were Isaac Luria Levi (1534–1572), born in Jerusalem, and Chajim Vital Calabrese (1543–1620).

The favourable position of the Jews in Palestine changed with the accession to the throne of Sultan Murad III (1574–1595). This Sultan was the first Turkish ruler to be hostile to the Jews. He is said to have given orders to exterminate all the Jews in his empire, an order, however, which was not carried out. The more the power of the Sultans was left in the hands of the harem, the Spahis and the Janissaries, the greater became the acts of violence, the extortions and cruelties of the pashas in the provinces. The position of the Jewish community in Jerusalem was often a desperate one. It was at that time that the famous Rabbi Moses Alschech, who had come to Safed from Venice, requested the Jewish community of the latter city to send money regularly to Palestine for the support of the poor, and the custom was soon imitated by the Jewish communities in Poland, Bohemia, Germany and Hungary. The moneys received were distributed among the deserving poor and the

[1] See Note 23 in Appendix.

institution became known as the *Halukkah* (distribution). To satisfy the cupidity of the pashas, the Jews were compelled to borrow money from the rich effendis at exorbitant interest, and if the money was not paid in time the Arabs invaded the Jewish quarter, sacking and pillaging. Although Sultan Murad IV (1623–1640), who erected the mausoleum over the tomb of Rachel, was favourably inclined towards the Jews, the latter nevertheless suffered under his reign from the cruel persecutions of the local potentate, Mohammed Ibn Faruch (1625–1627). He and his brother-in-law, Osman, imprisoned all the notable Jews of Jerusalem in order to extort money from them. Among the prisoners was the former Chief Rabbi of Prague, Isaiah Horovitz, who had come to the Holy Land in 1621. The Jews obtained the release of the prisoners by paying a heavy ransom, but no one now felt safe in the streets of the City of David. Numerous Jews fled to Tiberias, and particularly to Safed, to seek protection in the dominions of the famous Fakr-ed-Din, Prince of the Druses, who was master of the Southern Lebanon and Upper Galilee.

And yet, in spite of persecutions, cruelties and extortions, and the impossibility of earning a living in the Holy Land, Palestine still attracted the Jews from the Diaspora. After the cruel massacres of the Jews in the Ukraine under the Cossack hetman, Chmielnicki (1648–1649), a number of Jews from Poland sought refuge in the Holy Land.

Once more, as in the days of Rome, the Jews, in their desperate straits, sought consolation in Messianic hopes. As usually, the impulse came from the East, from the mystic and mysterious Orient, and especially from the Holy Land. In 1663 Shabbatai Zevi, the false messiah, came to Jerusalem. The more reasonable rabbis of Jerusalem refused to recognize him, but soon the oppressed and suffering masses greeted Shabbatai as their redeemer. The career, conversion to Islam and the death of Shabbatai Zevi are a tragedy, the tragedy of Jewry constantly deceived by false saviours and redeemers, but messianic enthusiasm and hope for redemption have never ceased among the Jews. They are ever ready to listen to the bugle-call of a new messiah, whether appearing in Oriental or European, mediæval or modern garb, and in all their hopes for redemption, in their dreams of a national or religious regeneration, Palestine, Zion, the Holy Land, the home of Jewish mysticism, has been and still is the goal of all those who are filled with the messianic idea.

The yearning and hope living in the hearts of the persecuted masses always turned, and turn, to the Holy Land, the ancestral home where the eternal wanderers expect to find redemption through the Messiah of the Lord. Sober reason may not approve, but the earnestness and energy often displayed in hugging a shadow compel respect and even admiration. At the news of the arrival of the Messiah in the person of Shabbatai Zevi, many affair occurred. When Tomasso, the guardian of a Capucine monastery in Damascus, disappeared, the Jews were accused of ritual murder. At the instigation of the monks, the Governor of Damascus, Sherif Pasha, allowed a general persecution of the Jews, which spread all over Syria. Thanks to the efforts of Adolphe Crémieux, Nathaniel Rothschild and Sir Moses Montefiore, Mohammed Ali ordered the liberation of the imprisoned Damascene Jews. Shortly afterwards the Pasha of Egypt had to give up Syria and Palestine and Sir Moses Montefiore obtained a firman at Constantinople which in future safeguarded the Turkish Jews against accusations of ritual murder.

A change in the position of the Jews in Palestine began in 1840 as the result of the intervention of the European Powers in Turkish affairs. The European consulates established in the Holy Land could henceforth assure the safety of life and property. The amelioration of the position of the Jews was also due to the efforts of the *Alliance Israélite* and of the Anglo-Jewish Association and, since 1882, to the Zionist movement, which encouraged the acquisition of land in the ancestral home and the settlement of Jews there.

The establishment of European consulates in Palestine, who watched over the safety of life and property, was a boon for the Jews of Palestine. The result was a steady immigration, especially from Russia, Poland and Rumania. The new immigrants settled mostly in Jerusalem and Safed and a few in Tiberias and Hebron. To settle in the open country and in places where no consulates existed was still somewhat dangerous. Great misery, however, prevailed among the Jews in the four holy cities of Jerusalem, Safed, Hebron and Tiberias. While the *Alliance Israélite* and the Anglo-Jewish Association were establishing schools and educational institutions in Palestine, Jewish philanthropists, like Sir Moses Montefiore and others, endeavoured to alleviate the material distress of their brethren in the Holy Land.

It was then that the idea of settling Jews on the land emerged in Palestine itself. Sir Moses brought the idea to Europe and tried to propagate it all his life, but without success. It was only in 1882, after the revival of the national idea, after the Russian pogroms of 1881 and 1882, that the idea of settling Jews as agriculturists and peasants on the sacred soil of the ancestral home received a new impetus. "Back to Zion" was the cry, and modern Zionism had made its appearance. Jewish colonization was started in 1882, but the efforts would have failed had it not been for the generous support of Baron Edmond de Rothschild. Jews were still flocking to Palestine, but they settled mostly in the towns. Nevertheless a productive element, not living on alms (*Halukka*), was introduced. It was the beginning of a peaceful reconquest of the Promised Land by Israel. The yearning for Palestine was also stirred among Yemenite, North African, Caucasian and Persian Jews, and their number in the country rose from 12,000 in 1850 to 35,000 in 1882 and to 85,000 in 1914. Palestine once more became an important cultural centre and the Hebrew language was revived.

Thus Palestine remained under Turkish rule for four centuries. From 1517 to 1856 only Moslems had the status and rights of full citizens under the Constitution of the Ottoman Empire. The Porte for over three centuries exercised but little direct control over the country, and the population lived under the overlordship of the pashas and beys in a sort of mediæval European system. In the course of the nineteenth century, under the pressure of European Powers, better conditions were secured for the non-Moslem population. The control of the Government at Constantinople over the independent authority of the provincial governors was strengthened and the Constitution of Syria and Palestine was more strictly defined.

Oppressive measures were certainly not wanting during the reign of Abdul-Hamid II (1876–1909), but the arbitrary power of the local chieftains had been broken and an organized administration, under the direct control of a governor appointed by the Porte, was introduced. Extensive establishments were maintained by foreign missions, foreign capital was invested in the country and foreign enterprise became prominent in commerce.

In spite, however, of the activity developed in the Holy Land, particularly by Jewish colonists, Palestine, in the first decade of the present century, was in a state of economic stagnation and financial strain. The results of the ruinous wars in which the Porte was engaged (1911–1912 with Italy and 1912–1913 with the Balkan States) made themselves felt all over the Ottoman Empire. Such was the state of the Holy Land when the European War broke out in August 1914.

CHAPTER XVII

PALESTINE A BRITISH MANDATORY COUNTRY
(A.D. 1917-1930)

The War of Liberation—Hopes and memories—Enthusiasm and imagination—The conquest of the Holy Land—The "Rise of Jerusalem"—A proclamation in seven languages—A National Home—Arabs and Jews—Nationalist dreams—Zionism—Diametrically opposed arguments—Religion and Economics—Capitalism and Democracy—Justice and Religion—The hopes of the Christian missionaries—Forcing the hand of Providence—A home for the spirit—The Jewish problem and the problem of Judaism—The opportunity of the Zionists—A Hebrew University—Arab claims and Zionist aspirations—The Balfour Declaration—A second Nehemiah—The Constitution suspended—The Mandate and the National Home—A feverish activity—A phase of transition—Development of agriculture—Desolation and cultivation—Report of Sir Herbert Samuel—British policy—Broken pledges—Difficulties and obstacles—Riots and pogroms—A Commission of Inquiry—The Wall of Wailing—A land of destiny—A country of limited possibilities—A way of living—A mixed civilization

ONE of the results of the European War has been the liberation of the Holy Land from Turkish dominion. Palestine was drawn into the vortex of the World War on November 5, 1914, when the Allies declared war on the Ottoman Empire, which had joined the Central Powers of Europe. The interest of Christian Europe in Palestine once more revived as in the days of the Crusades. The old magic name of the Holy Land was uttered by millions of lips—and hopes and memories centring round Jerusalem were recalled. Imagination was kindled and enthusiasm was set aflame. The coast of Syria and Palestine was blockaded by Allied warships, while the Turks made the country a base for operations against Egypt. On June 28, 1917, General Allenby assumed command of the Egyptian Expeditionary Force, collected from all quarters of the British Empire for the purpose of the conquest of the Holy Land, and in October he commenced his first attack against the Turkish forces in Palestine. On December 8, 1917, a converging movement was effected by the British forces, the advance was pressed, and on the morning of December 9, 1917, the British had isolated Jerusalem. At noon the city surrendered. All over the world the news was hailed both as a feat of arms and as the fulfilment of prophecy. People referred to the capture of the Holy City not as the "Fall" but as the "Rise of Jerusalem". General Allenby entered the City of David on December 11th, two days after its surrender, through the Jaffa Gate, and in the presence of the notables of the city a proclamation was read in English, Arabic, Hebrew, French, Italian, Greek and Russian. Jerusalem was placed under martial law, but the population was advised to pursue its lawful occupations.

In the meantime an event had occurred which was fraught with far-reaching consequences for the future destiny of the Holy Land.

On November 2, 1917, Lord Balfour (then Mr. Balfour), His Majesty's Secretary for Foreign Affairs, issued his now famous Declaration, which reads as follows: "His Majesty's Government view with favour the establishment in Palestine of a National

Home for the Jewish people, and will use their best endeavours to facilitate the achievement of that object, it being understood that nothing shall be done which may prejudice the civil and religious rights of existing non-Jewish communities in Palestine, or the rights and political status enjoyed by the Jews in any other country." On the 7th of November, 1917, the Allied nations issued a proclamation promising the nationalities freed from the Turkish yoke emancipation and self-determination, but Palestine could not be included in this proclamation on account of the promise given to the Zionists. The Arabs in the meantime raised a protest against the Balfour Declaration, and an Arab–Syro–Palestinian Congress proclaimed the Emir Feisal King of Syria and Palestine.

Zionism

It does not enter within the scope of this book to discuss Zionism, but as this Jewish movement is closely connected with the history of Palestine a brief summary will be necessary here.

Zionism is the Jewish nationalist movement, which aims at the establishment of Jews in Palestine on a national basis. Those who favour the movement differ widely in their reasons for doing so. For some it is mainly an economic and philanthropic movement, while for others it is religious and spiritual. Zionism is therefore supported by arguments often diametrically opposed to each other. Religious Jews who are in favour of Zionism believe that, by establishing a Jewish Home in Palestine, Judaism or the Jewish religion will be safeguarded, and Israel will be saved from assimilation. They consider Zionism as a religious phenomenon, and although it acts as a political movement they maintain that the success of Zionism greatly depends for its vitality upon the religious sentiment of the Jewish people which will be transplanted to the Holy Land. Jewish agnostics and free-thinkers, on the other hand, support the movement because they are convinced that only in Palestine, in their national ancestral home, will the Jews be able to maintain their national unity without requiring the bonds of a religion.

For these, as indeed for the majority of Zionists, Zionism is first and foremost a national movement, independent of religion, which is the private concern of the individual. Jewish intellectuals see in the movement an opportunity to develop the national genius of Israel in the Holy Land; they even cherish the dream of giving mankind a new Idea, a new and brilliant civilization. Jewish socialists are attracted to the movement by the social and economic possibilities latent in Zionism. They foresee the creation of a new state of society in the Old-New Land, the establishment of a social and economic régime based, not on Capitalism, but on Democracy, on Socialization, and even Communism. A good many Christians favour the movement both for reasons of justice and religion, while many anti-Semites see in the realization of the Zionist ideal an opportunity of getting rid of the Jews in a not dim and distant future. Christian missionaries hope that once a great number of Jews is gathered in the Holy Land it will be easier to convert them to Christianity, which there sprang from Judaism centuries ago.

A great many liberal Jews, however, are opposed to Zionism; they deny to Israel the name of a nation in the political sense, and consider the Jews only as a religious community. Zion is only a symbol, and the *national* ideal of Judaism is to *oppose the idea of nationality*. Judaism is progressive and evolutionary, and even during its first national establishment in Palestine it contained the seeds of universalism, which were destined to blossom forth and bear fruit in ages to come. Ultra-orthodox Jews look upon the Zionist movement as forcing the hand of Providence. For them the Restoration of the Chosen Race to Palestine is a religious hope, connected with the coming of the Messiah. Zionism without religion has therefore no *raison d'être*. Thus to some Zionism means the solution of the Jewish problem by creating a home for the Jewish people in Palestine, while to others the movement is the solution of the problem of Judaism. Palestine is "to become a rallying-point and an inspiration for Jews throughout the world whose genius could freely expand only in its ancestral home". Palestine is to be not so much a haven of refuge for the weary, wandering Jews as a home for the Jewish spirit.

A BRITISH MANDATORY COUNTRY

The Zionist movement is not a *creatio ex nihilo* of the nineteenth century, as some imagine. Ever since their dispersion the Jews have entertained the hope of returning to Zion or Palestine. During the long centuries of exile and the dark night of mediævalism, several attempts were made to bring the Jews back to the Holy Land. It was, however, during the nineteenth century, when the national movement among European nations became more intense, especially after 1859, that Zionism received a new stimulus. The nineteenth century witnessed the revival of Jewish race-consciousness and national feeling—sentiments strengthened by persecution, oppression and anti-Semitism. Moses Hess published his *Rom und Jerusalem* in 1862, and Leo Pinsker his *Auto-Emancipation* in 1882. The result was the movement of the Chovevei Zion (Lovers of Zion), which inaugurated Jewish colonization in Palestine for the purpose of ultimately reviving the Jewish people on the historic soil.

It was, however, in 1896 that political Zionism was founded by Theodore Herzl. He published a pamphlet, *Der Judenstaat*, and advocated an autonomous Jewish State, preferably in Palestine. He enlisted the sympathies of many Jews and convened a Congress at Basel in 1897. Here the Zionist political programme was adopted, and its purpose was "to establish for the Jewish people a publicly recognized, legally assured Home in Palestine".

During the European War the Jews, like all the

other inhabitants in Palestine who were looking to the Allies as their deliverers, had to suffer greatly from the Turkish officials, and particularly from Djemal Pasha, the Turkish Commander-in-Chief. But the advent of the World War had given the Zionist leaders, Dr. Chaim Weizmann, Nahum Sokolov and others, an opportunity to press a recognition of their claims to Palestine as their rightful historic Home. The Balfour Declaration was greeted with a shout of joy by the Jewries in the two hemispheres.

In March 1918 a Zionist Commission, headed by Dr. Chaim Weizmann, proceeded to the Holy Land, and on this occasion the foundation of a Hebrew University was laid on Mount Scopus.

Immediately after the British occupation of Palestine in 1917 and 1918 a military administration was established. The status of the country was, however, rather complicated, not only on account of Zionist aspirations and Arab claims, but also of Allied agreements. The Zionist activities were still hampered in the Holy Land, but an effort was made by the British Military Administration to restore the economic life of the country. In the meantime the Balfour Declaration, embodied in the Treaty of Sèvres, was endorsed by the Allied Powers at the Conference of San Remo (April 25, 1920). It was decided that Palestine should be entrusted to a Mandatory Power, and the Mandate was given to Great Britain. Soon afterwards the British Military Administration was superseded by a Civil

Government, and on July 1, 1920, Sir Herbert Samuel entered upon his duties as High Commissioner of the Holy Land. Since the days of Nehemiah he was the first Jew to become Governor of Palestine.

In 1920 an Advisory Council, nominated by the High Commissioner, was established. It consisted of ten British officials holding office under the Government of Palestine, and of ten representative Palestinians, seven Arabs (four Moslems and three Christians) and three Jews. In 1922 a Legislative Council was to supersede the Advisory Council and to consist of ten official members and twelve Palestinian members (eight Moslems, two Jews and two Christians), elected by popular suffrage. Objection, however, was raised by the Arab leaders, who maintained that they represented 90 per cent. of the population, and insisted that the Council should either consist of only elected members or that the Arab members should outnumber the official members. No agreement could be reached providing an acceptable basis for Arab co-operation. The British Government thereupon decided to suspend that part of the Constitution which refers to the Legislative Council, and temporarily to restore the old Advisory Council, which was to have been superseded.

On July 24, 1922, the Council of the League of Nations approved the British Mandate for Palestine, which came into effect on September 29, 1923.

LEAGUE OF NATIONS

MANDATE FOR PALESTINE

AND MEMORANDUM BY THE BRITISH GOVERNMENT RELATING TO ITS APPLICATION TO TRANSJORDAN,

APPROVED BY THE COUNCIL OF THE LEAGUE OF NATIONS ON SEPTEMBER 16th, 1922.

The Council of the League of Nations:

Whereas the Principal Allied Powers have agreed, for the purpose of giving effect to the provisions of Article 22 of the Covenant of the League of Nations, to entrust to a Mandatory selected by the said Powers the administration of the territory of Palestine, which formerly belonged to the Turkish Empire, within such boundaries as may be fixed by them; and

Whereas the Principal Allied Powers have also agreed that the Mandatory should be responsible for the putting into effect the declaration originally made on November 2nd, 1917, by the Government of His Britannic Majesty, and adopted by the said Powers, in favour of the establishment in Palestine of a national home for the Jewish people, it being clearly understood that nothing should be done which might prejudice the civil and religious rights of existing non-Jewish communities in Palestine, or the rights and political status enjoyed by Jews in any other country; and

Whereas recognition has thereby been given to the historical connection of the Jewish people with Palestine and to the grounds for reconstituting their national home in that country; and

Whereas the Principal Allied Powers have selected His Britannic Majesty as the Mandatory for Palestine; and

Whereas the mandate in respect of Palestine has been formulated in the following terms and submitted to the Council of the League for approval; and

Whereas His Britannic Majesty has accepted the mandate in respect of Palestine and undertaken to exercise it on behalf of the League of Nations in conformity with the following provisions; and

Whereas by the afore-mentioned Article 22 (paragraph 8) it is provided that the degree of authority, control or administration to be exercised by the Mandatory, not having been previously agreed upon by the Members of the League, shall be explicitly defined by the Council of the League of Nations;

Confirming the said mandate, defines its terms as follows:

Article 1.

The Mandatory shall have full powers of legislation and of administration, save as they may be limited by the terms of this mandate.

Article 2.

The Mandatory shall be responsible for placing the country under such political administrative and economic conditions as will secure the establishment of the Jewish national home, as laid down in the preamble, and the development of self-governing institutions, and also for safeguarding the civil and religious rights of all the inhabitants of Palestine, irrespective of race and religion.

Article 3.

The Mandatory shall, so far as circumstances permit, encourage local autonomy.

Article 4.

An appropriate Jewish agency shall be recognised as a public body for the purpose of advising and co-operating with the administration of Palestine in such economic, social and other matters as may affect the establishment of the Jewish national home and the interests of the Jewish population in Palestine, and, subject always to the control of the Administration, to assist and take part in the development of the country.

The Zionist organisation, so long as its organisation and constitution are in the opinion of the Mandatory appropriate, shall be recognised as such agency. It shall take steps in consultation with His Britannic Majesty's Government to secure the co-operation of all Jews who are willing to assist in the establishment of the Jewish national home.

Article 5.

The Mandatory shall be responsible for seeing that no Palestine territory shall be ceded or leased to, or in any way placed under the control of, the Government of any foreign Power.

Article 6.

The Administration of Palestine, while ensuring that the rights and position of other sections of the population are not prejudiced, shall facilitate Jewish immigration under suitable conditions and shall encourage, in co-operation with the Jewish agency referred to in Article 4, close settlement by Jews on the land, including State lands and waste lands not required for public purposes.

Article 7.

The Administration of Palestine shall be responsible for enacting a nationality law. There shall be included in this law provisions framed so as to facilitate the acquisition of Palestinian citizenship by Jews who take up their permanent residence in Palestine.

Article 8.

The privileges and immunities of foreigners, including the benefits of consular jurisdiction and protection as formerly enjoyed by capitulation or usage in the Ottoman Empire, shall not be applicable in Palestine.

Unless the Powers whose nationals enjoyed the aforementioned privileges and immunities on August 1st, 1914, shall have previously renounced the right to their re-establishment, or shall have agreed to their non-application for a specified period, these privileges and immunities shall, at the expiration of the mandate, be immediately re-established in their entirety or with such modifications as may have been agreed upon between the Powers concerned.

Article 9.

The Mandatory shall be responsible for seeing that the judicial system established in Palestine shall assure to foreigners, as well as to natives, a complete guarantee of their rights.

Respect for the personal status of the various peoples and communities and for their religious interests shall be fully guaranteed. In particular, the control and administration of Wakfs shall be exercised in accordance with religious law and the dispositions of the founders.

Article 10.

Pending the making of special extradition agreements relating to Palestine, the extradition treaties in force between the Mandatory and other foreign Powers shall apply to Palestine.

Article 11.

The Administration of Palestine shall take all necessary measures to safeguard the interests of the community in connection with the development of the country, and, subject to any international obligations accepted by the Mandatory, shall have full power to provide for public ownership or control of any of the natural resources of the country or of the public works, services and utilities established or to be established therein. It shall introduce a land system appropriate to the needs of the country, having regard, among other things, to the desirability of promoting the close settlement and intensive cultivation of the land.

The Administration may arrange with the Jewish agency mentioned in Article 4 to construct or operate, upon fair and equitable terms, any public works, services and utilities, and to develop any of the natural resources of the country, in so far as these matters are not directly undertaken by the Administration. Any such arrangements shall provide that no profits distributed by such agency, directly or indirectly, shall exceed a reasonable rate of interest on the capital, and any further profits shall be utilised by it for the benefit of the country in a manner approved by the Administration.

Article 12.

The Mandatory shall be entrusted with the control of the foreign relations of Palestine and the right to issue exequaturs to consuls appointed by foreign Powers. He shall also be entitled to afford diplomatic and consular protection to citizens of Palestine when outside its territorial limits.

Article 13.

All responsibility in connection with the Holy Places and religious buildings or sites in Palestine, including that of preserving existing rights and of securing free access to the Holy Places, religious buildings and sites and the free exercise of worship, while ensuring the requirements of public order and decorum, is assumed by the Mandatory, who shall be responsible solely to the League of Nations in all matters connected herewith, provided that nothing in this article shall prevent the Mandatory from entering into such arrangements as he may deem reasonable with the Administration for the purpose of carrying the provisions of this article into effect; and provided also that nothing in this mandate shall be construed as conferring upon the Mandatory authority to interfere with the fabric or the management of purely Moslem sacred shrines, the immunities of which are guaranteed.

Article 14.

A special Commission shall be appointed by the Mandatory to study, define and determine the rights and claims in connection with the Holy Places and the rights and claims relating to the different religious communities in Palestine. The method of nomination, the composition and the functions of this Commission shall be submitted to the Council of the League for its approval, and the Commission shall not be appointed or enter upon its functions without the approval of the Council.

Article 15.

The Mandatory shall see that complete freedom of conscience and the free exercise of all forms of worship, subject only to the maintenance of public order and morals, are ensured to all. No discrimination of any kind shall be made between the inhabitants of Palestine on the ground of race, religion or language. No person shall be excluded from Palestine on the sole ground of his religious belief.

The right of each community to maintain its own schools for the education of its own members in its own language, while conforming to such educational requirements of a general nature as the Administration may impose, shall not be denied or impaired.

Article 16.

The Mandatory shall be responsible for exercising such supervision over religious or eleemosynary bodies of all faiths in Palestine as may be required for the maintenance of public order and good government. Subject to such supervision, no measures shall be taken in Palestine to obstruct or interfere with the enterprise of such bodies or to discriminate against any representative or member of them on the ground of his religion or nationality.

Article 17.

The Administration of Palestine may organise on a voluntary basis the forces necessary for the preservation of peace and order, and also for the defence of the country, subject, however, to the supervision of the Mandatory, but shall not use them for purposes other than those above specified save with the consent of the Mandatory. Except for such purposes, no military, naval or air forces shall be raised or maintained by the Administration of Palestine.

Nothing in this article shall preclude the Administration of Palestine from contributing to the cost of the maintenance of the forces of the Mandatory in Palestine.

The Mandatory shall be entitled at all times to use the roads, railways and ports of Palestine for the movement of armed forces and the carriage of fuel and supplies.

Article 18.

The Mandatory shall see that there is no discrimination in Palestine against the nationals of any State Member of the League of Nations (including companies incorporated under its laws) as compared with those of the Mandatory or of any foreign State in matters concerning taxation, commerce or navigation, the exercise of industries or professions, or in the treatment of merchant vessels or civil aircraft. Similarly, there shall be no discrimination in Palestine against goods originating in or destined for any of the said States, and there shall be freedom of transit under equitable conditions across the mandated area.

Subject as aforesaid and to the other provisions of this mandate, the Administration of Palestine may, on the advice of the Mandatory, impose such taxes and Customs duties as it may consider necessary, and take such steps as it may think best to promote the development of the natural resources of the country and to safeguard the interests of the population. It may also, on the advice of the Mandatory, conclude a special Customs agreement with any State the territory of which in 1914 was wholly included in Asiatic Turkey or Arabia.

Article 19.

The Mandatory shall adhere on behalf of the Administration of Palestine to any general international conventions already existing, or which may be concluded hereafter with the approval of the League of Nations, respecting the slave traffic, the traffic in arms and ammunition, or the traffic in drugs, or relating to commercial equality, freedom of transit and navigation, aerial navigation and postal, telegraphic and wireless communication or literary, artistic or industrial property.

Article 20.

The Mandatory shall co-operate on behalf of the Administration of Palestine, so far as religious, social and other conditions may permit, in the execution of any common policy adopted by the League of Nations for preventing and combating disease, including diseases of plants and animals.

Article 21.

The Mandatory shall secure the enactment within twelve months from this date, and shall ensure the execution, of a Law of Antiquities based on the following rules. This law shall ensure equality of treatment in the matter of excavations and archæological research to the nationals of all States Members of the League of Nations.

(1)

"Antiquity" means any construction or any product of human activity earlier than the year 1700 P.D.

(2)

The law for the protection of antiquities shall proceed by encouragement rather than by threat.

Any person who, having discovered an antiquity without being furnished with the authorisation referred to in paragraph 5, reports the same to an official of the competent Department, shall be rewarded according to the value of the discovery.

(3)

No antiquity may be disposed of except to the competent Department, unless this Department renounces the acquisition of any such antiquity.

No antiquity may leave the country without an export licence from the said Department.

(4)

Any person who maliciously or negligently destroys or damages an antiquity shall be liable to a penalty to be fixed.

(5)

No clearing of ground or digging with the object of finding antiquities shall be permitted, under penalty of fine, except to persons authorised by the competent Department.

(6)

Equitable terms shall be fixed for expropriation, temporary or permanent, of lands which might be of historical or archæological interest.

(7)

Authorisation to excavate shall only be granted to persons who show sufficient guarantees of archæological experience.

The Administration of Palestine shall not, in granting these authorisations, act in such a way as to exclude scholars of any nation without good grounds.

(8)

The proceeds of excavations may be divided between the excavator and the competent Department in a proportion fixed by that Department. If division seems impossible for scientific reasons, the excavator shall receive a fair indemnity in lieu of a part of the find.

Article 22.

English, Arabic and Hebrew shall be the official languages of Palestine. Any statement or inscription in Arabic on stamps or money in Palestine shall be repeated in Hebrew and any statement or inscription in Hebrew shall be repeated in Arabic.

Article 23.

The Administration of Palestine shall recognise the holy days of the respective communities in Palestine as legal days of rest for the members of such communities.

Article 24.

The Mandatory shall make to the Council of the League of Nations an annual report to the satisfaction of the Council as to the measures taken during the year to carry out the provisions of the mandate. Copies of all laws and regulations promulgated or issued during the year shall be communicated with the report.

Article 25.

In the territories lying between the Jordan and the eastern boundary of Palestine as ultimately determined, the Mandatory shall be entitled, with the consent of the Council of the League of Nations, to postpone or withhold application of such provisions of this mandate as he may consider inapplicable to the existing local conditions, and to make such provision for the administration of the territories as he may consider suitable to those conditions, provided that no action shall be taken which is inconsistent with the provisions of Articles 15, 16 and 18.

Article 26.

The Mandatory agrees that, if any dispute whatever should arise between the Mandatory and another Member of the League of Nations relating to the interpretation or the application of the provisions of the mandate, such dispute if it cannot be settled by negotiation, shall be submitted to the Permanent Court of International Justice provided for by Article 14 of the Covenant of the League of Nations.

Article 27.

The consent of the Council of the League of Nations is required for any modification of the terms of this mandate.

Article 28.

In the event of the termination of the mandate hereby conferred upon the Mandatory, the Council of the League of Nations shall make such arrangements as may be deemed necessary for safeguarding in perpetuity, under guarantee of the League, the rights secured by Articles 13 and 14, and shall use its influence for securing, under the guarantee of the League, that the Government of Palestine will fully honour the financial obligations legitimately incurred by the Administration of Palestine during the period of the mandate, including the rights of public servants to pensions or gratuities.

The present instrument shall be deposited in original in the archives of the League of Nations and certified copies shall be forwarded by the Secretary-General of the League of Nations to all Members of the League.

Done at London the twenty-fourth day of July, one thousand nine hundred and twenty-two.

Certified true copy:

SECRETARY-GENERAL.

ARTICLE 25 OF THE PALESTINE MANDATE.

MEMORANDUM BY THE BRITISH REPRESENTATIVE

Approved by the Council on September 16th, 1922.[1]

Article 25 of the Mandate for Palestine provides as follows:

"In the territories lying between the Jordan and the eastern boundary of Palestine as ultimately determined, the Mandatory shall be entitled, with the consent of the Council of the League of Nations, to postpone or withhold application of such provisions of this Mandate as he may consider inapplicable to the existing local conditions, and to make such provision for the administration of the territories as he may consider suitable to those conditions, provided no action shall be taken which is inconsistent with the provisions of Articles 15, 16 and 18."

2. In pursuance of the provisions of this article, His Majesty's Government invite the Council to pass the following resolution:

"The following provisions of the Mandate for Palestine are not applicable to the territory known as Transjordan, which comprises all territory lying to the east of a line drawn from a point two miles west of the town of Akaba on the Gulf of that name up the centre of the Wady Araba, Dead Sea and River Jordan to its junction with the River Yarmuk; thence up the centre of that river to the Syrian frontier."

Preamble—Recitals 2 and 3.
Article 2. The words "placing the country under such political administration and economic conditions as will secure the establishment of the Jewish National Home, as laid down in the Preamble, and".

[1] See Minutes of the Twenty-first Session of the Council, *Official Journal*, November 1922, p. 1188.

Article 4.
Article 6.
Article 7. The sentence "there shall be included in this law provisions framed so as to facilitate the acquisition of Palestinian citizenship by Jews who take up their permanent residence in Palestine."
Article 11. The second sentence of the first paragraph and the second paragraph.
Article 13.
Article 14.
Article 22.
Article 23.
In the application of the Mandate to Transjordan, the action which, in Palestine, is taken by the Administration of the latter country will be taken by the Administration of Transjordan under the general supervision of the Mandatory.

3. His Majesty's Government accept full responsibility as Mandatory for Transjordan, and undertake that such provision as may be made for the administration of that territory in accordance with Article 25 of the Mandate shall be in no way inconsistent with those provisions of the Mandate which are not by this resolution declared inapplicable.

The Mandate for Palestine connotes practically two territories: Palestine proper and Transjordania. They are divided by a line drawn from a point two miles west of the town of Akaba, on the gulf of the same name up the centre of Wady Araba, the Dead Sea and the River Jordan, to its junction of the River Yarmuk, thence up the centre of that river to the Syrian frontier.[1] While to the west of this line the terms of the Mandate *in toto* apply,

---

[1] *Report of the High Commissioner of Palestine*, 1920–5, Colonial No. 15, 1925.

the articles relating to the establishment of a Jewish Home do not apply to Transjordania.[1]

The words "National Home" in the Balfour Declaration have never been clearly defined. The Zionists maintain that "National Home" means the ultimate establishment in Palestine of an autonomous Jewish Commonwealth; that Palestine will one day become the home and land of the Jews, as it had been theirs twenty-five centuries ago; that one day Palestine will be Jewish, as England is English, France French and Germany German.

Since 1918 the Zionists have developed a feverish activity in the country. With their resources and efforts they are helping to develop the Holy Land to the advantage of all it inhabitants. Zionists and even non-Zionists are taking a lively interest in the reconstruction of the ancient Homeland. They have improved economic conditions, thus benefiting both Jews and Arabs. After centuries of stagnation the Jews, especially under British rule, have brought new life to the country. Palestine is still in a phase of transition and in the throes of transformation, and such times are always full of trouble. Under the Turkish régime Palestine had remained undeveloped and under-populated. The methods of agriculture employed by the Arabs were primitive, while the areas of land cultivated could yield far greater product. Large cultivable areas were left untilled. The summits and hills suited to the growth of trees remained bare, nor was the

[1] See Mandate for Palestine.

abundance of water-power offered by the Jordan and the Yarmuk ever utilized. The Turkish laws had killed industries. From 1882 onwards the Jewish agriculturists developed the culture of oranges, cultivated the vine, drained the swamps and planted eucalyptus trees. Pleasant villages and prosperous cultivation now meet the eye where once were desolation and barrenness.[1]

Unfortunately there is still trouble in Palestine. Too many racial and religious interests have made the country a land of constant ferment and agitation. "There is too much diversity in the Holy Land," wrote Sir Herbert Samuel, "a diversity of religions, diversity of civilizations, diversity of physical characteristics." The Arabs still consider the Jews as intruders in their ancient Homeland, and pretend that promises with regard to Palestine previous to the Balfour Declaration had been given to them. A negative answer to this claim is, however, to be found in the White Paper, containing the correspondence with the Palestine Arab Delegation and the Zionist Organization, presented in Parliament in June 1922.

"It is not the case," it reads, "as has been represented by the Arab Delegation, that during the War His Majesty's Government gave an undertaking that an independent National Government should be at once established in Palestine." The

[1] See the High Commissioner's *Interim Report on the Civil Administration of Palestine during the period July* 1, 1920–*June* 30, 1921. Cmd. 1499, 1921.

claim of the Arab Delegation rests upon a letter dated October 24, 1915, written by Sir Henry McMahon, High Commissioner for Egypt, to the Sherif of Mecca, wherein the independence of the Arabs in certain territories was promised. In the White Paper, however, the British Government pointed out that the whole of Palestine west of the Jordan was excluded from the pledge of Sir Henry McMahon.

In July 1922 a lengthy declaration of British policy was issued, wherein it was stated that the development of a Jewish National Home in Palestine "did not mean the imposition of a Jewish nationality upon the inhabitants of Palestine as a whole". It meant only the development of the existing Jewish communities in Palestine with the assistance of Jews in other parts of the world, in order that Palestine may become "a centre in which the Jewish people as a whole may take, on grounds of religion and race, an interest and a pride". But, in order that this community should have the best prospect of free development and provide a full opportunity for the Jewish people to display its capacities, "it is essential that it should know that it is in Palestine as *of right* and *not on sufferance*". "That is the reason why it is necessary that the existence of a Jewish National Home in Palestine should be internationally guaranteed, and that it should be recognized to rest upon an ancient historical connection."

In August 1922 Mr. Winston Churchill, then

Colonial Secretary, defined the National Home in the sense of granting to the Jews "the right of establishing colonies, and educational, cultural, and industrial institutions in Palestine, as far as the present inhabitants of the country [i.e. the Arabs] will allow".[1]

In spite of all the statements and declarations of British policy in Palestine, in spite of all efforts at conciliation, the Arab leaders have never ceased to protest against the Balfour Declaration. In all their efforts to improve the prosperity of the country the Zionists have to fight against tremendous difficulties and obstacles. The Arab leaders try to impede the sale of land already owned by Moslems. Riots broke out on April 4 and 5, 1920, in Jerusalem, involving the loss of life and the pillaging of the city. A number of persons were arrested for instigation to disobedience by arming the populace. Among the Jews sentenced was Vladimir Jabotinsky, who had helped to raise a Jewish battalion for the British Army during the War. His sentence, however, was soon reduced, and he was released on July 8, 1920. In May 1921, Jaffa was the scene of violent conflicts between Moslems and Jews, while the Jewish colonies in the neighbourhood were subjected to attacks by Arab tribes. The alarm of the Moslem population at the Balfour Declaration has never abated. Lord Plumer occupied the post of British High Commissioner in Palestine from 1925–8, when he was succeeded by

[1] See White Paper; *Jewish Chronicle*, August 1922.

Sir John Robert Chancellor. During the time of his office a terrible conflict once more arose in the country between Moslems and Jews, and regular pogroms by Arab mobs occurred at Hebron and Safed, where old men, women and children were tortured, massacred or mutilated. In this conflict 130 Jews and 200 Arabs lost their lives. In October–December 1929 the British Government sent a Commission of Inquiry, headed by Sir Walter Shaw, which reported on the causes of the conflict. In January 1930 the Council of the League of Nations decided to nominate a special Commission for the purpose of investigating the question of the Wall of Wailing.

Conclusion

Such is the history of Palestine—a history covering forty centuries. It is the absorbing history of one of the most interesting countries in the world, still dear to millions of men and women of three faiths. It is a land of destiny, a land with a great past and, no doubt, with a great future in store for it. What that future may hide in its lap no one can tell. The age of prophecy belongs to the dim and distant past. To prophesy about Palestine, the classic land and birthplace of the ancient Prophets, in an age dealing in realities, would only be mere conjecture. Palestine has in turn been the "Promised Land", the "Conquered Land" and "the Land Lost". Will it one day become the "Land Regained"? Great things may be accomplished in the Holy Land by the Zionists, but will the enthusiasm continue long enough? Will the faith and sacrifice of Jewry for the upbuilding of the Holy Land be strong enough to develop the country and bring it within the compass of lands of modern civilization? The soil of Palestine is rich in hopes and dreams, but, alas! also in disappointments and disillusions. Will the ardour and spirit of the Zionists triumph over the disappointments? Will Palestine ever become as Jewish as England is English, or is it destined to enjoy the status of a British colony or dominion?

It has more than once been said that economically Palestine, the land "flowing with milk and honey", is a country of "limited possibilities". Politically one may even term it a land of "unlimited impossibilities"; but from the spiritual and religious points of view there is no end to the possibilities which may sprout on the mystic and mysterious soil of the Holy Land. Will its resettlement by Jews be an end in itself or only a means to an end? "A way to living or a means to keep alive?" Will Palestine remain the country of three faiths, or will one day a new idea, a new faith, a new Sermon be preached to Mankind from the tops of the hills of Judæa? Only future historians will be able to answer these perplexing questions.

The Civilization of Palestine

Palestine has never had a civilization of its own, nor could it ever have it. A country which through-from the West inaugurated an era of revival and renascence. But now, as in olden times, the stimulus comes, not from the natives, but from abroad. It is once more a foreign civilization which is being developed on the sacred soil of Palestine. Even the Zionists are introducing into the Homeland a Western European civilization with some reminiscences of the historic past. It is a hybrid civilization for the present, and it is difficult to venture upon any forecast for the future. And yet—just as the exodus from Egypt was the prelude to Sinai and the conquest of the Promised Land was a prelude to the Prophets and Christianity, so Zionism may prove to have been the prelude to a really Palestinian civilization.

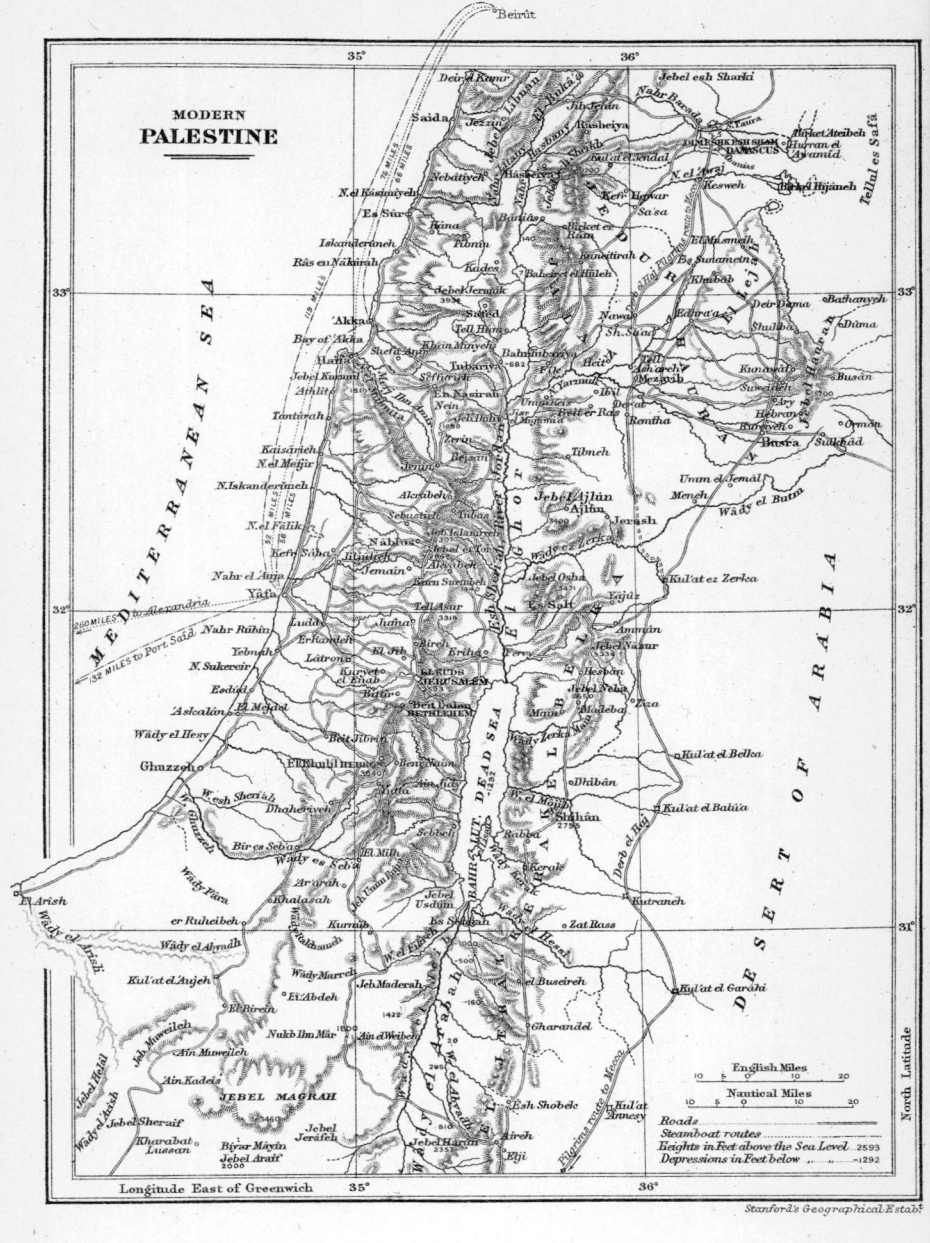

PRINCIPAL EVENTS AND IMPORTANT DATES IN THE HISTORY OF PALESTINE

B.C.

4000–3000	Megalithic period; Sumerians and Accadians. The Egyptians exploit the turquoise mines in the Sinai Peninsula.
2600	The Sumerians make conquests in Syria.
2500	The Amorites appear in history.
2100	King Khammurabi (Amraphel of the Bible) of Babylonia.
2000	Egyptian monuments mention Asiatics or Semites.
2000–1700	The Patriarchs.
1800	The Hittites appear in history.
1700	The Hyksos (Semitic nomads) take possession of Egypt.
1600–1500	The Hyksos are expelled from Egypt; Thutmose III brings Syria under Egyptian sway.
1500	Alliance of Syrian nations against Egypt.
1400	The Tell-el-Amarna period; first mention of Jerusalem and the Khabiri. The Hittites in Northern Palestine push back the Egyptians. The Hittites are pushed back by the Amorites.
1300	Ammon, Moab and Edom appear in history.
1300–1235	Ramses II.
1235–1215	Merneptah.
1220	Moses; Exodus; Joshua; Conquest of Transjordania.
1200–1000	The Judges.
1030	Samuel; Saul elected King.
1030–720	The political independence of Israel.
1030–1010	Saul King; he ruled over a united land (Israel and Judah).
1010–970	David; Jerusalem the capital of the entire Kingdom.
970–930	Solomon; building of the Temple.
930	The division of the Kingdom (after Solomon there were two kings, one of Israel and one of Judah).

HISTORY OF PALESTINE

930–908	Jeroboam, King of Israel; Sichem, the capital of the Northern Kingdom.
928	Pharaoh Shishak sacks Jerusalem.
890	The Aramæans appear in the history of Israel.
885–875	Omri; the foundation of Samaria.
875–853	Ahab, King of Israel.
842–814	Jehu, King of Israel.
781–740	Jeroboam II, King of Israel.
736–728	Ahaz, King of Judah, asks help from the Assyrians against Israel and Aram.
730–722	Hoshea, the best King of Israel, a vassal of Assyria.
727–699	Hezekiah, King of Judah, a vassal of the Assyrians.
722	Sargon conquers Samaria.
705–681	Sennacherib.
701	Siege of Jerusalem.
637–607	King Josiah; Reforms; battle of Megiddo.
608–597	The Egyptians rule in Judah.
586	Nebuchadrezzar captures Jerusalem.
586–537	The Babylonian Captivity.
537–332	The Persian dominion.
538	The First Restoration.
520–516	The Temple rebuilt.
458	The Second Restoration.
	Ezra; the proclamation of the Law (444).
	Nehemiah; the Samaritans (432–420).[1]
333	Alexander the Great conquers Syria.
320	Ptolemy I, King of Egypt, seizes Syria and Palestine.
312	Beginning of the era of Seleucidæ.
301	Palestine a dependency of Egypt; battle of Ipsus.
264–248	Fight between Syria and Egypt for the possession of Palestine.
217	The battle of Raphia.
198	Antiochus III conquers Palestine.
175	Antiochus IV makes an attempt to Hellenize the Jews.

---

[1] For the dates, see Note 11 in the Appendix.

PRINCIPAL EVENTS

167–140	Rise of the Maccabæans.
165	The Feast of Dedication.
150	Jonathan an ethnarch.
141	Simon hereditary High-priest and Prince of Judah.
140–163	The rule of the Hasmonæans.
139	The political independence of Judah recognized by the Roman Senate.
135–104	John Hyrcanus; Judaization of the Edomites.
129	Judæa an independent State.
103–76	Alexander Jannæus; Judaization of Upper Galilee.
76–67	Salome Alexandra; the rule of the Pharisees; the Sanhedrin.
67	Civil war between Hyrcanus II and Aristobalus II.
63	Pompey besieges and captures Jerusalem.
63–6 A.D.	Roman Protectorate.
47	Herod in Galilee.
40	The invasion of the Parthians.
40–37	Antigonus.
37–4	Herod the Great.
19	The Temple of Herod.
4	Judæa a Roman province under procurators.
A.D.	
41–44	Agrippa I, King of the Jews.
44–66	The government of the Roman procurators.
66–73	The Jewish War.
70	The fall of Jerusalem.
73	Fall of Massada.
132–135	The Revolt of Bar-Kochba.
135–138	Persecution of the Jews under Hadrian.
165–210	Judah Hanasi.
200	The Mishnah.
429	Abolition of the Patriarchate.
614–628	The Persians masters of Palestine.
636–638	The Arabs conquer Palestine and capture Jerusalem.
1099	The Crusaders capture Jerusalem.
1187	Saladin conquers the Holy Land.
1210	About 300 French and English Rabbis settle in Jerusalem.

HISTORY OF PALESTINE

1260	Syria and Palestine devastated by the Mongols.
1267	Nachmanides comes to Jerusalem.
1492	Jews exiled from Spain and Portugal come to Palestine.
1517	Palestine conquered by the Ottoman Turks.
1570	Don Joseph Nasi rebuilds Tiberias.
1628	The persecutions of Ibn Faruch.
1700	Judah Hassid comes to Jerusalem. Fakr-ed-Din.
1798	Napoleon in Palestine.
1832–1840	Palestine under Egyptian rule; Mohammed Ali.
1837	Earthquake at Safed and Tiberias.
1840–1917	Palestine under Turkish rule.
1840	The Damascus affair.
1917	The British enter Jerusalem.
1918	Palestine a Mandatory country of Great Britain.
1922–1925	Sir Herbert Samuel High Commissioner of Palestine.
1925–1928	Lord Plumer High Commissioner of Palestine.
1929	Massacre of Jews by Arabs.
1930	The Shaw Commission; the White Paper (Cmd, 3692).

BIBLIOGRAPHY

THE best bibliographical works on the literature dealing with Palestine are:

RÖHRICHT. *Bibliotheca geographica Palæstinæ,* containing a number of works from 333 to 1878.

Zeitschrift des Deutschen Palaestina Vereins up to 1895.

THOMSEN, P. *Die Palaestina—Literatur.* Leipzig, 4 vols. (1908–1927).

In addition to the books quoted in the text the following works have been consulted for the present volume:

BAEDEKER. *Palestine and Syria.*

BEZOLD. *Oriental Diplomacy.* 1892.

BRUGSCH. *A History of Egypt under the Pharaohs.* 1881.

BUDGE and BEZOLD. *The Tell-el-Amarna Tablets.* 1892.

BUHL. *Geographie des alten Palaestina.* 1896 (very valuable).

Cambridge. *Ancient History.* Vols. 1–4.

CONDER. *Heth and Moab.* 1889.

CORNILL. *History of the People of Israel.* 1898.

DERENBOURG. *Histoire de la Palestine.* 1867.

DUBNOW, S. *Weltgeschichte des jüdischen Volkes.* Berlin. Vols. i and ii (good bibliography).

ERMAN. *Life in Ancient Egypt.* 1894.

GRAETZ, H. *Geschichte der Juden.*

GUTHE. *Geschichte des Volkes Israel.* 1899.

HOGARTH. *Authority and Archæology.* 1899.

KENT. *History of the Hebrew People.*

KITTEL, R. *Geschichte des Volkes Israel.* 1912–1922 (very valuable).

KRAUSS, S. *Vierjahrtausende jüdischen Palästinas.* 1922.

LEHMANN-HAUPT. *Israel, seine Entwickelung im Rahmen der Weltgeschichte.* 1911.

HISTORY OF PALESTINE

MACALISTER. *The Philistines.* 1914.

MASPERO, G. *The Dawn of Civilization.* 1895.
    The Struggle of the Nations. 1897.
    The Passing of the Empires. 1900.

MCCURDY. *History, Prophecy and the Monuments.* 3 vols. 1894–1901.

MEYER, E. *Geschichte des Altertums.* 1884.

MÜLLER, W. M. *Asien und Europa nach altägyptischen Denkmälern.* 1893.

MUNK, S. *La Palestine.* 1845.

PETRIE, FLINDERS. *Syria and Egypt from the Tell-el-Amarna Letters.* 1898.

PIEPENBRING. *Histoire du Peuple Israel.* 1898.

RADAU. *Early Babylonian History.* 1900.

SAYCE. *The Races of the Old Testament.* 1891.
    The Early History of the Hebrews. 1897.

SCHRADER. *The Cuneiform Inscriptions and the Old Testament.* 1885–1888.

SMITH, G. A. *Historical Geography of the Holy Land.* 1898.

SMITH, G. *History of Babylonia.* 1895.

SODEN. *Palästina und seine Geschichte.* 1918.

VINCENT. *Canaan d'après l'exploration récente.* 1907.

PERIODICAL PUBLICATIONS

Biblical World. 1896–1897.
Contemporary Review. 1896.
Journal Asiatique.
Journal of the American Oriental Society.
Palestine Exploration Fund, Quarterly Statements.
Revue Biblique. 1899.
Revue des Etudes Juives. Vols. 1–50.
Scribner's Monthly. 1894.
Zeitschrift der deutsch-morgenländischen Gesellschaft.
Zeitschrift des deutschen Palästina Vereins.

APPENDIX

NOTES

(1) *Rephaim* has been considered to be the name of the early giant races in Palestine. The word, however, is also used in the sense of the "dead", the "lifeless" (Ps. lxxxviii. 10; Job xxvi. 2, and elsewhere). It has therefore been rightly suggested that *Rephaim* means "extinct giants". The old giants were still thought to be haunting the ruins and deserts of East Canaan (see Driver, *Deut.*, 40, and Schwally in *Z.A.T.W.*, 1898, 132 ff.; see also R. Kittel, *Geschichte des Volkes Israel*, 1912, i. 35).

(2) There are striking similarities between the Law of Israel and the Code of Khammurabi. Whether the Law of Israel is directly dependent upon the Code of Khammurabi, or whether both are to be traced to a common older Semitic source, is a question which has not yet been solved. In any case, the ethical and religious superiority of the Jewish Law is admitted by all scholars (see Jirku, *Altorientalischer Kommentar zum alten Testament*; see also Dubnow, *Geschichte des jüdischen Volkes*, i. 57 ff.).

(3) Up to within a very recent period this king was identified with the Pharaoh of the Oppression, while his son, Merneptah II, was believed to be the Pharaoh of the Exodus. Scholars, however, are now inclined to place the Exodus earlier, i.e. under Merneptah I or between 1480 and 1470 B.C.; Professor Mahler is of opinion that the Exodus took place in 1335 B.C.

(4) The origin and first use of the word *Ibrim* is still a matter of doubt, and numerous explanations have been propounded. The word *Ibri* has usually been derived from *Eber*, meaning "ford", "pass", and the Hebrews were, therefore, supposed to have been the "men from beyond the river". R. Kittel explains the words "from beyond the river" in a wider sense, namely, "wandering tribes". Many scholars are inclined to identify the *Ibrim* or Hebrews with the *Khabiri*.

(5) The late Professor Nöldeke was the first to declare in

1869 that criticism had forever disproved the claim of *Genesis*, ch. xiv, to historicity. In the light, however, of what has been revealed through the decipherment of the cuneiform inscriptions, scholars like R. Kittel do no longer hesitate to declare the chapter to be a record of historical events.

(6) The tendency is now towards an earlier date. See, however, Dubnow, l.c., 460–461; see also Mahler, *Handbuch der jüdischen Chronologie*, 1916; McCurdy, *History, Prophecy and the Monuments*, ii. 204; and *Cambridge Ancient History*.

(7) There is a difference in the presentation of the Conquest in the Books of Joshua and Judges. In our narrative we have followed Wellhausen and Dubnow.

(8) According to Biblical Criticism Jerusalem did not become the central sanctuary of the nation before the time of Deuteronomy, i.e. in the seventh century B.C.

(9) The Edict of Cyrus affected not only the Jews, but all the subjects of the king, and the famous proclamation giving permission to the Jews to return to their homes was a boon conferred also upon other nations. There were many cities whose gods and peoples had been deported to Babylon and both the one and the other were restored by Cyrus, as is evident from a cylinder inscription. "The gods who inhabit them I restored to their seats, and made for them a dwelling-place there for ever. All of their people I gathered and returned them to their homes." Cyrus, who professed himself to be a worshipper of Bel-Merodach and Nebo (cylinder inscription composed in 549 B.C.), had no particular sympathy with either the Jews or monotheism, but politically the return of the Jews to their homes was advantageous to him. He thus hoped that the returned exiles would be in a position to defend the border-land against Egypt (see also McCurdy, l.c., iii. 410 and 414).

(10) For the history and religion of the Samaritans we refer the reader to the following books: Montgomery, *The Samaritans*, London, 1907; M. Gaster, *The Samaritans*; and A. S. Rappoport, *La Liturgie Samaritaine*, 1901.

(11) Scholars are not unanimous as to the date of the arrival of Ezra in Jerusalem. While orthodox Jewish historians

NOTES

place the event in the year 458, the majority of Christian scholars contend that Ezra came to Jerusalem in the seventh year of the reign of Artaxerxes II (and not of Artaxerxes Longimanus), i.e. in 397 B.C. Some scholars place the event in the year 433, i.e. during the second visit of Nehemiah (see A. Van Hoonacker, *Nehémie et Esdras*, Paris, 1890; *Biblical World*, October 1899; see also Dubnow, l.c.).

(12) As a distinct party the Pharisees became known during the latter half of the second century B.C., in the reign of John Hyrcanus, but their tendencies may be traced back to the Chasidim or Hassidæans, the "pious" who were opposed to extreme Hellenization. The Hassidim had joined Judas Maccabæus until it became clear to them that the aims of the Hasmonæans went beyond religious freedom and that they aspired to national-political independence. The Hassidæans constituted the democratic "People's party" and became the progenitors of the Pharisaic party.

(13) Judaism, potentially a universal, was in reality a national religion. As a result of the establishment of the theocratic State after the return of the exiles from captivity and the arrival of Ezra, the Pharisees had erected a barrier between the Jewish and the surrounding nations. The hope of the ancient Prophets of ever turning Judaism into a world religion seemed thus to have been lost for ever. Gradually, however, the idea gained ground that only *individualistic* and not national religion, i.e. personal faith and belief, could pave the way for universalism. On the other hand, the long struggle with Rome convinced many Jews that it was a lost battle they were fighting, a superhuman effort. Only a God-sent Messiah could save the nation. The question now arose: Was this Messiah to be a political or a religious Redeemer? The answer to this question led to a parting of the ways in Jewish thought. While some clung to the idea of a national Messiah, a scion of the House of David, others expected a Messiah who would be the Redeemer, not of the nation, but of the individual, of the human soul. Religion, they maintained, had been given to man as an individual and not to the nation. Man ought, therefore, to be brought nearer to God independently of the destinies of the nation. The precursors

of the expected Messiah announced his coming; he would come, however, not to save the nation, but to redeem the human soul. The Kingdom of God, they proclaimed, had other foundations than the Temple, the Holy City and the Jewish nation. The faith and morality of the individual had nothing to do with political freedom or national independence. It was, in a word, individual redemption, and not national salvation, which the followers of the new movement expected from the Messiah. It was, indeed, a parting of the ways—and Christianity was born. It must, however, be pointed out that even within the limits of Jewish nationalism tendencies towards individualism or individualistic religion are to be found in the doctrines of the Essenes and in those of *Hassidism*, the religious current of the eighteenth century (see Ed. Meyer, *Ursprung und Anfänge des Christentums*, 1921–1923; Dubnow, l.c., ii. 523–561; and 579–584 with full bibliography; see also Rappoport, *Labour, Social Reform and Democracy*, xi. and xii.).

(14) *Apocalypses* are revelations of hidden things given by God to someone of His chosen saints, or written accounts of such revelations. The chief object of Apocalyptic Literature was to solve the difficulties connected with a belief in God's righteousness and the suffering condition of His servants on earth. Apocalyptic Literature arose among the Jews between 170 B.C. and 100 A.D.—and later on among the Christians. Jewish Apocalyptic Literature continued down to the close of the Middle Ages. Traces of Jewish Apocalyptic Literature are found in Ezekiel, Joel and Malachi, but the earliest proper Jewish Apocalypse is the latter part of the Book of Daniel, while the best-known Christian Apocalypse is the Book of Revelation (see Schürer, iii. 182).

(15) See Note 13.

(16) During the reigns of the pagan emperors the Jewish religion was tolerated by Rome because the Jews themselves were tolerated and considered as a separate nation. The privilege of exercising their religion freely was extended, not only to the Jews in Palestine but also to those who were Roman citizens. The Emperors explained this exceptional attitude on the part of Rome by the national character of the Jewish cult. That was the reason why Judaism remained

NOTES

a *religio licita* (see Juster, *Les Juifs dans l'Empire Romain*, 1914, i. 244-247).

(17) One of the greatest heroes of the Spirit in those times was Jochanan ben Zakkai. He obtained from Vespasian the permission to settle at Jabneh and to found there a school of learning. This fact, namely, the establishment of a house of learning on the ruins of the political independence, has been interpreted in a different manner by various historians. What Jochanan ben Zakkai really established at Jabneh was not so much an academy as a centre for the Jewish *nomocracy*, i.e. a national centre after the loss of the political independence of the Jews.

(18) Eusebius was a semi-Arian, so-called because he would not at first accept the formula of Athanasius.

(19) The Fiscus Judaicus was the tax of two drachmas (didrachmon) introduced by Vespasian in the place of the annual tribute of half a shekel paid by all Jews for the Temple at Jerusalem. The Emperor diverted the national tribute of the Jews to the Temple of Jupiter Capitolinus—and the tax existed still in the third century.

(20) The *Mishnah*, or repetition, is the text of the Talmud in contradistinction to the *Gemarah*, or commentary upon the *Mishnah*. The rabbis whose sayings are recorded in the *Mishnah* are called *Tannaïm*, or traditionists. The *Mishnah* contains the teaching of the rabbis till about A.D. 200. The text was collected, and edited by Rabbi Judah the Holy (Ha-nasi, or Hakaddosh) towards the end of the second century, while the *Gemarah*, or completion, finished about A.D. 600.

(21) The system of critical notes on the external form of the Biblical text goes back to the Palestinian schools and began in Pre-Maccabean times. It was brought to a close by Ben Asher and Ben Naphtali in the tenth century.

(22) Punctuation originated in all probability in the sixth and seventh centuries,

(23) *Kabbalah* is the term used since the eleventh and twelfth centuries for the system of esoteric theosophy and Jewish religious philosophy.

INDEX

Abd-al-Malik, 254
Abdi-Khiba, letters of, 102, 104
Abdul-Hamid, 322
Aber Nahara, satrapy of, 180
Abimelech, 132
Abraham, 65, 119
Abu-Bekr, 244
Accad, 54
Acre, siege of, 308
Actium, battle of, 26
Ælia Capitolina, 230
Agade, 63
Agrippa I, 209
Ahaz, King, 160
Ahmose, King, 90
Ajalon, Gulf of, 29, 105
Akhetaten, 100
Albinus, procurator, 213
Alexander Jannæus, 198
Alexander the Great, 181
Ali Bey, 306
Allenby, Lord, 325
Alliance Israélite, 320
Alschech, Rabbi Moses, 315
Altaku, battle of, 164
Amarna, *see* Tell-el-Amarna
Amenemhat, wall of, 80
Amenhotep, King, 90, 100, 110
Amorites, the, 55
Ammurabi, *see* Khammurabi
Ammurapi, *see* Khammurabi
Amraphel, King, 65
Amurru, the, 53
Anastasi I, papyrus of, 113
Anglo-Jewish Association, 320
Anti-Lebanon, 22
Antioch, capital, 184
Antiochus Epiphanes, 188
Antiochus IV, 197
Antipater, 198
Apachnas, 86
Aphek, 135
Apophis, 86
Apurru, the, 124
Arabah, 25
Arabia, 52
Arabs, claims of, 346; Northern, 174; in Palestine, 242, 246
Aramaic, spoken in Palestine, 178
Archæology, Palestinian, 35
Arculf, Bishop, 268

Aretas, King, 198
Arioch, King, 65
Aristobulus I, 197
Artaxerxes Ochus, 180
Ashurnasirpal, 147
Assyria, Empire of, 155
Athaliah, Queen, 152
Aton, god, 100
Auaris, city of, 87
Azuri, King, 161

Baasha, King, 146
Babylonia, in Palestine, 59, 62, 67, 68
Balfour Declaration, 325
Barak, victory of, 130
Bar-Kochba, 231
Beibars, Sultan, 290
Belibus, King, 165
Benhadad, 148
Benjamin of Tudela, 296
Beth-Shean, 128
Boghaz-keui, discoveries at, 100, 112
Bordeaux pilgrim, the, 266
Burides, dynasty of the, 285
Burjite dynasty, 292

Caligula, Emperor, 210
Canaan, conquest of, 133
Carchemish, battle of, 170
Cave age, the, 38
Chajim Vital Calabrese, 315
Chalcedon, the Council of, 225
Chancellor, Sir John R., 348
Charlemagne in Holy Land, 270
Chedorlaomer, 65
Chmielnicki, 316
Chosroes, 239
Christianity, birth of, 211
Civilization, Greek, in Palestine, 351
Civilization of Palestine, 349
Clermont-Ganneau, 38
Colonization in Palestine, 321
Commission, Zionist, 330
Congress, Zionist, 329
Constantinople, capture of, 294
Crémieux, Adolphe, 320
Cromlechs, 47
Cup-marks, 47
Cyrus, King of Persia, 171

INDEX

Daher, Sheikh, 304
Darius Hystaspes, 174
David, lament of, 138
Dead, burning of the, 45
Dead Sea, the, 25
Deborah, Song of, 69, 131
Diospolis, 30
Djezzar Pasha, 306
Dolmens, 47
Dome of the Rock, 255
Dur-Yakir, city of, 162

Egypt, interest in Palestine, 60, 74, 97
Elah, King, 146
Elamites, the, 54
Erech, 59
Eretz Israel, 20
Esar-haddon, 167
Exodus, time of the, 123
Ezekiel, 181
Ezra, 174

Fakr-ed-Din, Emir, 302
Fatimids, the, in Palestine, 258
Feudalism in Palestine, 285
Fiscus Judaicus, 231
Flinders Petrie, 36

Gabinius, proconsul of Syria, 201
Galilee, picturesqueness, 31
Garstang, Professor, 41
Gaza, battle of, 182
Gessius Florus, procurator, 213
Gezer, city of, 37, 69, 350
Ghor, the, 21
Gideon, 131
G'lil Ha-Goyim, 173
Godfrey of Bouillon, 281
Goshen, land of, 120

Hadadezer, 142
Hadrian, Emperor, 230, 233
Halukkah, the, 316
Hanno, King, 158
Haremheb, tomb of, 120
Hasmonæans, the, 192, 202
Hassidim, arrival of, in Holy Land, 318
Hebrews, oppression of, 120
Helena, Queen, pilgrimage of, 226
Hellenism in Palestine, 181, 186, 187

Heraclius, Fast of, 239
Heraclius, King, 228
Hermon, Mount, 22
Herod Antipas, 208
Herod, King, 204
Herzl, Theodor, 329
Hess, Moses, 329
Hezekiah, King, 161
Hiku-Khasut, 84
Hilkiah, high-priest, 168
Hinnatouni, 109
Hiram, King, 140
Hisham, Caliph, 257
Hittites, the, 69, 108
Hobah, 65
Holagu, Mongols under, 289
Horimes, the, 46
Horites, the, 46
Horns of Hattin, battle of, 287
Hoshea, King, 158
Huleh, Lake, 24
Hyksos, the, 84

Ibrim, the, 118
Ilubdi of Hamath, 159
Isaac Hacohen Shuleil, 313
Isaac Luria, 315
Isaiah, 154, 161
Islam, victory of, 241
Israel, spiritual individuality of, 181
Israel stele, the, 123
Israelites in Palestine, 118
Ituræa, 197

Jabin, King of Hazor, 127, 129
Jabotinsky, V., 347
Jael, 130
Januamu, 111
Jebus, city of, 139
Jechiel, Rabbi, 297
Jehuda Hassid in Holy Land, 318
Jephthah, vow of, 132
Jeroboam, 143
Jerubbaal, 131
Jerusalem, Assizes of, 282; capture of, 139; fall of, 216; siege of, 170; "rise of", 325; See of, 225
Jews, the theocracy of, 175; renaissance in Babylonia, 175; national consciousness awakened, 176; at Marathon, 180; assimilation, danger of, 185; nation expired

politically, 218; position in Palestine, 236; pilgrimages to Holy Land, 275; massacres in Europe, 296; expulsion from Spain and Portugal, 298; messianic enthusiasm, 317
Joab, general, 139
Jochanan ben Zaccai, 234
John Hyrcanus, 197
Joppa, capture of, 96
Jordan, the, 23
Joseph Kara, 314
Joshua, 126
Juda I, 235
Judah Halevy visits Palestine, 277
Judaism, a *nefaria secta*, 236
Judaism and paganism, 214
Judas Maccabæus, 192
Julian the Apostate, 237
Junds, Syria divided into five, 251
Justinian I, 238

Kabbala, the, in Palestine, 315
Kadesh-Barnea, 126
Kadesh-Barnea on the Orontes, 112
Kaina, Lake, 93
Karkar, battle of, 148
Karnak, temple of, 91, 113
Kassites, the, 54, 67, 88, 117
Kedem, land of, 80
Kengi, land of, 59
Ketbogha, general, 289
Khabiri, the, 98, 99, 102, 107
Khammurabi, Code of, 65, 120
Khari, *see* Horites
Kheops, *see* Khufu
Kheta-Sar, 111
Khnumhotep, tomb of, 82
Khufu, King, 76
Kinahna, 20
Kinnereth, Sea of, 24
Kirjath-Anab, 111
Kishon, River, 23, 130
Kotuz, Sultan, 289
Kudur Lagh-ghamar, 67

Lachish, 36, 69
Lagash, 59
Laish, graven image of, 133
Lamentations, Wall of, 275
Larsa, 59
Lugalsaggizi, King, 63, 75
Luria, Isaac, *see* Isaac

Macalister, researches of, 37
Maccabæns, *see* Hasmonæans
Maimonides visits Holy Land, 277
Maketa, *see* Megiddo
Malachi, 181
Mamelukes, the, 289
Manasseh, King, 166
Mandate for Palestine, 332
Manetho, history of, 85
Marathon, Jews at, 180
Mariamne, wife of, Herod, 206
Maritime Plain, the, 29
Marriages, mixed, 177
Masjid-al-Aksa, the, 251
Masorah, the, 294
Megalithic monuments, 49
Megiddo, battle of, 91, 95, 169; plain of, 30
Melukha, King, 150
Menhirs, 47
Meri-ka-ra, 78
Meri-ra-pepi, 76
Merneptah, 122, 123
Merodach Baladan, 162
Merom, Lake, 24; waters of, 127
Meroz, the people of, 131
Mesha, stone of, 148
Messiah, idea of the, 211
Micah, 154
Migrations, Semitic, 64
Mishnah, the, 234
Mitanni, Kingdom of the, 88, 108
Moab, mountains of, 25
Mohammed, 243
Mohammed Ali, 308, 310
Mohammed Ibn Faruch, 316
Mohar, Travels of a, 113
Mongols in Syria, 289
Montefiore, Sir Moses, 320
Monuments, megalithic, 49
Mosque, the, of Omar, 251
Murad IV, Sultan, 302
Mysticism in Palestine, 317

Nabatæans, the, 242
Nabopolassar, 169
Nachmanides in Holy Land, 297
Napoleon invades Syria, 307
Naram Sin, 63, 75
National Home, the, 344
Nebuchadrezzar, 170
Necho, King, 169
Negeb, the, 23
Nehemiah, 174

INDEX

Nezib, battle of, 311
Nicæa, Council of, 274
Nineveh, 157
Nippur, 59

Obadiah, 181
Omar, Mosque of, 251
Omri, King, 147, 149
Osmanlis capture Constantinople, 293

Palæolithic age, 43
Palermo, the annals of, 75
Palestine—term of, 19; earthquakes in, 26; unique position of, 32; Exploration Fund, 35; archæology of, 35; coveted by Egypt, 74; under Persian domination, 172, 178, 179; after death of Herod, 207; a Moslem possession, 250; air of, 276; divided into five pashaliks, 300; home of mysticism, 317; British policy in, 346; future of, 349
Patriarchate, the, 234, 237
Pharisees, the, 193
Philistines, land of the, 19
Philistines, the, 135, 139
Pilgrimages to Holy Land, 261
Pinsker, Leo, 329
Pithom, 121
Plumer, Lord, 347
Poetry, liturgical, in Palestine, 295
Pompey in Palestine, 199
Procurators, Roman, in Palestine, 209
Ptolemies in Palestine, 183, 184
Pul, King, 156

Rabbis, Palestinian, 235
Ramoth, City of, 148
Ramses II, 112, 114, 121
Raphia, battle of, 186
Rehoboam, 143
Renaud de Châtillon, 282
Rephaim, the, 46
Restoration, the Jewish, 175
Retenu, the land of, 79
Rezon, King, 142
Rome, rule of, in Palestine, 200

Sabako, King, 158
Sahure, King, 76
Saladin, Sultan, 286

Salome Alexandra, 198
Samaria, 22
Samaritans, the, 151, 173
Samsie, Queen, 159
Samuel, Sir Herbert, 45
Sardanapalus, 167
Sargon, 75
Sargon of Agade, 63
Saul, King, 138
Sebaste, city of, 206
Selim the Grim, conquest of Palestine, 299
Sellin, researches of, 39, 40
Semites, term of, 51; script of, 72
Sennacherib, King, 164
Seti I, 111
Shabbatai Zevi, 317
Shalmaneser III, 147
Sharon, 29
Shaw, Sir Walter, Commission of Inquiry, 348
Sheshank, King, 144
Sheshbazzar, 173
Shiloh, tabernacle of, 127
Shishak, *see* Sheshank
Shophetim, the, 128
Shulkhan Arukh, the, 314
Sinsariskum, King, 168
Sinuhe, the Romance of, 79
Sisera, 129
Sokolov, N., 330
Solomon, King, 140
Subbiluliuma, King, 100
Suleiman II, 301
Sumer, people of, 54, 58

Taanach, city of, 39, 69
Tanis, city of, 87
Tehutia, general, 96
Tell-el-Amarna, letters of, 69, 70, 100, 123
Tell-el-Hesy, 36
Temple, the, of Herod, 206
Thutmose, King, 67, 90, 113
Tiberias, academy of, 294; Lake of, 24
Tidal, King, 65
Tiglath-Pileser, 150
Tirhakah, King, 167
Torah, the, national constitution, 177
Transjordania, 343
Troglodytes in Palestine, 46
Tzimiscus, 258

367

Ukush, Sultan, 63
Umma, the *patesi* of, 63
Ur-Kasdim, 120
Ur-Nina, 62
Uru-Kagina, 63
Urusalimu, the King of, 110
Usertsen of Egypt, 79
Uzziah, King, 153

Vespasian, 216

Wadi Magharah, 75
Weizmann, Dr. Ch., 330
White Paper, the, 345

Yaman, King, 161
Yarmuk, battle of, 248

Zedekiah, King, 171
Zerubbabel, 173
Ziftha, 92
Zimri, 196
Zimrida, 36, 103
"Zion, Back to", 321
Zionism, 326
Zionist Commission, 330
Zoan, city of, 89
Zoba, Kingdom of, 145